A History of Mexico

Sir Nicolas Cheetham

Mexico:
A Short History

Thomas Y. Crowell Company
New York · *Established 1834*

First published in the United States of America in 1971.
Originally published in Great Britain under the title
A History of Mexico.

Copyright © 1970 by Sir Nicolas Cheetham

Printed in Great Britain

L.C. Card 76–136101
ISBN 0–690–53389–6

Contents

List of illustrations

Preface

I was moved to write this book by wide though unsystematic reading about Mexican history, mostly in secondary sources, and by my own personal experiences derived from six years' acquaintance with Mexico at two distinct periods. On the first occasion I stayed two years as Second Secretary at the British Legation and on the second I was lucky to have been appointed Ambassador and to stay for four years. The various claims on a diplomat's time always conspire to thwart him from gaining as thorough a knowledge as he would wish of the country in which he is working, but he does generally find good opportunities for travel, and I myself managed somehow to visit all the thirty-one States and Territories of the Republic. During these journeys I became deeply absorbed in the fascinating evidence of three thousand years of historical development which is to be met at every turn of the road, and very conscious of my own fundamental ignorance of Mexico's past. Even when I began to think I knew something about it there was always a new and exciting discovery to upset my previous ideas and drive me to start learning afresh. Although quantities of books have been written about Mexico, it struck me that there was still a need for a plain but balanced version of its history from the earliest to the most modern times, and that is what I have attempted to provide. I would hope that it may serve as a useful introduction to Mexico for the increasing numbers of people who are now visiting it on pleasure or for reasons of business.

Eyford, 1969

Chapter One The Early Civilisations

Origins

When the Prince of Wales passed through Mexico in 1966, *The Times* reported him as having visited 'the Aztec pyramids of Teotihuacán'. The august newspaper failed to realise that in attributing these famous monuments to the Aztecs it was committing a fearful schoolboy howler, as if it had referred to the Roman builders of the Parthenon, or to Sir Christopher Wren as the architect of Canterbury Cathedral. In fact the pyramids had been abandoned centuries before the Aztecs ever reached the Valley of Mexico, the goal of their long migration from the north.

The light-hearted error by *The Times* correspondent is typical of the vagueness still prevailing abroad about the origins of the Mexican nation, although the mysterious and fascinating history of pre-Columbian Mexico has been laid bare by scholars and archaeologists from many countries. Two thousand years of more or less coherent history produced a teeming and brilliant stone-age civilisation on Mexican soil. But they were preceded by many millennia of prehistory about which only an obscure outline of fact is discernible.

Indeed the movements and settlements of early man on the American continent have given rise to plenty of brisk argument between the learned and the not so learned. Opinions have differed strongly on the fundamental questions—if man did not originate on the American continent just as he originated, by way of a whole succession of pre-human and sub-human species, on the other continents, how did he reach America, and when? To cut a long and complicated story short, the controversialists on this subject have been divided into two schools of thought, known as the

Americanists and the Diffusionists. These agree with one another only on the point that man did not gradually evolve in America as he did in, say, Africa or Asia. On the contrary, he appeared on American soil as fully-fledged Homo Sapiens. What the controversy is concerned with is the source of the migrations which brought him to America.

The Americanists' theory is quite simple. They say that the whole of the continent, from arctic Canada to Tierra del Fuego at the extreme southern point of South America, was peopled from eastern Asia, or more exactly what is now northern China or eastern Siberia. They assume that America was slowly penetrated by successive waves of immigrants who began to cross from one continent to the other twenty thousand years ago (and perhaps much earlier still) using the land bridge which at that time no doubt existed over the Bering Strait. The indigenous population of America, the so-called American 'Indians', who were in undisputed possession of the continent when the Europeans arrived in the early sixteenth century, sprang from this and no other source. Thus the great civilisations which emerged on the west coast of South America, as well as in Central America and Mexico, were developed by the descendants of these immigrants from Asia, by their own talents and quite independently of any physical immigration or cultural influence from other parts of the world.

The Diffusionists, for their part, are quite ready to accept the Mongoloid origin of the vast majority of the immigrants. They do not, however, think it reasonable to suppose that the elaborate cultures of Indian America grew and flowered in isolation and unaffected by developments in other continents. They have assembled a great deal of evidence designed to prove that contacts were made in historical times across the Pacific between Asia or Oceania and the American continent, and that cultural and racial influence from overseas can be traced on American soil. All sorts of affinities, in language, customs and the arts, are quoted in support of this theory, which is made to sound quite plausible despite the enormous difficulties of navigation in primitive times across the immensities of the Pacific.

Although some of the diffusionist arguments are plainly fanciful or even crackpot, it is impossible not to be attracted by them. It would be thrilling, for instance, to establish beyond doubt the reality of trans-Pacific voyages or of a relationship between the art forms of south-east Asia and those of the Mayan civilisation. But while Diffusionism appeals powerfully to the imagination, the proofs which it adduces to support its claims are usually rather slender. They are apt to belong to the realm of romantic conjecture. Reluctantly one is bound to admit that the Americanist approach is more scientific and therefore more credible. It is safer to go along with the majority of scholars and accept its conclusions, based as they are on painstaking, if sometimes tedious, anthropological research. For the experts have followed the marks of the immigrants on their painful southward march since the end of the last ice age. It would seem that recent discoveries tend to show that the process of the human penetration of America was a lengthier one than the earlier Americanists ever supposed.

Most American Indians have a characteristically Mongoloid appearance, especially if they have little or no admixture of European blood. An Englishman who recently worked among Tibetan refugees was struck, on his first visit to Mexico, by the physical resemblance between his Tibetans and the Indians living in villages near Mexico City. The same general physical type is found among the indigenous inhabitants of the whole continent, although the author has to confess to some doubts about the origin of the Chaco Indians of Paraguay and of the inhabitants of the Amazonian jungles, who look so primitive that they must have evolved, one is tempted to think, in primitive times directly from their native swamps. Basic uniformity of race, however, permits of infinite variations, and the extent to which the migrants have become differentiated among themselves in the course of so many thousands of years of wandering and sojourning in America is a fascinating study even in the Mexico of today, when the character of the race has been so profoundly modified.

Mexico is still a mosaic of Indian peoples. Within a short distance of its huge and sophisticated modern capital, there is no difficulty in distinguishing the Nahuas, descendants of the Aztecs and related tribes, from, for example, the Otomis or the Tarascans. All three peoples possess distinct physical traits and speak (besides Spanish) totally distinct native languages with no points of resemblance of structure or vocabulary. This multiplicity of separate languages is indeed one of the most baffling peculiarities of the pre-Columbian scene. One cannot imagine how this enormous variety could have possibly come to exist within a comparatively restricted area. In the south of Mexico, especially in the states of Oaxaca and Chiapas, the proliferation of peoples and languages becomes even more fantastic. Each secluded mountain valley seems to contain a group, sometimes a very small one, boasting its own identity and strong individuality. The awesome geography of the region has tenaciously resisted the modern tendency towards assimilation.

But we are going too fast. Many thousands of years were to pass before the scattered groups of hunters and fishers which by 10,000 BC were already roaming the territory now known as Mexico coalesced into anything resembling the complex of nations and tribes identifiable in historical times. We may assume that this shifting population, though constantly strengthened over a long period by fresh arrivals from the north, remained very sparse. Until the early Indo-Americans hit upon the cultivation of the maize plant, the human element cannot have bulked very large in the grandiose landscape of Mexico. The natural environment was scarcely affected by the presence of man in insignificant numbers.

That environment must have been wild and beautiful beyond the dreams of the imagination. The tourist of the twentieth century can only admire the skeleton of its former magnificence, but even so it is not too difficult to form a picture of what the country looked like in the pre-agricultural age. The low-lying coastal regions were of course covered by virtually impenetrable jungles and we may safely assume that the nomadic tribes of the time would at first have had little inclination to confront the obvious dangers and hardships in those tropical fastnesses. But on the high plateaus of the centre of the country, and wide plains of the north, conditions were much more propitious for human existence. Instead of the forbidding desiccation which today blights so large a range of Mexico, the wandering tribes found an entirely lush and well watered country, heavily forested in parts and merging in others into green and grassy plains which we know only as desert or semi-desert. During the long epoch which preceded the invention of agriculture many variations of climate took place; some periods were drier and warmer than others. The cold periods produced extensive caps of snow and ice on the higher mountain ranges. And accompanying these variations, sometimes intensive, sometimes spasmodic but never entirely absent, came outbursts of seismic activity, pitting the landscape with thousands of volcanic cones and scarring it with the tumbled flow of lava.

This country supported an abundant animal and vegetable life off which primitive men lived with comparative ease for countless generations. At first food supplies were virtually inexhaustible, for nature had provided the primitive weapons and traps of the nomadic hunters with the widest possible choice of victims. These ranged from the mammoth or ancient elephant, through the bison, camel and wild horse and many varieties of deer, to innumerable small mammals, some of which survive today. Thus the early inhabitants were primarily eaters of meat, fowl and fish.

Near Mexico City itself the subsoil has yielded up the skeleton of a mammoth with an obsidian knife or spear point embedded in a rib, and in the vicinity were found human remains clearly establishing the fact that palaeolithic man on the central plateau of Mexico was engaged ten thousand years ago in the pursuit of the greatest of all prehistoric beasts. The evidence may be seen and studied in the little village of Tepexpan, on the way to the pyramids of Teotihuacán. But this vivid reminder of an elephant hunt is, curiously enough, a solitary flash of human interest illuminating a vast darkness of ignorance and conjecture. Although conditions in Mexico must have closely resembled, in all essential respects, those prevailing in palaeolithic Europe or Africa, traces are so far totally lacking in this part of America of artistic activity similar to that with which we have become so familiar in the caves of southern France and Spain, or among the rocks of the Sahara. Nevertheless it would be very rash to assume that discoveries of this kind will not one day be made, and throw a much needed light on the development of the forgotten nomad tribes.

Meanwhile we can only guess, with a certain degree of confidence, that by 2000 BC the first steps in agriculture had been taken, and that maize, beans and other plants were being cultivated around the lakes of the Valley of Mexico and in other favoured sites. One theory put forward to explain the switch to agriculture in Mexico is that a reduction in the stocks of animals suitable for hunting, perhaps due to climatic reasons, drove the inhabitants, under the pressure of necessity, to cultivate the soil. This does not, however, seem to be an entirely satisfactory supposition, for there is no doubt that wild life remained plentiful throughout the whole period of indigenous civilisations, and only dwindled rapidly after the Spanish Conquest. Whatever force there may be in the straightforward economic explanation, it makes equal sense to ascribe the change to the operations of a natural law of human inventiveness, according to which, when conditions are suitable, this particular transformation of the human way of life becomes inevitable. In Mexico these conditions happened to be fulfilled at some date towards the end of the third millennium BC.

The Archaic or Pre-classical Period

In the so-called archaic or pre-classical period Mesoamerica—that is the territory stretching from the north-central regions of modern Mexico well into the interior of Central America—emerged from the mists of palaeolithic pre-history and evolved a settled neolithic civilisation. At least fifteen hundred years of such evolution paved the way for a classical period coinciding very roughly with the first thousand years of the Christian era. The classical civilisations which sprang up at that time at a number of widely distant centres throughout the area were extremely complex and diversified. But they were all essentially extensions of the cultures of the preceding archaic age. They were superimposed on its very simple foundations. Despite their rich cultural elaboration they introduced no new element foreign to, or uncharacteristic of, the Stone Age. Indeed they represented the apogee of the Stone Age which never reached such heights in any other part of the world. Hence the importance of the archaic period in the formative sense. Fortunately it is a period which has revealed plenty of evidence to the archaeologists and is daily revealing much more as the search proceeds. Any generalisations about it are therefore bound to be tentative and susceptible to being upset at any moment by significant new discoveries.

At this point it may be useful to insert a chronological table. This cannot pretend to more than approximate accuracy, but it is hoped that it will serve as a useful framework for dating the complicated panorama of pre-Columbian times.

CHRONOLOGICAL TABLE

Archaic Culture 1500 BC—beginning of Christian era
    VALLEY OF MEXICO
    (a) Copilco, Zacatenco   1200–600 BC
    (b) Ticomán, Cuicuilco, Tlatilco   600–100 BC
    OLMECS (Southern Vera Cruz and
    Tabasco, spreading into Central Mexico)   800 BC–AD 100

CLASSICAL CULTURE
    (a) TEOTIHUACAN   100 BC–AD 800
        The great pyramids were built between

Teotihuacán: Great Pyramid

(*J. Allan Cash*)

Ceremonial buildings at Chichén Itzá (Yucatán)   (*J. Allan Cash*)

AD 100 and 300 and the golden age
lasted from about AD 200 to 700.

(b) MAYAS
   (i) 'Old Empire'   AD 100– 900
   (ii) 'New Empire'   AD 900– 1500
(c) XOCHICALCO   AD 600– 1000
(d) TOTONACS (El Tajin)   AD 600– 900
(e) ZAPOTECS (Monte Alban)   AD 300– 900

TOLTECS (Tula)   AD 900– 1224

MIXTECS (Oaxaca)   AD 1000– 1500

AZTECS   AD 1325– 1521

The archaic culture flourished by the lakes of the Valley of
Mexico and in the adjoining regions. It also grew up in the
western part of the country and, to a more significant extent, in
the coastal districts lying along the Gulf of Mexico. Although the
greatest cultural advance at this stage of development was to be
made between the great rivers entering the Gulf on either side of
the isthmus of Tehuantepec, earlier material progress can be more
easily followed in the Valley sites, Copilco, Tlatilco, Zacatenco
and others. Here people lived in sparse and straggling communities of mud huts thatched with reeds, cultivated their
primitive crops and eked out their existence by age-old methods
of hunting and fishing. By European standards their range of
domestic animals seems strangely restricted. They had no cattle,
horses, donkeys, goats, sheep, pigs or chickens. Dogs were kept
for eating as well as for more obvious purposes: ducks and
turkeys were ubiquitous as they are today. But here the list stops,
as indeed it stopped in 1519 when the first European animals were
brought to the country.

At some moment during the second millennium they learned to
make pottery, which gradually became more elaborate in shape
and colour. Their nascent artistic sense was manifested in great
numbers of clay statuettes of people (or rather of women) and
animals. There is no reason to suppose that these little figures,
which so greatly amuse and intrigue us today, served any religious
purpose: as elsewhere, they satisfied the basic human love of
representation. Domestic implements and utensils, some of which
are used by modern villagers in exactly the same form for the
preparation of the same simple food, were made of stone; and
ornaments of stone or bone.

The physical appearance of these folk can be reconstructed from their skeletons. It did not differ in any marked respect from that of the Indians of Moctezuma's time, who themselves were the close ancestors of the Indians of 1968. We may picture them therefore as stocky, brown and athletic, dark-haired and smooth-skinned, and wearing the scantiest of clothing woven from cotton or the fibre of the maguey cactus.

Their social, political and religious institutions were of the most rudimentary kind. It is hardly likely that their basic social organisation applied to more than a small group of families inheriting a particular locality. Their religion did not probably transcend the sort of fertility cult which is normally celebrated in primitive agricultural communities, coupled with simple funerary rites for the dead. It also looks as if these modest communities were essentially pacific, except for sporadic scuffles between rival groups for the possession of land or hunting grounds. However the spear, the arrow and the knife of these neolithic warriors, especially when tipped with the razor-sharp obsidian so plentifully present in the volcanic soil, were deadly enough whether employed against animals or men.

For many centuries no change can be discerned in the slow rhythm of life dictated by the gathering of food and the crude struggle with the environment. Then, with the advent of the last millennium BC, the pace begins to quicken. The population increases, society becomes more complex, the first signs appear of political and religious organisation and of sophisticated culture. The process is rapid and continuous. It is tempting, but as usual unrewarding, to ask what was the stimulus that evoked so lively a response from the Indians of Mesoamerica at this crucial period of their development. So far as the Valley of Mexico is concerned, the climatic factor is again invoked. It is claimed that the dwellers by the great lakes were driven by persistent droughts, and a consequent shrinkage in the water levels, to improve their agricultural techniques and to elaborate their hitherto fragmented social life. But whatever the cause of this sudden expansion of human energy, it rapidly produced remarkable results.

As has already been mentioned, the swiftest progress during this period was made on the Gulf of Mexico by the inhabitants of what is now southern Vera Cruz and Tabasco. It is a hot and steamy region, where sluggish rivers wind through interminable swamps and the hills are covered with luxuriant jungle. In this uncompromising terrain lived the Olmecs, traditionally reputed

18

to be the founders of Mesoamerican civilisation, and the first people in the area to have bequeathed to us a series of impressive monuments. The origins of this mysterious race are obscure. What is certain is that they flourished exceedingly on their own ground for the best part of a thousand years, and that their influence radiated over much wider territories.

The principal sites in the Olmec homeland are called La Venta, Tres Zapotes and San Lorenzo. Here were found the finest examples of the colossal and sometimes grotesque sculpture which is the hallmark of Olmec art. Enormous basalt heads, each weighing several tons, stare enigmatically at the visitor (not only at the sites themselves, because the Mexicans have a passion for reproducing them in museums and in public gardens); their exaggeratedly negroid features seem to have no kinship with the clearly marked traits of the American Indian. Nor can we guess for what strange religious or ceremonial purpose they were devised. The stone was quarried as far as 60–80 miles from the sites where the statues were found and was presumably transported most of the way by water. Even so the labour involved must have been stupendous; it can only reflect the existence of a

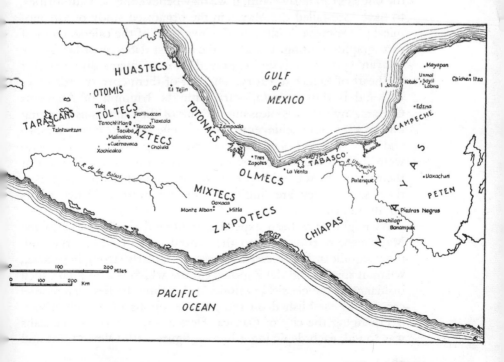

strictly disciplined society obeying the directions of a ruling hierarchy and conforming to a highly developed religion. The Olmecs built no monumental stone temples, although the plain structures of earth of which their ceremonial centres were composed were symmetrically planned and aligned and embellished with massive stone altars and stelae.

Besides the giant basalt heads the Olmec sculptors produced smaller figures of great variety and refinement in many kinds of stone and notably in jade. Foremost among the subjects represented is the jaguar, an animal which exercised a peculiar fascination over the Olmecs. They seem to have revered it as a deity, or rather as the symbol of their nation, with an even greater devotion than the Aztecs showed, in later times, for the eagle. Often the jaguar appears in bizarre combination with the human form, or else the features of a purely human figure subtly but terrifyingly suggest the jaguar's snarl. When their expressions are not thus ferociously contorted these plump, jolly, naked Olmec men are irresistibly sympathetic. Women do not seem to have been represented at all.

In addition to their other social, religious and artistic advances the Olmecs can fairly claim, if we may believe the best authorities, to have forestalled the Mayas in the organised study of astronomical phenomena, leading to the invention of the calendar and of pictographic writing. Certainly the earliest dates recorded by the 'Mayan' system are found engraved on monuments discovered at the heart of Olmec territory. The first of them corresponds to 31 BC, and is thus contemporary with the triumph of Augustus Caesar. Anyhow it is pleasant to think of the Olmecs as bringing off this crowning achievement on the eve of their disappearance and of the absorption of their cultural heritage by the peoples who were about to build the classical civilisation of Mesoamerica. For their influence was widespread and as the archaeologists pursue their search they are finding more and more evidence of its ramifications.

As might have been expected, it filtered southward into the Maya area, northward into the central part of Vera Cruz and, more significantly, westward. It was particularly strong in Oaxaca, where it sparked off the Zapotec culture which was to attain such brilliance in the classical period. At this time the first ceremonial centre was established on the great acropolis of Monte Albán, overhanging the city of Oaxaca. Here a series of big stone slabs was found, each depicting a human figure with Olmec traits and in a typically Olmec attitude. Some of them bear date glyphs. They are known as 'Los Danzantes' and can be admired on the site. Traces of Olmec influence have also been discovered further west in Guerrero, as far as the Pacific coast, but much remains to be learned about the extent of this penetration and of its relation to the other early cultures of this wild and largely unstudied region.

On the central plateau Olmec influence made itself felt in the Valley of Mexico as well as in Puebla and Morelos. It is especially reflected in the pottery and clay figures from the site known as Tlatilco in the Federal District, which has produced an extra-ordinarily rich hoard of superior artistic quality. This vital element implanted in the receptive soil of the Valley supplemented and enriched the already existing culture and eventually resulted in a happy fusion. While the artistic impulse was inspired chiefly from outside, it is impossible to judge whether the parallel process of social and religious development owes more to one element or the other. But there is no doubt that the society of the Valley was regulated, just as in the Olmec area, by a priestly caste which imprinted on it a highly ceremonial stamp.

The chief cult was evidently that of Huehueteotl, the god of fire, who is represented as an old man. For the first time in Meso-american history religious monuments with some architectural pretensions were built and one notable example has survived. This is the so-called pyramid of Cuicuilco, also in the Federal District. It is actually a cone-shaped mound about 70 feet high, originally of earth but later rebuilt in adobe roughly faced with stone. Primitive, awkward and bulky, it nevertheless earns respect as the ancestor of the innumerably more sophisticated structures with which the Mexican landscape was studded in ancient times, as thickly as it is now dotted with domed churches. Indeed the traveller is tempted to see a pyramid under every hillock which looks even faintly artificial.

The interest of the Cuicuilco mound is enhanced by its romantic situation, for it is half-embedded in the lava flow of the Pedregal, a tumbled waste of volcanic rock resulting from an eruption which overwhelmed the region towards the end of the pre-classical era. It is rather a pity that the solitary grandeur of the site has recently been disturbed by a network of noisy highways and its proximity to the new Olympic village. It is an indication of what the Pedregal may still conceal, and conceal for ever.

The Classical Period

We have now arrived at the brink of the classical era. There is of course no clear dividing line between it and the preceding archaic or pre-classical age, in terms either of precise dating or of any abrupt change in life and habits on the part of the population. It should never be forgotten that all the main tendencies which became apparent during the first age are merely accentuated or elaborated during the classical. There was no sudden break and one period merges almost imperceptibly into the other. While the beginning of the Christian era furnishes a convenient date for memorising a new situation, it should not be imagined that the classical culture began to bloom at its principal centres at the same moment, or that it fell into decay simultaneously throughout Mesoamerica. We are entering a period characterised by complexity and diversity, by increased inter-communication between regions and by other advantages conferred by the imposition of broadly similar norms of life on densely settled populations over an enormous territory. Neolithic civilisation reaches its zenith at Teotihuacán, in the Mayan cities, at Monte Alban and in the coastal districts of Vera Cruz.

Teotihuacán lies thirty miles from the centre of modern Mexico City. The immense layout of its ceremonial buildings is described (not without inaccuracies) by all the guide-books. The visitor will duly note the generous scale and geometrical exactitude of the planning. He will find that the biggest pyramid has a base larger than that of the great pyramid of Egypt, though it invites no such comparison in terms of height. He will admire the temples in the so-called Citadel and murals and sculptures of the 'Palace of Butterflies'. If he has the time, he will be well advised to study the ceramics, jewellery and other *kleinkunst* in the museums of Teotihuacán and Mexico City. But if he is of an enquiring mind, he will have a lot of questions to ask about the origin, history and fate of the great city and its people. Such questions are hard to answer accurately, because virtually the only evidence on which we can attempt a coherent account of the rise and fall of Teotihuacán is that provided by archaeology. The Teotihuacanos left no written records, apart from a few hieroglyphic inscriptions; we have no idea what language they spoke; the actual course of their history is unknown to us. The Aztecs, who were familiar with the grass-grown ruins of the city, regarded it as the abode of superhuman beings. Luckily the archaeological findings are extensive and justify solid deductions.

The site of Teotihuacán was occupied for about a thousand years. The first inhabitants were contemporary with the people who built Cuicuilco; they were probably indigenous to the central plateau and not immigrants. About AD 100 they began to develop their city in spectacular fashion and to build the principal existing monuments, to be much modified in succeeding centuries. From about the third to the sixth century the city continued to expand and flourish in peaceful magnificence. Thereafter it started to decay; in the eighth century it was destroyed by barbarians from the north, its civilisation collapsed and its ruins were abandoned except by squatters.

In its heyday it was governed by a priestly caste devoted to elaborate religious observances and to the practice of astronomy. They directed the worship of a whole pantheon of individual gods; many of these cults survived into a later age. The presiding deity was Tlaloc, god of rain, fertility and agriculture; he is prominently represented in the art of Teotihuacán and his name is still commemorated in one of the high mountains overlooking the valley. It would surely be wrong, however, to think of the priests as entirely absorbed in ceremonies and abstruse calculations. Ruling over a population which must have numbered hundreds of thousands, they had their practical responsibilities. The evidence is that they acquitted themselves well in their task of maintaining a stable and prosperous society over so long a period.

One example of their practical ability is their town-planning. Teotihuacán was designed on a rectangular grid which applies not only to religious precincts but also to the quarters which housed the mass of the traders, artisans and workers. It also possessed an excellent drainage system. The splendour, and the sumptuous state in which its rulers lived, depended on a carefully organised economy. Traders carried the products of its workshops for hundreds of miles, towards the civilised south and the barbarian north and west. In addition, the organisation of agriculture must have presented so populous a society with new and peculiar problems, especially at periods when tens of thousands of men were employed on building the monuments and were therefore economically unproductive. The failure of a single maize harvest was sufficient to bring the community to the edge of disaster. Hence the emphasis placed by its religion on rainfall and irrigation, even though the land was then incomparably richer in water than it is today. The forests were also far more extensive and the lakes, teeming with fish and wildfowl, were near at hand. Nevertheless the danger of famine was always present and it is possible that the fall of Teotihuacán was caused or hastened by economic weakness. In other words, a top-heavy community had outrun its means of subsistence.

This, however, is a matter of speculation. Other factors were probably at work as well. It would also be interesting to have a clear conception of the extent of territory politically controlled or dominated by Teotihuacán. It probably included the whole of the Valley of Mexico and the neighbouring regions of the present states of Mexico, Hidalgo, Tlaxcala and Puebla. Conditions were similar throughout this area and the population homogeneous. Archaeology has already revealed many traces of the Teotihuacán culture in the vicinity of Puebla and it is fairly certain that before long this fertile plain will be proved to have been an essential adjunct or component of the theocratic state of Teotihuacán. Very real rewards are already greeting the excavators at Cholula and other places.

The sway exercised by the priest-rulers of Teotihuacán was pacific. There is no sign that it was a tyranny enforced by repression, or that society as a whole was at all war-like. In this respect no greater contrast can be imagined between its ethos and that of the Aztecs, who lived in a continuous state of hostility with their neighbours and whose existence was bound up with the deliberate waging of war. One cannot help wondering how Teotihuacán managed to endure so long without the protection of a warrior class. If fighting men there were, they do not seem to have played a dominant role. Teotihuacán was in fact an open city, tremendously wealthy and with no bellicose traditions. As such it was surely calculated to invite attack from northern tribes which had not yet emerged from the nomadic stage.

Yet this did not happen until Teotihuacán had been granted nearly a thousand years to fulfil itself. When the barbarians struck, it is more than likely that internal decadence had set in. Previously it had been the men of Teotihuacán who had thrust their civilising influence into the barbarian lands, establishing settlements in remote places. But as they grew less dynamic or lost faith in themselves, their culture lost its glamour for outsiders, who turned from admiration to aggression. Once the destructive forces of nomadism had been released, the old civilisation was doomed. In a welter of conjecture about causes one fact stands out clearly: the city was sacked and burned and never recovered.

Possibly the barbarians were joined in the work of destruction by what Toynbee would call the internal proletariat, revolting against the oppression or incompetence of their rulers. It is not surprising that so static a civilisation should eventually stagnate and end in sudden disaster. One looks in vain for a parallel in the old world, but ancient Egypt, which was culturally static but historically most eventful, lasted even longer and died a natural death in extreme old age. At Teotihuacán a millennium of significant human activity passed away without a single recorded fact or name. There followed in central Mexico a long period of confusion and semi-barbarism.

The Mayas created in the south of Mesoamerica an even richer and more varied civilisation than the people of Teotihuacán did on the central plateau. Moreover, it appeals more strongly to our interest and imagination because we know more about it, because its monumental remains are so numerous, impressive and widespread and because Mayan history covers so long a time-span. The Mayas have been described as the heirs of the Olmecs, and from a chronological point of view at least this designation fits neatly, since Mayan development begins almost at the same moment as the Olmec culture vanishes. The first date inscribed on a Mayan stela comes from Uaxactún, a city lying on the borders of Guatemala and British Honduras. It corresponds, according to the earliest reckoning, with AD 68 (the end of Nero's reign), while the last date recorded at the same site is AD 889. No date inscriptions later than AD 900 have been found at any of the cities in the same area.

Mayan civilisation did not, however, conveniently disappear, as at Teotihuacán, with the end of the classical period. For reasons which will be discussed later, it shifted its axis from one region and group of cities to another and took on a new lease of life. With remarkable flexibility and resilience, it absorbed elements from Central Mexico and was not dead, though sadly decadent, when the Spaniards arrived and extinguished it. In other words, it was in continuous evolution from the archaic period until the early sixteenth century. Even after the Conquest it did not altogether lose its identity. Indeed the Mayas have preserved their distinctive character more successfully than any other of the Indian peoples of Mexico until the present day. The traveller in Yucatán often has the impression that he is no longer in Mexico. In their language, names, dress and customs and above all in their physical type, the modern Mayas are different from their fellow citizens to the north and they have maintained in their traditions a natural and unbroken connexion with their remote past.

The Maya area was very large. It comprised not only the Yucatán peninsula and the territory covered by the states of Campeche, Tabasco and Chiapas, but also parts of the modern Central American countries as far south as Nicaragua. The first cities appear to have been founded in the Peten, a district shared between British Honduras and Guatemala. Further groups sprang up to the south and east and particularly along the Usumacinta river. Here are located some of the most famous sites, such as Bonampak, Yaxchilán, Piedras Negras and Palenque. They and dozens of others lie buried in the tropical rain forests. The whole area has only been superficially explored and no one knows what the archaeological map will look like when the jungle has been finally opened up and forced to reveal its secrets.

It seems incredible that these almost impenetrable recesses should ever have been so tamed by Mayan persistence and ingenuity that they became capable of supporting great populations with a creative minority leading an elaborately sophisticated existence. The Mayas must have been uncommonly efficient organisers of human effort to overcome this formidable environment. Their technical equipment was still neolithic and in their agriculture they were necessarily dependent on primitive and impermanent methods which consisted of burning and cultivating successive strips of jungle and passing to others when they became exhausted. The cities alone gave cohesion and stability to Mayan society. Whereas at Teotihuacán planned residential quarters were grouped around the ceremonial core of the city, the Mayan centres were purely religious and administrative. Each consisted of an impressive complex of monumental buildings, laid out on an imperial scale and frequently covering a vast area. They were linked together by water and by a system of causeways which allowed extraordinarily swift traffic between the centres of the region.

The Mayas excelled as stoneworkers, both architecturally and decoratively. Their temples and palaces display great variety of design, contrasting with the somewhat monotonous mutiplication of the pyramid, large and small, in Central Mexico. The pyramid and the stepped platforms as a base for temples are of course common in the Mayan world as well, but the Mayas show a lively inventiveness in their styles which has no counterpart further north. They built rectangular structures, diversified with courtyards and galleries; they invented the corbelled arch and experimented cleverly with roof designs. They were true architects, not mere pilers up of balanced masses. Though sometimes guilty of clumsiness, their sense of proportion is usually excellent. At its best Mayan architecture achieves an exquisite harmony, as at Palenque where the lay-out triumphantly avoids the heavily monumental.

These buildings are often profusely ornamented with formal motifs and with sculpture in low relief. The finest examples of the sculptor's art are again found at Palenque, where they recall the delicate but firm lines of archaic Greece. Each city has produced its quota of carved stelae representing important and gorgeously attired personages engaged in solemn functions. They are also inscribed with hieroglyphic texts which, if we could only read them, would no doubt explain the whole significance of the events commemorated. But unfortunately we can only interpret the date glyphs.

While there is something inhuman about the stiff ceremonial attitudes of these dignitaries, with their enormous feathered head-dresses, massive jewellery, distorted skulls and lips and ears pierced and bulging with ornaments, a more sympathetic impression of the same people can be derived from the unique murals of Bonampak (the originals are perishing from exposure but have been brilliantly copied in the Mexico City museum). In these frescoes the participants in the ceremonies are seen not singly but as performers or spectators in whole scenes, and the effect is naturalistic as well as extremely colourful. The Mayan notables spring to life and abandon their hieratic postures. They reveal themselves not as mysterious priests but as fat epicureans enjoying to the full the pomps and pleasures of their privileged state. If Bonampak makes the rulers seem less remote, the everyday life of the Mayas in the classical period is presented to us even more directly by the thousands of figurines recovered from the cemeteries of the island of Jaina, which lies off the coast of Campeche. They portray with the freest realism men and women of all ages and classes in the greatest variety of attitudes and occupations. Seldom has so accurate a mirror been held up to a past age which in other respects proves so enigmatic.

As Mayan hieroglyphs cannot be deciphered, the history of the so-called 'Old Empire' will never be reconstituted. The word 'empire' is a misnomer and the political organisation is more likely to have consisted of a sort of theocratic league loosely held

27

together by the common interest of the ruling caste. This was ranged in an intricate hierarchy of priests, astronomers, administrators and soldiers. War was perhaps the least significant of these activities; Mayan society was oriented towards peaceful pursuits and war would have interfered with the serious business of life—agriculture, building, the propitiation of the gods and, above all, the study of mathematics and the recording of astronomical data.

The gods of the Mayan pantheon were as carefully arranged as the rulers in hierarchical order. Deities of the sky and underworld, of creation, of nature and of agriculture, each had its due of worship and sacrifice, though the latter was not carried to excess with human victims. At the same time the religious concept was fused with the mathematical. We have to imagine an élite of specially selected and dedicated intellectuals who, century after century, accumulated an astonishing fund of exact knowledge. In a society which had failed to invent the wheel, they were absorbed in the perfections of number and the conjunction of the stars. They did succeed in inventing a calendar which is unsurpassed for precision, but in general the intellectual achievement of the astronomers was considered more as an end in itself than in relation to any practical value. All social and artistic effort was subordinate to it. But, perversely enough, it is the art and architecture of the Mayas that has survived, while we can hardly begin to penetrate the secrets of the philosopher-mathematicians.

Towards the end of the classical period a sudden and baffling disaster befell the Mayas. For reasons which have never been adequately explained, all the cities of the 'Old Empire' were deserted by their inhabitants and swallowed up by the jungle from which they are at last being painfully reclaimed. A thriving civilisation was arrested, or committed suicide, as it was in full swing. Many theories have been advanced for this bizarre turn of events—social upheaval and civil strife; overpopulation and exhaustion of the soil; fatal epidemics; superstitious forebodings inducing a sense of doom; none seems entirely convincing. But whatever the cause, the effect was catastrophic and organised society was extinguished. Perhaps the annihilation or expulsion of the ruling caste sufficed to produce utter chaos. Nevertheless, as has already been mentioned, Mayan culture was transplanted to the soil of the Yucatán peninsula where it flowered with renewed vigour.

Although Yucatán was already Mayan territory, it had hitherto led an obscure and marginal existence. All this was changed by the arrival of the refugees from the south, bearing with them the traditions of their culture and accomplishments. It was presumably a small but creative element of the population that dared and survived the journey. The result was the foundation of many new cities, the development of which spanned the transition (artificial as it is) between the classical and post-classical periods. The most important group centred on Uxmal, just south of the modern capital of Merida.

Uxmal itself is very large and monumental; there seems to be no end to the enormous buildings looming out of the scrub. When associated with its satellite cities of Kabah, Sayil and Labná, it formed an almost continuous complex of ceremonial centres, gleaming white expanses joined by crowded causeways and stretching to the horizon, serving a busy and closely cultivated region like a huge market garden. What the architecture lacks in refinement as compared with the cities of the south, it fully makes up in grandeur; it conveys an overwhelming impression of opulence and power.

Indeed power, accompanied by increasing violence, is the keynote of the new Mayan age. There is a spirit of competition and aggression in the air. In Yucatán it took concrete form as the intrusion of a northern people of recent barbarian origin, the Toltecs, about whom more will be said in the next section. According to the traditions of both peoples, a migration or at least a major expedition of Toltecs reached Yucatán about the year 1000. Profiting from the internal dissensions of the Mayas, they seized and settled the country round the city of Chichén Itzá, which they dominated for a long time. At this period Toltec influence was paramount between Central Mexico and the Gulf and the occupation of Chichén Itzá was probably the furthest point reached in force by this enterprising folk.

The legend has it that the adventurers were led by Quetzalcoatl (in Mayan Kukulcán), the 'Plumed Serpent'. This is the half-mythical, half-historical King of the Toltecs whose personality and fabled exploits made such a powerful impact on the imagination of the peoples of the high plateau. At all events the Toltec settlement in Yucatán is a solid historical fact. Chichén Itzá rapidly became the leading city of the area. In it the Toltec element fused with the Maya and was eventually assimilated. The Toltecs introduced their own vigorous art and architecture, superb examples of which may be seen at Chichén Itzá alongside and in combination with the native Mayan styles.

29

Less happily, they also brought with them their warlike habits, thus initiating a long era of strife and slow decline. It is true that the fabric of civilisation was slow to crumble; the early Maya-Toltec period was one of great magnificence. For two or three centuries it held together, especially when the three cities of Chichén Itzá, Uxmal and Mayapán joined together in a league to impose peace. But the decadence is only too evident in the ruins of Mayapán itself which, though extensive, are quite devoid of aesthetic interest. While the Aztecs were at the height of their power, the Mayan world was dissolving in a chaos of savage tribal wars. When the Spaniards came on the scene all they found was the wreck of a civilisation, a ruined and disunited country. All the same, they had to fight hard to conquer it and suffered many setbacks. Fortunately they were sufficiently interested in the dying Mayan culture which they saw around them to record at considerable length the chronicles of the conquered people.

Other Classical and Post-Classical Cultures: the Zapotecs; El Tajín; Xochicalco; the Toltecs

In order to complete this survey of Mexico before the Aztecs it is necessary to describe four further regional centres of power and culture in classical and post-classical times. Each has its peculiar quality but the last and most important, the Toltec monarchy, is also significant as helping to bridge the gap between the fall of Teotihuacán and the emergence of the Aztec empire. The three other cultures are the Zapotec in Oaxaca, that of El Tajín in Central Vera Cruz and that of Xochicalco in Morelos.

The Zapotecs, despite these outside influences in the formative stage, made their own distinctive contribution to Mesoamerican culture. Their heyday corresponds almost exactly with the classical age in Teotihuacán and the Mayan 'Old Empire'. Their homeland was, as it is now, the broad fertile valley of Oaxaca and the mountains which border it. The country towns and villages were governed from the sacred hilltop of Monte Albán, the grandest ceremonial site in Mexico. Its architecture, always elegant and never pretentious, does justice to the lightness of the air and the incomparable mountain setting.

In their political organisation the Zapotecs conformed to the now familiar pattern of a theocracy staffed by a ruling and priestly caste. They were active traders and excelled in the crafts, particularly as potters and jewellers. Much of their art was devoted to the cult of the dead; the flanks of Monte Albán are honeycombed with the elaborate tombs of great personages, some decorated with wall paintings. All were found stocked with funerary urns of much beauty and originality; they are shaped to represent the dead in their richest ceremonial dress but often with startlingly realistic features.

So far as we can judge from their remains, the Zapotecs were a happy and self-sufficient folk, free from upheavals and violent changes. For nearly a thousand years they lived undisturbed in their valley. After about AD 800, however, they lost ground to the Mixtecs, a mountain people dwelling to the north of them, who began to encroach on their territory. The Mixtecs had not shared in the intellectual achievements of their neighbours; they were neither astronomers nor, before they occupied the valley, architects. But as craftsmen, and particularly goldsmiths, they were superior, witness the splendid treasure of one of their chieftains which was discovered in a Zapotec tomb appropriated by the invaders. They also worked beautifully in silver, jade, bone, rock crystal and (a significant innovation) copper. Perhaps it was their advances in technique that helped them to push the Zapotecs into the corners of their former domain and to occupy Monte Albán.

Another Mixtec speciality was the making of pictographic codices on which they crudely but colourfully recorded their traditions and the genealogies of their leaders; some of these survive in museums. This strange but gifted race deserved a better fate. They have long retreated into their mountains, where they eke out a precarious living in some of the harshest country in Mexico. The Zapotecs, on the other hand, are again the dominant race in the valley. They are an industrious and prosperous people, proud of having produced Benito Juarez, the hero of the modern Mexican nation.

From an historical point of view, there is little to tell about either El Tajín or Xochicalco. But it would be a mistake to pass over in silence these two great cities of the classical period. El Tajín lies in the heavily forested country of central Vera Cruz, and incidentally within the area of one of Mexico's richest oilfields. Until a few years ago it was almost entirely engulfed in jungle and even now, when there is no difficulty about access to the site, much of it remains unexplored. Its architecture—especially the famous 'niched' pyramid—has a character of its own but also shows traces of Mayan influence; indeed the inhabitants of the region (later to be known as Totonacs) were related to the Mayas. Their lively sculpture, of which there is a good collection in the Jalapa museum, specialises in gay and smiling figures reflecting a relaxed view of life. They also seem to have been particularly addicted to the ritual game which was played all over Mesoamerica.

Xochicalco, by contrast, stands on a bare hill-top on the edge of the plain of Morelos, with sweeping views over the surrounding mountains, a minor Monte Albán. Its builders have left no clues to their identity, but from the style of their sculpture they too had links with the Mayas. A more obscure problem is that of their affinities with Teotihuacán, for it is inconceivable that two centres of such importance could have flourished for so long side by side without impinging one on the other. Certainly the frieze of plumed serpents in relief encircling the base of the main temple at Xochicalco strongly recalls the serpent heads of the 'temple of Quetzalcoatl' at Teotihuacán. Archaeological evidence points to the survival at Xochicalco of a religious and cultural tradition which was transmitted by its rulers to the recently arrived Toltecs. It is also possible that it was through Xochicalco that the Toltecs conceived the urge to venture into the Mayan world.

With the advent of the Toltecs we enter a period when written records begin to take the place of archaeology as the principal source of our knowledge. The prestige of the Toltec monarchy in the Nahua-speaking parts of central Mexico was so great that it long outlasted the fall of the monarchy itself. During the confused times which followed, and throughout the Aztec domination, claimants to Toltec ancestry were held in the highest regard. Thus after the Conquest Indian chroniclers committed the Toltec traditions to writing, and though these annals naturally contain a large admixture of legend, they are by no means all story-telling. Below the fantasy there is a solid basis of fact. We are beginning to deal with real persons whose names we know and who led a real historical existence.

The Nahua tribes which destroyed Teotihuacán subsequently settled all over the Valley of Mexico and the surrounding regions mingling with the previous inhabitants. The leader who was chiefly associated with this phase of the conquest and assimilation, Mixcoatl, founded the Toltec kingdom at Culhuacán, now a village on the outskirts of Mexico City nestling under the sacred hill known as the Hill of the Stars. Here he was murdered and his throne usurped. But his infant son Topiltzin was smuggled away across the Ajusco mountains into Morelos where, according to

'Temple of the Warriors' at Chichén Itzá   (*J. Allan Cash*)

Detail from 'Temple of the Warriors'   (*J. March-Penney*)

The great plaza on the top of Monte Albán.

tradition, he was brought up by the priests of Quetzalcoatl at Xochicalco.

All his life Topiltzin was to remain a devotee of this god, who in his double form (the quetzal bird and the snake) symbolised, among other manifestations of duality, the morning and the evening star. When he came to manhood he set out to regain his father's throne and having accomplished this task, refounded the kingdom at Tula, in the state of Hidalgo. Here he reigned for nineteen years. These events took place in the second half of the tenth century.

The reign of Topiltzin was subsequently remembered by the Nahua peoples as a golden age of peace and plenty. As the high priest of Quetzalcoatl, whose name was soon substituted for his own, he did his best to tame the more barbarous tendencies of his subjects, to encourage agriculture and to promote the civilised arts in which he himself had been educated as a young man. The cult of Quetzalcoatl was developed at the expense of the worship of Tezcatlipoca, the traditional Toltec war god, with its emphasis on human sacrifice.

In later ages all sorts of superhuman feats and magical qualities were attributed to the King: the sixteenth century Spanish friar, Bernardino de Sahagun, in his marvellous *Historia General de las Cosas de Nueva España,* refers to him quaintly as 'otro Hercules gran nigromantico'. Like so many reformers, he was ahead of his times, and in due course a violent reaction against his rule was provoked by the priests of Tezcatlipoca. Eventually it proved too strong for Topiltzin-Quetzalcoatl, who was forced to abandon Tula. After a period of wandering between central Mexico and the coast, he is reputed to have headed the Toltec expedition to Yucatán, of which we have already taken note. But before he left he promised his followers that he would return, and foretold the calendar year in which this would happen. Since this turned out precisely to be the year in which Hernán Cortés landed at Vera Cruz, and the legends portrayed Quetzalcoatl as bearded and white-skinned, it is no wonder that in the year 1519 the emperor Moctezuma, a keen student of the traditions, was extremely perturbed.

Topiltzin left behind him a splendid capital, the ruins of which (despite their close proximity to the giant chimneys of Associated Portland Cement Ltd) are still tremendously impressive in a somewhat crude way. Toltec architecture and art, though receptive to Mayan influences, lack the refinement of the classical age. The huge Atlantean warrior statues which dominate the main temple of Tula typify the aggressive military spirit which defied the efforts of Quetzalcoatl and remained the distinguishing feature of Toltec society. Under a new dynasty it maintained its supremacy for another 150 years. The last King, Huemac, was unable to stem further nomad pressure on his northern boundary and fled from Tula in 1168. By the middle of the following century the last Toltec lordships in the Valley of Mexico had been overwhelmed by the exuberant wave of barbarism.

Chapter Two   The Aztecs

The nomads who took over the Toltec domain in the thirteenth century are known generically as Chichimecs, and this name continued to be applied to barbarians on the fringe well into Spanish times. They moved en masse into the settled country from their hunting grounds in the north and northwest. They had, however, long felt some civilising influences; indeed they were capable of building occasional towns and villages of unhewn stone, such as can be seen at La Quemada in Zacatecas. They were also capable of combining, for the purpose of invading the Toltec area, under a single chieftain, Xolotl, who headed the grand assault on the last Toltec defences in 1224.

Xolotl founded a Chichimec dynasty which maintained a separate identity, though later acknowledging Aztec overlordship, until the Conquest, but he did not establish a unitary state. Once the defences had been breached, the invaders tended to split up into small tribal groups, each occupying a separate point of vantage in the Valley. Here they fused with the remnants of the Toltecs and with the great mass of the indigenous population, among whom the newcomers from the north must always have been in a minority. Inevitably the groups were in conflict with each other; wars and skirmishes became endemic. But at the same time the Chichimecs quickly turned to permanent agriculture and the practice of the arts of peace which was to produce, in the century before the Conquest, the final flowering of Indo-American culture.

The small principalities or lordships were scattered thickly over the valley floor, a whole batch being contained within the area now comprised in the Federal District. Some groups settled further afield, for instance at Tlaxcala on the edge of the Puebla plain, and round Cholula which had been a centre of population since the Teotihuacán period. Xolotl himself chose Tenayuca, the site of an extant pyramid which goes back in its earliest form to Chichimec days. Another important lordship was Culhuacán, whose dynasty boasted Toltec descent and therefore enjoyed much prestige. In some cases a group would wander for many years before it could assert its ownership of a suitable piece of territory.

This was the fate of an insignificant tribe called the Aztecs. Tradition depicts them as a band of skin-clad archers who appeared primitive even by Chichimec standards and could only support life by hiring themselves out as mercenaries to the warring dynasts. They derived their name from Aztlán, a mythical island in the north which they regarded as the cradle of their race, but were also commonly known as 'Mexicans'. They were at first led by four chiefs who were at the same time priests of the tribal god Huitzilopochtli, whom the Aztecs worshipped as their special patron and as the personification of the sun in his glory.

The Aztecs pursued this precarious and vagabond existence for about a hundred years. Towards the end of the thirteenth century they found a temporary home on the hill of Chapultepec, where the palace of Maximilian stands today. They did not, however, succeed in staying there. Harried by the rulers of Culhuacán and Atzcapotzalco, they were forced to take refuge in the swamps bordering Lake Texcoco. The chronicle, in recounting their expulsion and final settlement with a wealth of legendary detail, attributes their disasters as well as their eventual salvation to the guiding hand of Huitzilopochtli. It tells how the priest of the god, appropriately named Cuauhcoatl (Eagle-Serpent) announced to the despairing Mexicans the divine message that they should establish themselves on a small island in the marshes, at the place where the eagle, now the emblem of the Mexican nation, was discovered perched on a tenochtli cactus and devouring a snake. This dramatic episode is dated to the year 1325.

The watery location of what was to become the great city of Mexico-Tenochtitlán was uninviting enough; at least it was not calculated to excite the jealousy of the numerous settlements already flourishing on firm ground around the shores of the lake. The Aztecs began by putting up a humble sanctuary to Huitzilo-pochtli on the exact spot where his great temple was subsequently to stand. They then faced the problem of adapting themselves to a semi-aquatic life and to wresting their livelihood from the lake itself.

This they did with such remarkable success that in little over a century they transformed what first resembled a prehistoric Swiss lake-village into something as marvellous, in Spanish eyes, as Venice. In the early days they created their fields and gardens artificially by piling mud on wattle rafts; they traced canals, dams, bridges and causeways; they traded the products of the lake with their neighbours on dry land for food and building materials. It was a drab and laborious way of life which called for the highest degree of discipline and determination on the part of rulers and people alike. As the generations passed, the prodigious effort of construction and organisation began to pay off: the city grew larger, more solid and more beautiful. It attracted artisans and merchants from all sides. Meanwhile the warriors, fighting first in the service of others and then on their own account, steadily and relentlessly extended the Aztec domain. Right from the start we have the clear impression of a purposeful and closely-knit control bent on achieving the paramountcy of tribe and nation.

From their lakeside retreat the Aztecs were well placed to watch the dissensions of their neighbours and to profit from them when occasion arose. In the mid-fourteenth century the main rival powers in Anahuac were the Chichimec dynasty, descendants of Xolotl, and the Tepanecs of Atzcapotzalco, whose original home had been near Toluca, to the west across the Sierra de las Cruces. The Tepanecs were the stronger and more aggressive. The Aztecs found it politic to pay them tribute and to serve them as mercenaries, and it was in this capacity that they helped in the destruction of independent Culhuacán and the expulsion of the Chichimecs from Tenayuca, whence they retired to Texcoco on the opposite side of the lake.

The Aztecs long enjoyed the advantages of being on the winning side. For over sixty years the Tepanecs were ruled by Tezozomoc, an able and unscrupulous leader who anticipated the Aztec monarchs of the fifteenth century in his ambition to dominate the whole of Anahuac and the neighbouring region of Morelos. During all his campaigns he was accompanied by his faithful dependants and allies, the Mexicans, who thus acquired a unique experience in pursuing a scheme of armed conquest. Tezozomoc was also a pastmaster of that type of astute diplomacy which consisted of playing off one party against another in a world of fragmented sovereignties and jealous intrigues. The latter part of his reign was occupied with a protracted struggle with Texcoco, during which period Ixtlilxochitl, King of the Chichimecs, resisted him bitterly and for a time successfully. In 1418, however, he was finally defeated and slain and his lands annexed.

His heir, Nezahualcoyotl, was driven into exile, and it seemed that Tezozomoc's goal of empire had been fulfilled, but the old man died in 1426 without having had much time to enjoy his triumph. His two sons were incapable of holding together a realm which had been built and maintained solely by the King's genius for war and diplomacy and was too flimsy to survive his death. It was the Aztecs who stepped straight into the power vacuum which then ensued.

We have seen how in the early years they had been governed by the four priests of Huitzilopochtli. In 1376, however, they were moved to elect a King. Their choice fell on one Acamapichtli (1376–95), who was said to be connected with the former lords of Culhuacán and thus possessed a claim to Toltec descent. He was succeeded by his son Huitzilihuitl (1395–1417). Both were in effect client-princes of their Tepanec overlord, and the third King of the Aztecs, Chimalpopoca (1412–27) was actually Tezozomoc's grandson. Unfortunately for him, he chose the wrong side in the contest for the succession between Tezozomoc's sons, and was ignominiously hanged by the victor. But no harm was done to the Aztec state. The notables promptly filled his place by electing Itzcoatl (1427–40), the son of Acamapichtli by a slave-girl.

Itzcoatl turned out to be a great king who paved the way for the transformation of Mexico-Tenochtitlán from a struggling principality into a wide-stretching empire. The first step was to deal with the remnants of the Tepanecs. This task was accomplished by the Aztecs in concert with the resurgent Chichimecs of Texcoco and with Tlacopán (the modern Tacuba), and the victory was sealed by the conclusion of an offensive and defensive alliance between the three cities which was to last until the Conquest. In the event Tenochtitlán swiftly outshone both her partners; Tlacopán lapsed into a mere suburb of the capital while Texcoco developed on different lines.

Tenochtitlán, on the other hand, immediately took the political and military lead. Under Itzcoatl, Aztec hegemony was substituted for the former Tepanec power in the Valley and the surrounding country, and the region of Anahuac consolidated as the base for future Aztec expansion into the non-Nahua lands to the east and south. Henceforth there was to be no doubt about the submission of the quarrelsome little cities of Anahuac to Aztec will. One curious anomaly, however, survived for some years within the very framework of the Mexican state. This was the independent existence of Tenochtitlán's twin city, Tlatelolco, which by its origins was as Aztec as Tenochtitlán itself but had managed to assert a separate political status under its own King. So long as the twin cities acted in harmony this illogical arrangement could continue undisturbed, but with Tenochtitlán aspiring to an imperial position it was clearly irritating for its ruler to have to tolerate even a nominally independent sovereign established nearer to his palace than Westminster is to the City of London and in control of the Cities' most thriving commercial centre. But it was not until 1473 that the Emperor Axayacatl picked a quarrel with the last King of Tlatelolco and had him hurled to death from the top of its pyramid.

Itzcoatl was succeeded by his nephew Moctezuma I Ilhuicamina (1440–69), the first Aztec ruler who deserves to be described as 'Emperor'. It was he who relentlessly launched the Aztec armies into a career of planned conquests outside the central plateau. The Aztecs first moved against the Totonacs of the Gulf Coast and their neighbours to the north and north-west, the Huaxtecs, a nation of the same stock as the Mayas inhabiting tracts of coastal and mountain country in the states of Vera Cruz, Puebla, Hidalgo and San Luis Potosí. The control of these regions was vital to the Aztecs as a source of agricultural and luxury products, in which they were extremely well endowed. Also their peoples, culturally sophisticated and pacifically inclined, were in no position to withstand ruthless aggression. Thus they were methodically subjected during the fifties of the century by a series of campaigns which left Tenochtitlán permanently enriched by the tribute of these brilliant and beautiful tropical lands. In the sixties a further drive was initiated in the direction of Oaxaca.

These conquests did not only gratify the Aztecs' lust for domination and material wealth: they also satisfied the strange compulsive need of their religion for sacrificial victims in the shape of prisoners of war. For the devotees of Huitzilopochtli, the welfare and glory of Tenochtitlán depended uniquely on the strength of the sun-god, which could only be nourished and renewed by human blood. The wider the growth of the Aztec state, the more insatiate the god's demands became. Already, in 1455, the inauguration of his grand new temple by Moctezuma, the first of the great imperial builders, was celebrated by the immolation of thousands of Huaxteca captives, and these ritual slaughters increased in scale as the century progressed.

The prevalence of human sacrifice among the Aztecs is the greatest stumbling-block to our appreciation of their culture. It shocks us nearly as much as it did the Spanish conquerors, who were notoriously unsqueamish in other respects, in spite of our efforts to understand Aztec religion and psychology and not to see things in black and white. Human sacrifice was practised throughout Mesoamerica in classical times, though on a restricted scale; there is, for instance, little or no trace of it at Teotihuacán. The peoples of Nahua stock, however, seem to have had a greater addiction to it. We have already seen how Quetzalcoatl failed in his attempt to keep it in check among the Toltecs. As for the Aztec religion, it would be unrecognisable without the essential element of propitiating the gods with human victims. The Aztecs worshipped a great variety of deities—their own tribal gods, the gods of earlier peoples with whom they had mingled and of others whom they had conquered. Most of these required human sacrifice in one form or another; for example infants were drowned in honour of Tlaloc the rain-god.

So far nothing distinguishes Aztec customs from the rites celebrated by other agricultural societies at a roughly similar stage of development. But the lives of the people were regulated to an unparalleled extent by religious observances, superstitious dread and astrological predictions; they firmly and universally believed that if the prescribed rites and practices were neglected, the processes of nature controlled by the gods would simply cease to function and the world would come to an end. But when all due allowances have been made, there is something unusually revolting—an unhealthy graft on the familiar growth of nature-worship—about the grand immolations of men in honour of Huitzilopochtli; one feels that a practice, barbarous though comprehensible and certainly not unknown in other parts of the world, had got thoroughly out of hand. It may well be that the chosen warriors of the Nahua region, once they were made captives, regarded death on the altar, where black-robed priests tore their hearts from their living bodies, as a natural and honourable fate, and looked forward to a future existence as attendants on Huitzilopochtli in the guise of humming-birds. Nevertheless one doubts whether the mass of miserable prisoners, grabbed at the taking of newly conquered or rebellious towns, and hauled in thousands to the sacrifice at the temples of Tenochtitlán, were animated by any sentiments except terror and despair.

The death of a single victim, drugged and bedecked with flowers and finery, at the festival of a nature-god, is a ritual which we can understand with little difficulty: it is otherwise with the butchery of ten thousand men rounded up after a battle. Only the massacres of a Tamerlane (who slew in cold blood without the excuse of religion) seem to us more senselessly savage. But what worried the rulers of Mexico was not the waste of lives but the risk that the gods might not receive their due quota of victims and visit their displeasure on the land by way of natural disasters. Hence the institution of a curious procedure known as the 'flowery war' (xochiyaoyotl), by which the lords of the triple alliance and of certain independent cities entered into a compact to conduct perfectly artificial hostilities, at times when they were normally at peace, for the sole purpose of procuring prisoners for sacrifice.

Nezahualcoyotl, King of Texcoco, was not primarily interested in warfare, although his soldiers took part in the Aztec campaigns and his small realm benefited from their conquests. He preferred to leave the main work of imperial aggrandisement to his allies, or confederates, the Aztec sovereigns. On regaining the Chichimec throne in 1428 he devoted himself to the well-being of his subjects and the encouragement of civilised ways. He won fame as a poet, a lawyer, a religious innovator and as a builder and engineer. For many years after his death and after the Conquest, men looked back to his long reign as a kind of twilight golden age, evoking the half-forgotten legends of Quetzalcoatl and contrasting vividly with the harsh glories of the masters of Tenochtitlán. But tradition has not exaggerated the achievements of this remarkable man. They are too solidly attested for doubt. Moreover he is fortunate in having as his chronicler one of his own descendants, Ixtlilxochitl, who compiled a valuable history in Spanish of his Chichimec ancestors. He emerges from these writings as the most interesting and versatile personality of his times.

Under his rule Texcoco became the second capital of the empire and the main source and inspiration of its cultural life. Beautifully sited in the narrow plain between the lake and the forested ranges which separate the Valley of Mexico from the Puebla uplands, just south of the ruins of Teotihuacán, it was sufficiently removed from Tenochtitlán to protect its identity and to exert its own influence. It was the acknowledged centre of learning and intellectual activity, the seat of a court of appeal for the whole empire, which was presided over by the King, and of an academy of letters, music and science founded under royal auspices. The Texcocans were proud of their handling of the rich and supple Nahuatl language, in which they claimed to surpass all their neighbours. They were fascinated by the power of the spoken word, especially as manifested in the most decorative eloquence and in delicately lyrical, allusive poetry.

The surviving verses reveal Nezahualcoyotl as profoundly conscious of the dignity and duties of kingship, but at the same time imbued with a grateful and philosophic pessimism, a disinterested spectator of the convulsions of his age. In his personal religion this detached habit of mind led him to superimpose on the fantastic Mexican pantheon his own austere conception of an unknown supreme creator without attributes, rites or sacrifices. This cult was, however, reserved for his chosen intimates and he was too wise to reject polytheism or oppose popular practices. So far as his public attitudes were concerned, he was the benevolent father of his people and the munificent patron of the arts, but also the sternest of lawgivers. So strict were his statutes that he felt compelled to have his heir and favourite son executed for adultery. He lived in magnificent style; the splendour of his court, the size and variety of his buildings, fully rivalled those of Tenochtitlán. On the hills behind his capital he laid out an immense park, planted with exotic trees and stocked with rare animals and birds. Water was channelled by aqueducts into an ingenious system of ponds and cascades, of which a faint trace survives on the dry hillside. Equally ingenious, and of great practical utility, was the long dike built across the lake from north to south to protect the city of Tenochtitlán from flooding; this was designed by the King for the benefit of his fellow-sovereign the emperor Moctezuma I.

His son and successor, Nezahualpilli, inherited his father's refined and intellectual tastes, but not his force of character, and the prestige of the Texcocan monarchy declined in quite a *fin de siècle* atmosphere of luxury and decadence. Meanwhile the Aztec emperors had lost none of their energy. Under the three successors of Moctezuma I, Axayacatl (1468–81), Tizoc (1481–86) and Ahuitzotl (1486–1502), the wars of expansion continued without interruption.

Whereas his predecessors had extended Mexican power in the direction of the Gulf, Axayacatl chiefly campaigned much nearer home. It was a peculiarity of the Aztec empire that it allowed free centres of resistance to subsist within a hundred miles or less from

42

the capital while the Mexican grip was being fastened on very much remoter areas on the coast or even south of the isthmus of Tehuantepec. Thus, beyond the volcanoes, Popocatepetl and Ixtaccihuatl, the republic of Tlaxcala and the cities of Cholula and Huejotzingo preserved their independence to the end. That the Aztecs tolerated this untidy situation can in part be explained by the requirements of the 'flowery war'; it was convenient to have an enemy available not too far away in case there was an embarrassing shortage of captives for sacrifice and there was no time to obtain them from the frontier provinces. But there is also no doubt that there existed in the independent cities of the plateau and their warrior folk a very real spirit of resentment and hostility towards the Aztecs. The Tlaxcalans in particular refused to be overawed; they were inspired by a genuine hatred for the enemies who hemmed them in from every side. Also the very outskirts of Tenochtitlán were not immune from a sudden attack from the men of Huejotzingo, who might cross the high pass between the volcanoes and raid into the valley by the same route as Hernan Cortés was to take.

Another such focus of independence was the valley of Toluca on the opposite side of Tenochtitlán. Here the Matlatzincas, a tribe related to the vanquished Tepanecs, maintained themselves in a group of towns clustering around another snow-capped volcano, the Nevado de Toluca. It was Axayacatl who reduced them to subjection. The Aztecs then found themselves up against much tougher opponents in the shape of the Tarascans. This nation, which had no kinship with the Nahuas and spoke a completely different language, inhabited a vast region in the states of Michoacán and Guanajuato, a fertile and temperate country of lakes and pine-covered mountains, highly volcanic and very beautiful. They had developed quietly on their own lines since the archaic period as a people of peasants and fishermen, without ever attaining a high level of culture. But they knew how to defend themselves; they were politically united and militarily a match for the invading Aztecs. This time the Aztecs were soundly beaten and never again attempted to swallow up their big neighbours to the West.

The defeat was a severe humiliation for Axayacatl. But he and his successors were intelligent enough to cut their losses. Thereafter hostilities with the Tarascans were confined to frontier skirmishes, and garrisons watched each other nervously from barriers of rude forts aligned in the mountains between the two states. The Tarascans, who were not of an aggressive disposition, did not attempt to retaliate.

The short-lived Tizoc and his successor Ahuitzotl were more ambitious and successful in their conquests. In the latter's reign the Aztec dominions were widely enlarged to the south until they reached the highlands of Guatemala and the fringes of the Mayan country. The reign of Ahuitzotl was marked by the worst excesses of Mexican imperialism. He has left a sinister reputation for ferocity and oppression, and it is recorded of him that he celebrated the reconstruction of the great twin temple of Huitzilopochtli and Tlaloc in 1487 by the sacrifice of twenty thousand prisoners in one day. So brutal was his treatment of the subject peoples that the word 'ahuizote' has survived in modern Mexican Spanish as signifying a bitter visitation or scourge. He gives an impression of overweening arrogance and ruthless efficiency. On his accidental death in 1502, the Aztec empire had reached the summit of its power, and despite rumblings of discontent it was a superb heritage for the next ruler, Moctezuma II Xocoyotzin.

Moctezuma was the son of Ahuitzotl. Before his election as emperor by the dignitaries of the realm he had occupied the high military post of *tlacochcalcatl*, a command generally reserved for members of the imperial family and future emperors, and which had given him frequent opportunities to display military prowess. It had also assured him a place in the emperor's inner Council. Besides being an experienced soldier and administrator, he was famed for his devotion to the gods and his punctiliousness in carrying out the rites and ceremonies. He is said to have been chosen as supreme ruler out of sixteen possible candidates. The omens were therefore favourable for another glorious reign, but one unmarred by the tyrannical conduct of an Ahuitzotl, for Moctezuma was of an altogether milder nature.

In fact his government was destined to be plagued by a series of revolts by angry or desperate tributaries, which were duly suppressed by the Aztec armies. But of the catastrophe which was to overwhelm the empire seventeen years later there was no hint in the air. The Aztecs were totally unaware that on the accession of Moctezuma a Spanish governor was already ruling in the island of Hispaniola (Santo Domingo), with jurisdiction over all territories in the Indies which might be discovered and conquered for his sovereign.

It is time to attempt a picture of this doomed society at its zenith. Two centuries of dynamic effort had changed the Mexican community beyond recognition. A small tribe had turned into a great state, an intricate organisation built on primitive foundations. The bands of rude hunter-warriors had transformed themselves into the sophisticated overlords of dominions stretching for hundreds of miles from the centre of government and embracing a veritable mosaic of peoples of different origins, speech and culture. They had created a military and administrative machine of extraordinary efficiency to dominate and control these territories. They had overcome formidable difficulties of geography and climate as well as the basic handicap of a technology which had not risen above the neolithic level. It should never be forgotten in estimating the achievements of the Aztecs that at the height of their development they still possessed no vehicles or draught animals.

The heart of the empire, and the masterpiece of Aztec endeavour, was the capital, Tenochtitlán. Together with its suburbs and satellite settlements it probably contained a million people at the beginning of the sixteenth century, roughly the same as the population of Mexico City in 1940. A traveller coming over one of the passes into the valley would have seen the shores of the lakes and surrounding country thickly studded with townships, each with its core of solid stone houses and brilliantly painted pyramidal temple, and with more modest villages of adobe and thatch set among the maize fields which sloped upwards to the forest's edge. The city itself presented a strictly geometrical appearance; it protruded into the lake in the form of a great square, joined to the mainland by three broad causeways leading north, south and west and protected on the east by Nezahualcoyotl's dike. Its traffic was carried mainly by canoe along the broad, straight canals, which either occupied the whole space between the houses lining them, as in Venice, or shared it with a street. They were spanned by a multitude of wooden bridges. Thus the city was divided into rectangular blocks.

The houses were generally of one storey; only the palaces of the imperial family and of the notables had two. No windows overlooked the street; consequently all the activities of the household were carried on in the interior patios and on the flat roof tops, both of which were embellished with gardens. Only the finer houses were built of stone and wood; the common sort were of white-washed adobe. Furniture, even in the grander establishments, was of the barest and the plainer dwellings contained virtually nothing but pottery and matting. But patios and rooms were bright with gay awnings and curtains, while the Indian love of flowers spread a mantle of colour over the whole scene. Above the low roofs towered the steep pyramids of the temples, crowned with gaudily painted shrines.

For administrative purposes the city was divided into four large quarters. Within these divisions, however, the basic unit was the *calpulli*, a word which is best translated as 'parish'. Each *calpulli* had its communal land, its temple and its council with an elected chief or president. Evidently this was a survival of the primitive social organisation of the Aztecs when they first settled in the valley. In the sixteenth century the chief was charged with a variety of exacting duties: he was responsible to the head of the Emperor's civil household for collecting taxes, for keeping the register of land and property and for providing a labour force for minor public works. In fact he and his subordinate officials had begun to resemble civil servants in a centralised bureaucracy rather than the democratically chosen representatives of the citizens.

The magnificence of Tenochtitlán was concentrated in its central plaza, which followed almost exactly the layout of the 'Zócalo' of modern Mexico City. Eminent among its fine buildings, the new palace of Moctezuma II stood on the site of the present National Palace, which was the seat of the Viceroys in colonial times and now houses the offices of the President and the Minister of Finance. The life of the Mexican empire flowed continuously through its spacious halls and courtyards. It revolved around the person of the supreme ruler, the Uei Tlatoani, just as the life of France in the seventeenth century centred upon the palace of the Sun-King at Versailles. Here the Emperor sampled the pleasures of his harem and dispensed lavish and unending hospitality to his subjects.

But the imperial dwelling-place was first and foremost the focus of administration, civil and military, for the Aztec realm. Moctezuma was personally a conscientious man devoted to the duties of his position. Not that he despised the amenities that fell to his lot, his choice foods, adornments and jewels, the exotic tribute of the provinces, his women, his hunting preserves, his gardens, aviaries and zoo; but apart from his due delight in the externals of power his whole life was dedicated to the fulfilment of his responsibilities as monarch. His was a full-time job that brooked no intermission. Indeed there is no record of his ever having quitted his capital or its environs in the course of his reign.

He left his campaigns to his chief captains and did not even indulge in formal progresses throughout his dominions. All his days were filled and circumscribed by an arduous and exact routine. As supreme judge, administrator and warlord, he unwearyingly conducted the business of empire and took all major decisions.

Moreover, although he ranked neither as god nor high-priest, the awe and reverence which he inspired invested him with a kind of semi-divinity and a delegated responsibility for the working of the will of the gods of Anahuac. The punctilious observance by the Emperor of the proper rites and ceremonials was regarded as crucial for the welfare of his people. He himself laboured, with dutiful humility, to fulfil this role of intermediary. The perfect autocrat in all his mundane acts, he dreaded the consequences of making a false step in relation to the forces of destiny which governed the nation. Devout to the point of superstition, he was exaggeratedly sensitive to the need of propitiating the gods and to the warnings of astrology and divination. And until the final test came, these qualities earned him deep respect.

In matters of administration his authority was upheld by an elaborate official hierarchy and intelligently delegated. Immediately below him, the chief honours devolved on a dignitary known as the Ciuacoatl (literally 'Serpent-Woman'), whose function was to deputise for the Emperor, whenever the occasion demanded, in his essential duties as head of State, to take decisions in the sovereign's name and to act as sovereign during an interregnum. He presided over the select council of empire which chose the new Emperor.

On the civil side, the principal official or secretary of state was called the *Uei Calpixqui*. He acted as head of the Emperor's household, as superintendent of the numerous bureaucracy of the capital, and as controller of the army of tax-gatherers charged with raising the tribute from the subject peoples of the empire. He was a very great functionary indeed and his emissaries, the subordinate *calpixquis,* though much dreaded and hated, demanded unquestioning obedience in the provinces. Once collected and stored in the palace and its dependencies, the revenue was the responsibility of the High Treasurer or Steward, the *Petlacalcatl,* who, like the other leading administrators, was served by a complicated organisation of officers and clerks.

Parallel to the administrative system functioned an equally complex judicial organisation, for the Aztecs, after graduating from their primitive ways, had developed a highly legalistic turn of mind and litigious habits. The judges were kept hard at work, and the harsh penalties they inflicted were equalled by the severity with which they were pursued if they were found guilty of corruption or arbitrary behaviour. As already mentioned, the higher court was presided over by the King of Texcoco himself. All this bureaucratic and legal activity called for the careful keeping of records in pictographic writing and resulted in the accumulation of vast official archives. If this mass of manuscript had not perished, practically in its entirety, at the Conquest, along with all but a fragment of the Aztec literary heritage, historians would now have available the most ample and detailed documentation of the social and political life of the Mexican nation.

Outside the capital, the emperor's authority was wielded by governors of towns and districts who might either be Aztec lords (*tecuhtli* is the title in Nahuatl) or, in the case of the subject peoples, their former rulers and chiefs who had been absorbed by the imperial system and made responsible to Tenochtitlán for the behaviour of their own folk. These governors possessed very wide powers, civil, military and judicial; their establishments were in effect a microcosm of the imperial court. They enjoyed a great number of privileges and immunities to compensate them for their onerous duties and the dangers of their position. The frequent revolts which disturbed Moctezuma's reign testify to the risks inherent in high office in the provinces groaning under the exactions of imperial *calpixquis*. Nevertheless these arduous offices were highly honorific and profitable; they also tended to perpetuate themselves in the same families.

The survival of the empire depended on the constant assertion of Aztec power and superiority in war. Consequently the military establishment had to be an even more highly organised and efficient instrument than the civil. Every Aztec citizen was expected to bear arms and to regard the profession of warrior as the most honourable service which a Mexican could perform. From childhood on he was encouraged to excel in personal bravery and military skills. Military service was a universal obligation for free men.

At a very early age the boys were sent to an institution known as the *telpochcalli* ('house of the young men'), where the principal object of their education was to train them as soldiers. When they had finished their training the youths were tested in battle, and their future prospects as warriors depended on the proficiency

48

they displayed. If the worst came to the worst, they were relegated to civil life. However a dazzling series of rewards was open to promising soldiers; they could aspire to the highest positions in the state. As they rose in rank the perquisites—lands, booty, slaves—increased in value. They became entitled to wear magnificent clothing and distinctive ornaments.

The military hierarchy was crowned with a galaxy of high officers with resounding titles, such as the *tlacatecatl* (senior commander in the field) and the *tlacochcalcatl* (responsible for organisation and supply). The dignitaries were usually drawn from the imperial family itself, but in practice as well as theory a man of humble origin could rise to the higher commands by virtue of his valour and efficiency. There were plenty of occasions for him to give proof of his talents, whether it was a matter of a stiff campaign against unconquered tribes or desperate insurgents, or of the ritual business of the 'flowery war', when it was the number of prisoners that counted, conducted as a grim tournament in which the stakes were earthly glory or the most honourable of deaths.

The élite of Mexican fighting-men were enrolled in two orders of knighthood (to use a European term), the Eagles and the Jaguars, who went into battle wearing fantastic feathered headdresses or the pelts of the beasts whose ferocity they strove to emulate. A headquarters of these orders, dating from the early sixteenth century, has been discovered at Malinalco, in wild mountain country between Mexico and Cuernavaca. This splendid site, decorated with eagle and jaguar emblems, conveys an overwhelming impression of the dignity and pride of these dedicated warriors. Led by such men, a Mexican host in battle order presented a fearsome spectacle. Its effect on the less martial tribes of Indians was shattering. The massed regiments, impeccably arrayed, surged forward beneath a swirl of feathers and banners, to the deafening accompaniment of drum beat, the moan of conch shells and the scream of whistles. If the enemy did not yield straightaway to panic—and thus provide the desired quota of captives—the weapons they had to face in close combat were formidable enough, though belonging in essence to the stone age. At close quarters the most deadly work was done by the *maquihuitl*, a wooden club studded with obsidian blades, which was the Mexican equivalent of a sword and capable of inflicting terrible wounds. Missiles were discharged by the javelin-thrower or *atlatl*, the bow and the sling. Protective devices, on the other hand, were not very effective, being confined to wooden targes and armour of padded cotton.

The priestly caste enjoyed at least equal prestige with the military, as was natural in so pious a community. While the warriors extended the empire and defended it against external risk, the *tlamacaxquis* (priests) protected it against supernatural menaces and the inevitable doom which was certain to overtake the world unless averted by skills which only the clerical sooth-sayers understood. They also had the function of setting a moral standard for society and establishing it by precept and example. They were consequently very numerous and their influence was all-pervasive.

Their hierarchy was if anything more elaborate than its civil and military counterparts. It was headed by the high priests of Huitzilopochtli and Tlaloc, who enjoyed equal status. They jointly controlled the great temple and ranked among the Emperor's most trusted counsellors. Each minor deity of the Mexican pantheon was similarly served by a high priest; each temple was staffed by resident clergy and a host of ecclesiastical dependents. Among the high personages of the church were a treasurer, who managed its vast estates and movable property, and a kind of nuncio who represented its interests in day-to-day business at the emperor's court. Finally the organisation and co-ordination of religious affairs as a whole lay in the hands of a national figure of immense importance, the *Mexicatl teohuatzin* or high chancellor.

In effect, the ecclesiastical establishment of the Mexican empire resembled that of the mediaeval church in Europe, and that was how it appeared to the more objective Spanish writers after the Conquest. While horror-struck by the bloody practices of the Aztec religion, they could not help admiring the discipline and abnegation of its priests, devoted as these qualities were to the cult of the devil.

For although the temples were rich, and their wealth was being constantly augmented by imperial generosity and the spoils of conquest, the clergy were as individuals bound by effective vows of poverty and celibacy. They lived up to the standard they them-selves imposed. Boys—and in some cases girls—were dedicated to the gods in early youth and placed under the care of temple priests. If these novices showed proof of a true vocation, they were admitted to a *calmecac*. This was a key institution in the Aztec community, since it provided a ritual link between the clergy and the lay ruling class. It served both as a religious school for candidates for the priesthood and as a training college for the sons of noblemen. While the young plebeians were receiving their military and civil training in a *telpochcalli,* the children of the lords—the *tecuhtlis*—underwent an even more rigorous preparation for their duties in life in a *calmecac* under priestly supervision. They were obliged to live in conditions of extreme austerity and were subjected to harsh discipline and penances, both spiritual and physical. At the same time they were formed in the intellectual accomplishments of their age and schooled in ceremonial manners. The whole object of their education was to produce a supply of leaders for state service.

The novices who shared their lot were destined for a different though no less exacting career, and were required to exercise for all their days the same severe virtues as had been inculcated in the *calmecac.* The more intelligent of the *tlamacaxquis* could look forward to responsible office in the Church bureaucracy or as teachers in the *calmecacs.* It was they, too, who were the repositories of learning and of the national traditions. But the great majority were employed in the performance of the complicated and unceasing rites and ceremonies of the Aztec religious calendar, in the celebrations of festivals and sacrifices, in the study of the heavenly bodies and in the practice of divination. The activities of individual Mexicans, as well as official decisions, hung largely on astrological predictions: consequently a whole category of priestly specialists were kept busy in the production of advice in the very broad field where the supernatural impinged on the conduct of ordinary business. Inevitably this function was abused by the less reputable practitioners of magic arts, and even today sorcery, divination and medicine are inseparably connected in the mind of the Mexican Indian.

We have seen that the primitive Mexicans had been free and equal within their strict tribal and theocratic framework, but that this simple state of affairs had changed quickly under the stimulus of their expansion. In 1500 Aztec society no longer pretended to be egalitarian. As the dominant race in Mesoamerica the Aztecs had evolved a class structure based on the privileged position of the administrator, the warrior and the priest, which had fully justified itself in terms of external triumphs. Nor were its successes achieved to the detriment of internal harmony and social cohesion. There is no evidence that if the Conquest had not taken place or had been indefinitely delayed, the Aztec state would have succumbed to social stresses and strains. Disaster overtook it when it was still healthy and gaining in vigour.

Indeed the Aztec nation, as distinct from the subject peoples which might resent Aztec rule but were powerless to challenge it, was well satisfied with its lot. Its citizens were proud of belonging to a master race. They joyfully accepted a settled order of things to which they could envisage no alternative. Barring a cosmic catastrophe which might admittedly be inflicted by divine forces if precautionary measures were not taken to avert them, nothing could disturb the serene continuance of state and society as they knew it, under the protection of the gods and the sway of the benign Emperor.

It is true that the privileged castes enjoyed enormous advantages, which in different circumstances might have caused jealousy and dissension. But it is equally true, and essential to an understanding of Aztec society, that their privileges were regarded as inseparable from their duties. There was no question of an aristocracy wasting its days in idle dissipation. Honours and wealth depended on merit and on the ability of the individual to maintain an exacting standard of service. For those who failed to make the grade justice was severe and the imperial displeasure swift and crushing, even for the most exalted *tecuhtli*.

Moreover the governing élite was being constantly recruited from below; there was no obstacle to the promotion of a talented commoner, once he had proved his worth, to the highest offices. Such promotion was accepted in theory and frequently occurred in practice. Naturally the *pillis* or young noblemen, the sons of the aristocracy of service, had the advantage of a good start over the commoners. Other things being equal, they had a better chance of winning the available rewards, and the evidence suggests that in the early sixteenth century a trend towards a hereditary oligarchy was being established. On the whole, however, society was still sufficiently fluid, and the educational system sufficiently flexible, to prevent social discontent. There is no trace of this sort of strife in the native chronicles, but plenty of warning for those in authority who neglected their duty.

Equally conducive to social harmony was the fact that all Aztecs (with the exception of an insignificant class of slaves, captives spared from the sacrifice or debtors pledged to their creditors) were free men with clearly defined rights and obligations. They were at least equal before the gods and the law. The commoners (*macehualtin*) had their own place and stake in society; they were no serfs, subject to arbitrary treatment by the state or individual masters. By virtue of his membership of the *calpulli* each had his share in the communal lands, guaranteed for his lifetime and subject to forfeiture for misbehaviour only. His children received the basic education through which they might, if gifted, attain honours and riches. In return for these elementary but important rights, he was liable to taxes and to various forms of civic and military service, all more or less onerous. Three quarters of the Mexican population consisted of these peasants, modest, frugal and hard-working, and it was on them that the stability of the empire ultimately depended. So did its economic prosperity, for the thickly populated region of Anahuac could never have maintained its supremacy if its soil had not been efficiently and productively worked.

Resting as it did on a firm agricultural base, the economy was enriched by the immense tribute accruing from the provinces. This was paid in every conceivable type of produce from the conquered lands. Everything—foodstuffs, building materials, textiles in bulk, gold, jewels, rare stones, spices, feathers, skin, live and dead birds and animals and many other commodities— was carried on the backs of thousands of porters, trotting docilely along the interminable trails leading to the capital. It would be impossible to put a value on the empire's revenues, since the Aztecs did not use money or any other convenient unit of calculation. Various commodities were currently accepted as a medium of exchange and taxes were counted in lengths of cloth. But in terms of goods the income from tribute was very large indeed; stored in the imperial treasuries or distributed to the deserving, it endowed the naturally austere Mexicans with a standard of living which they could never have reached as a non-imperial people.

It also provided the means of livelihood for an army of artists and craftsmen. In the capital and other towns these formed an important class of freemen, tightly banded together in guilds and holding themselves apart from the ordinary citizens. They were known as *toltecas,* which implies that their skills had been inherited from an older civilisation and transmitted through successive generations of artisans. Their high reputation is not belied by the excellence of their less perishable products as revealed by any and every excavation in Mexico City. Socially their exclusiveness lent them a prestige superior to that of the communal farmers, although there was no essential difference in their legal status.

Even more exclusive, and not fitting into any other category of Aztec society, was the merchant class. These merchants, or *pochteca*, must be distinguished from the petty barterers of the market-place. They were traders on the grand scale, the big bourgeois of the Aztec world. Their function was to exchange the produce and manufactures of Anahuac for the exotic goods which could only be obtained in the necessary quantities from across the southern border of the empire. For this purpose they had to fit out expeditions to these remote and dangerous lands whose inhabitants, though not averse to profitable trading, were fundamentally hostile and suspicious of Mexican encroachments. These merchant adventurers were organised in companies or guilds operating from the cities of the high plateau, according to a tradition which originated in Tlatelolco, Tenochtitlán's twin city, before its absorption into the empire. Every year great caravans of porters, under *pochteca* leadership and escorted by strong contingents of armed men, would set out for the southern frontiers.

The distinction between a commercial venture and a foray into untamed country in search of booty was indeed a thin one. Frequently the expeditions became engaged in stiff encounters with the local tribes, in which they seem to have showed the prowess of professional warriors. The imperial authorities were duly delighted when the *pochteca* emerged victorious from these obscure jungle battles. They were naturally by no means averse to using the merchants for spying out the frontier territories and preparing the way for Aztec expansion into hitherto un-garrisoned country. Successful capitalists, relying on the benevolence of a government and the efficiency of their own operations, reaped a plentiful reward. Their trade was extremely lucrative and amassed great wealth in the hands of private individuals.

It may seem odd that the state should tolerate, let alone encourage, the existence of so influential a closed caste which hardly fitted into the hierarchical scheme, and whose members derived their riches from private enterprise and not from state service. The *pochteca* were however protected against the jealousy of the grandees, provided that they kept within their station and did not flaunt their affluence. Even the most prosperous of them found it prudent to wear threadbare clothing in public and to affect a modest demeanour. When at home they lived in separate quarters, governed by their own regulations, worshipping their own gods and exempt from the duties of ordinary citizens.

Their profession was hereditary, like that of the craftsmen. It was the same sort of situation that prevailed in Jewish communities in Europe and the Middle East which were encouraged for economic reasons so long as they did not advertise their prosperity. The rise and increasing importance of a middle class towards the end of the Aztec era is a most interesting phenomenon; one wonders on what lines it could have developed further within a hierarchically organised society.

On the eve of its destruction Aztec civilisation was by no means in decline. The empire, far from teetering to its fall, had never been stronger. Revolts of the subject tribes were sternly suppressed and they had no real chance of reasserting their independence. They smarted under Aztec exactions but could do nothing about it. Although Moctezuma's reign had not seen any notable expansion of the Mexican realm, and there had so far been no repetition of the aggressive campaigns of his predecessors, there is no reason why conquests should not have been resumed by a new and more dynamic emperor. Outside the Mexican sphere, there was no other native power in Mesoamerica capable of challenging the Aztecs, much less of putting an end to their dominion. On the west and east respectively of the Valley of Mexico, the Tarascan Kingdom and the republic of Tlaxcala maintained an independence based on mutual respect or special reasons, but there was no danger to Tenochtitlán from either quarter. Nor did any threat impend from militant barbarians beyond the northern frontier, where the wild Chichimecs roamed as they had done for many centuries. The well-organised Aztec armies could chastise them with the utmost ease if their raiding parties overstepped the mark. To all appearances the empire was at the apex of its power, or had not yet even reached it.

We have also seen that the structure of society was sound and did not contain the seed of internal decay. It was held together by an unquestioned, fatalistic religious discipline, a strong consciousness of national superiority and an innate feeling for order, justice and the dignity of the individual. These admirable qualities were not of course displayed in the relations of the Mexicans with their subjects and neighbours. In this field they only too often exhibited a strain of brutal prussianism of the Ahuitzotl type, a compound of arrogance and a distorted (to our minds) sense of religious compulsion. But it should be recognised that the life of Anahuac was a well regulated and smoothly functioning mechanism perfectly suited to the needs of its people.

Nor is there any sign that internal stability was likely to be undermined by economic weaknesses. The land was intensively cultivated and supported a much larger population than at any time before the mid-twentieth century and the diet of the people, though simple, was healthy. The elementary rules of cleanliness and hygiene were strictly observed (every citizen regularly went to the steam bath or *temazcalli*, even if he did not have one in his house), and it was left to the Europeans to introduce lethal epidemics. Famine was indeed not unknown—there had been several disastrously lean years in the reign of Moctezuma I—but it had ceased to be a serious menace since the Aztecs had laid their hands on the best maize-growing lands between the capital and the Gulf coast. At the moment there was sufficiency for all and a superfluity for the minority. In these circumstances an agricultural economy virtually unchanged since the days of Teotihuacán might have lasted indefinitely without the Indians ever receiving the necessary mental stimulus for inventing the wheel or the plough, or for developing metallurgical skills.

The Aztecs were pre-eminent as craftsmen but their performance in the fine arts did not equal the achievements of the classical cultures. They had nothing original to contribute, for example, in the way of architecture, although the monuments of Tenochtitlán imposed by their size and number. They were at their best as sculptors. The temples and other public buildings were filled with reliefs and free-standing statues. Even the scanty remnant of these which has survived the Conquest is tremendously impressive. In the mass they must have been overpowering in their effect, if too heavy and barbaric for our taste. We may find the great set pieces —the Aztec calendar, the huge statues of the deities with their elaborate carving and savage imagery, the ferocious representations of imperial victories—less satisfying than the simple but altogether delightful stone coyotes, eagles or tortoises, half stylised, half naturalistic, which welcome us in the Mexico museum. The paintings in fresco which also adorned the city have perished, but we can derive a faint idea of what they were like from the pictographic manuscripts that have survived. In general there is a certain rigidity about Aztec art which makes one suspect that it was unlikely to have developed new forms of expression.

The picture presented in the preceding paragraphs is of a vigorous and healthy, but nevertheless static society. For it is hard to resist the conclusion that, despite its strength and brilliance, it had reached a dead end. It was incapable of change; either it remained as it was, or it must disappear in the sort of cataclysm predicted by Mexican astrologers. The common tendency is to deplore the Spanish conquest as having put an end to a unique and valuable civilisation, as if this could have somehow been indefinitely preserved, like a fly in amber, a neolithic curiosity surrounded by an alien world changing at an ever increasing rate.

Such an attitude is understandable but quite unrealistic. Obviously the ancient Mexican world was destined to collapse at the first clash with invaders possessing a greater technical capacity and a more adaptable intellectual outlook. It mattered little whether the death blow was administered by the Spaniards, English or the French (to name the European powers in the running). Moral condemnation of the Conquest should be directed, when appropriate, to the methods employed, not to the fact itself. One suspects that if the conquerors of Mexico had been sixteenth-century Englishmen, the process of destruction would have been even more radical and horrible than it was when carried out by Spaniards. The wonder is that the Conquest had so many mitigating features, that so much of the Indian heritage survived to mingle with the exotic currents that flowed from Europe. It is this intermingling of the two cultures, after the appalling vicissitudes of the invasion, that makes the study of Mexican colonial history so fascinating.

A strait only one hundred miles wide separates the north-east corner of the Yucatán peninsula from the western tip of the island of Cuba. Given a fair wind, the passage to the mainland was no problem for the caravels which had regularly braved the Atlantic crossing since Columbus made his epic voyage in 1492. All the same, a quarter of a century went by between the discovery of America and the first Spanish landing on Mexican soil.

The Catholic Kings, Ferdinand and Isabella, had of course no idea of the immense territories which the Spanish Crown might acquire as a result of this and later discoveries. They were far more deeply concerned with the conquest of Granada, the last stronghold of the Moors in their Iberian homeland, which fell to their armies in the same year. Nevertheless the royal authority was duly established in the Indies with Hispaniola (the present Haiti and Santo Domingo) as the headquarters of the Viceroy and Governor-General and the main field for Spanish colonisation. Using Hispaniola as a base, the colonists—those who preferred adventure to the exploitation of estates by Indian forced labour or had been unable to get themselves estates—prepared to explore and subjugate other lands in or beyond the surrounding seas. They frequently attached themselves to the expeditions which continued to be organised in the mother country. In the earlier years exploration was chiefly directed towards the eastern and northern seaboards of South America and the isthmus of Panama (Darien). So far nobody suspected the existence of a continent lying directly to the west.

In 1509–10 two such ventures in the Panama region suffered terrible hardships and losses and nearly came to grief altogether.

Eventually Balboa, the first to look upon the Pacific, succeeded in founding a colony. The Viceroy of the Indies, who happened to be Diego Colón (son of the discoverer) then decided to concentrate on territories close to his base. First Puerto Rico was occupied, and in 1511 an expedition was despatched under Diego Velázquez to conquer Cuba. This task was soon accomplished, for the inhabitants offered little resistance. In 1512 Ponce discovered Florida, far to the north-west. But it was not till 1517 that the Spaniards set foot on the Mexican mainland.

In that year a landowner in Cuba named Francisco Hernández de Córdoba, with the blessing of Velázquez (now appointed Governor of the island) collected a party of one hundred and ten men and sailed with three ships towards the west. He was swept by a storm into the Gulf of Campeche and after three weeks' battering made a landfall on the west side of Yucatán. Almost at once the Spaniards came across a stone-built city and an Indian population with a notably high standard of civilisation and a far fiercer disposition than the helpless Caribs whom they were accustomed to enslave. The local Mayas were not cowed by the outlandish appearance of the intruders or by their superior armament. Wherever the Spaniards attempted to land they were attacked and forced to retreat to their ships. Finally they were thoroughly beaten, with the loss of half their number killed, in a pitched battle near the present city of Campeche, where, according to tradition, Mass was celebrated for the first time on the Continent. After this disaster they had no choice but to sail back to Cuba, where their leader died of his wounds.

Velázquez, however, refused to be discouraged. Despite his obesity which was considered quite a joke at the time, he was an active and ambitious man, anxious to gain credit for winning new lands for the Crown, as well as profit for himself. He lost no time in recruiting a new force of 240 men and four ships, which he placed under the command of his kinsman Juan de Grijalva. They left Santiago de Cuba in January 1518 and arrived, after three days sailing from the western end of Cuba, at Cozumel, the large island off the eastern coast of Yucatán which has lately become famous as a tourist resort. Finding it deserted, they crossed to the mainland, where to their astonishment they caught sight of the houses and temples of a city which one of their number described as being the size of Seville, gleaming white on the cliff's edge. It was an eloquent tribute to Mayan civilisation, splendid even in decadence, and the ruins of the city in question, Tulúm, are still very impressive. But Grijalva found the Mayas as truculent as those encountered by Hernández de Córdoba on the other side of the peninsula. Again a bloody battle took place, and again the Spaniards retired to their ships. They proceeded cautiously round the corner of Yucatán and down the coast, passed Campeche and came to Tabasco, a flat, marshy country intersected by innumerable creeks and rivers. Here Grijalva parleyed inconclusively with the Indians, who were obviously preparing another hostile reception for him, using as his interpreters two natives of Yucatán who had been taken prisoner in the previous expedition. After an exchange of gifts he wisely sailed away.

The squadron coasted slowly northward until it reached the latitude of Vera Cruz. The Spaniards beheld with wonder, glittering in the western sky, the perfect snowy symmetry of the highest mountain in Mexico, Citlaltepetl or the Pico de Orizaba. Their progress was observed, with equal wonder, by watchers on the coast, and when they arrived at the mouth of a river (probably the Papaloapam) they were met and courteously greeted by a flotilla of canoes. This time the Indians were agreeable and hospitable: the Spaniards were feasted and presented, at their own request, with a quantity of gold. The Aztec officials who directed this entertainment sent messengers speeding to Tenochtitlán to announce the extraordinary news and to convey to their emperor their first impressions of the strangers (with whom they were unable to converse because the interpreters did not understand Nahuatl).

Grijalva, for his part, seems to have realised that his expedition had run up against a formidable power with which he had neither the initiative nor the resources to deal. In any case he lacked the persistence to go any further in his enterprise. He sent one of his captains, Pedro de Alvarado, to report to Velázquez and ask for guidance. But before this could reach him he decided to break off the expedition altogether and followed Alvarado back to Cuba. Velázquez, however, reacted with vigour to the fiasco of Grijalva's expedition. Before the year 1518 was out, another had been mounted. This time the leader was a very different character from the indecisive Grijalva. His name was Hernán Cortés.

Cortés was a native of the town of Medellin in Extremadura. He was born in 1485 of a family of modest gentlefolk. In 1499 he was sent to the University of Salamanca, where he studied grammar (that is, Latin) for two years as a preparation for taking his degree in law. But to his father's disappointment he grew disgusted with academic life and suddenly quit the University. For the next three years he appears to have led a vagabond existence up and down the highways of Spain, uncertain whether to enlist for service in the Italian wars or to try his luck in the Indies. Having opted for the latter, he missed a first convoy in 1502 owing to an amorous scrape.

Eventually he embarked in 1504 and after a difficult voyage arrived in Santo Domingo. He brought with him no material assets, but he had courage and natural charm in plenty, besides quick wits, a good basic education and more than a modicum of ambition. He also carried a family recommendation to the Governor-General, Nicolas de Ovando. Thanks to this connexion a post was soon found for him as Notary Public of a small settlement called Azúa; he was also presented with farmland and a draft of Indian labourers. It seems that despite his failure to take a degree, Salamanca had furnished him with the necessary rudiments of legal training. Here he remained for some years, dividing his time between his job, his farm and a number of more or less disreputable love affairs. He did not leave Santo Domingo until Velázquez invited him to join the expedition of 1509 to Cuba as his personal secretary and also in the capacity of King's Treasurer. These appointments produced a significant improvement in his fortunes, as well as some dangerous moments. During the next decade his life revolved round his peculiar and complicated relationship with Velázquez, who regarded him alternately with cordial favour and irritated distrust.

The trouble began with a dispute over a girl, Catalina Xuarez, whom Cortés had seduced but was reluctant to marry, thus incurring the Governor's disapproval. More serious was the secretary's tendency to become involved in intrigues against his chief in the turbulent period of the settlement of Cuba. Whatever the rights and wrongs of the matter may have been, Cortés was clapped in prison and was lucky to escape summary execution. He succeeded, however, in breaking out of gaol and accomplished the double feat of reconciling himself with the girl's irate father, having agreed to marry her, and of restoring himself to the good graces of the equally infuriated Velázquez. It was an achievement that speaks volumes for his charm and ability to wriggle out of the most awkward situations. He went on to become Alcalde or chief magistrate of the important town of Santiago, which meant that he was now a personage to be reckoned with on the island.

From the security of this post he watched the abortive ventures of Hernández de Córdoba and Grijalva. If, as is probable, he had already conceived the ambition to be a conqueror, he was well placed to profit by their experience and to learn to avoid their mistakes. By 1518 he judged that the moment he had been waiting for had arrived, and he readily accepted Velázquez' proposal that he should lead the new expedition. He was then thirty-three, popular, successful and well versed in colonial politics. But he possessed no military experience to speak of and his talent for the higher statecraft was as yet unsuspected. Fortunately he was supremely self-confident and was fast developing the gift of inspiring confidence in others.

The months preceding the departure of his expedition were rich in intrigue. Velázquez was convinced that Cortés had the right qualities to succeed where the others had failed. But he wanted the glory and profit for himself; so he had to try to ensure that he did not lose the spoils either to his superior, the Governor-General, or to his commander whom he could never entirely trust. The problem for Cortés, on the other hand, was to keep in favour with all the higher authorities while awaiting an opportunity of throwing off his subordination to Velázquez. He exerted himself to attract the best men to his banner and staked his personal fortune on the enterprise. He also adroitly arranged that the instructions from Velázquez to himself should be drafted with the maximum of ambiguity and give him, in effect, a free hand to conquer and settle whatever territories he considered ripe for occupation.

As time went by and the preparations neared completion, Velázquez took fright and tried to call the whole thing off. But it was too late for him to intervene effectively. Enthusiasm for Cortés was running high in the colony and he could afford blandly to disregard the Governor's protests and orders. He stood out to sea on 18 November 1518. When all his forces had approached their rendezvous, and the armada finally left Cuban waters, it consisted of eleven ships with five hundred and eight soldiers, one hundred seamen, sixteen horses and fourteen cannon. It was not until mid-February that, following the example of Grijalva, Cortés landed in Cozumel.

The company of adventurers mustered there by their untried leader consisted of about the toughest human material which the Spanish Indies could produce. Some were veterans of the Italian and Moorish wars; others had seen hard service across the Atlantic. Of the captains, Alvarado, Montejo and Dávila had accompanied Grijalva. Bernal Díaz del Castillo, who was to become most famous among the common soldiers and to write the history of the Conquest in extreme old age, had narrowly escaped with his life both in Darien and in Yucatán. Such men were not easy to handle. Though accustomed to military discipline, they were also Spaniards, critical and anarchic individualists only too ready to repudiate a commander who did not know his job. There was also a strong element among them more inclined to Velázquez than to himself. He had made a good start, but could not afford to put a foot wrong. Had he shown signs of weakness at the inception of the enterprise, or had behaved arrogantly and inequitably, he would not have lasted a month. Luckily he possessed an unerring talent for combining iron firmness with the most gracious tact and affability. He soon established a hold on the imagination and affections of his men. As for his ulterior intentions, he was an adept at keeping his own counsel but gradually infecting the soldiers with his aims and enthusiasms. When the time was ripe to march on Tenochtitlán, he had welded them into a deadly instrument of aggression.

In the meantime he followed the same route as Grijalva, but with better fortune. At Cozumel he picked up a Spaniard named Aguilar, one of the only two survivors of a party of Spaniards from Jamaica who had been cast upon the Yucatán coast eight years before. The other, Guerrero, refused to be rescued; he was quite content with his new life as a Mayan chieftain, married and the father of the first children of mixed (mestizo) race in Mexico.

On 12 March, Cortés arrived off Tabasco, where he found the natives determined to resist a landing. Aguilar was sent to reason with them, but in vain. In the subsequent battle the Spaniards deployed their artillery and the little troop of horse with devastating effect; the Indians were routed and consented to parley. Cortés mounted for their benefit a ceremony of taking possession of the country in the name of Charles the King-Emperor, but he had no more intention than Grijalva of staying there. He set out to sea again after graciously accepting the Indians' apologies and presents, among which were twenty girls. These ladies were promptly baptised and distributed among the captains. One of them turned out to be the daughter of a Mexican (Nahua) notable who had been traded into servitude among the Mayans. Being of a different class from the others, she was distinguished with the title 'Doña', tacked on to her baptismal name Marina, and handed over to Alonso Hernández Puertocarrero, a man of noble birth and a particular favourite of Cortés. She was destined to play a crucial as well as a romantic part throughout the Conquest. In its early stages she and Aguilar had to work together as interpreters whenever Cortés wished to communicate with speakers of Nahuatl. His words were rendered into Mayan by Aguilar and by Marina into her own language. In such a roundabout manner the vital transactions of the coming months were conducted.

Easter saw the Spaniards established in an insalubrious camp among the sand dunes near the future site of Vera Cruz. Here they were at once brought face to face with the local Aztec authorities and with a succession of special emissaries from Moctezuma himself. A complicated process of probing and negotiation then began which lasted until mid-August. This period was one of desperate tension for both the Emperor and Cortés.

Moctezuma gave orders that the Spaniards should be amicably and hospitably received while his agents collected information about them and their reports were digested and interpreted by his political and spiritual advisers. It was of course most important for him to establish whether the newcomers—or their leader— were of divine origin. If they were gods, there was a chance that they might be suitably propitiated and persuaded to go away, although this job might well tax the ability of the most experienced of priestly magicians; for if Cortés were really Quetzalcoatl, would he not insist on claiming the long-abandoned heritage of the Toltecs? But if the strangers were adjudged not to possess the divine attributes, and merely to rank as alarmingly powerful human beings, there was also a good chance that they might be successfully dealt with by diplomacy or force. The trouble was that Moctezuma could not make up his mind one way or the other. For a start he despatched a cargo of carefully chosen as well as costly gifts to test Cortés' reactions: they included the masks and characteristic regalia of three major gods, Tezcatlipoca, Tlaloc and Quetzalcoatl, besides a dazzling assortment of jewels and golden objects.

Cortés failed to solve the Emperor's problem for him by assuming or clearly rejecting a divine role. The gifts, however, opened his eyes to the opulence of the Aztec civilisation. He grasped immediately that unimaginably valuable prizes awaited him beyond the mountains. From the first he was at pains to impress the Mexicans with the invincibility of his arms and the power of his master the King-Emperor. He also informed them that he wished to go up to Tenochtitlán and greet Moctezuma in

64

VERACRUZ

17th Century Spanish Painting of the Conquest of Mexico

(Ministry of Public Building and Works)

CONQUISTA DE MEXICO POR CORTES. A⁷

17th Century Painting of the Conquest of Mexico. Artist unknown

(Ministry of Public Building and Works)

person. From the horrified reception of his proposal and the repeated arrival of fresh embassies bearing more splendid presents he deduced that the imperial authority might be feeble and vacillating.

An even more interesting indication that all was not well within the Aztec empire came from the Totonacs of the neighbouring city of Zempoala, ruled by the famous 'fat *cacique*' who appealed to the Spaniards not only as a useful ally but also as an endearing figure of fun. The Totonac envoys spun a long tale about Mexican oppression which fell on receptive ears. They were promised Spanish protection and, as it happened, the assurance was immediately put to the test by the appearance of five arrogant Mexican tax-collectors (*calpixques*). At first the Zempoalans were so frightened that they prepared to accede to these officials' demands that they should sever their connexion with the white men and provide forthwith twenty victims for sacrifice to the Aztec gods. Later, stiffened by Spanish support, they plucked up courage, bundled the *calpixques* into prison and would have immolated them had Cortés not secretly abducted them and sent them up to Tenochtitlan with a polite word to the Emperor.

Having thus adroitly attached the Totonacs to his cause without openly aligning himself with them against the Aztecs, he proceeded forcibly to convert them to the true faith; their idols were cast down and their shrines purged. Mass was celebrated by Father de Olmedo, chaplain to the expedition, and the proceedings were crowned by a present from the *cacique* of six Totonac girls. The ugliest, being the niece of the chieftain, Cortés was obliged to take for himself.

So far his relations with the native powers had developed not unfavourably. A more exciting drama, however, was played out within the ranks of the Spaniards themselves. Inaction, disease and fear of the unknown were having a dispiriting effect on the soldiers, who had lost thirty of their number from various causes. There was a very natural urge to return to Cuba with the spoil already acquired, and this was exploited by those who considered that Cortés was exceeding the powers granted by his commission from Velázquez. Cortés saw that unless he quickly repudiated the Governor's supremacy and put an end to faction among his troops he would never succeed in marching inland. On the other hand, he was reasonably sure that most of his men were eager to support him in establishing a permanent settlement on the mainland. Whether they, or even Cortés, fully understood the

E

implications of this course in terms of subduing Aztec resistance is another matter.

The turning point in his struggle with apathy and opposition from the supporters of Velázquez was the decision to found a city, which his critics were not strong enough to block. It was a popular move and flattered the imagination of the soldiers. So the first Spanish town in Mexico, 'La Villa Rica de la Vera Cruz', was created with the solemn observance of the proper legal forms. The new citizens duly appointed their magistrates; they then proceeded to declare null and void the instructions from Velázquez to Cortés and to elect the Governor's former deputy as their Captain-General, with full military and legal powers. This meant that Cortés was henceforth directly responsible to the King and could not be held to account by any intermediate authority.

It was a tricky operation and concluded just in time, for a ship fitted out for the venture, but not finished when Cortés sailed, struggled in with the news that Velázquez had been specifically granted rights of mainland settlement. Cortés thereupon decided to send a ship directly back to Spain carrying a justification of his actions to the King as well as the royal share, or fifth, of the treasures hitherto collected. As Captain-General he too had the right to a fifth, while his captains and soldiers would now receive their normal due according to the rules with which Cortés, the former Royal Treasurer in Cuba, was perfectly familiar. On board the ship which sailed for Spain was his confident Puerto-carrero, the man to whose care he had entrusted the by now indispensable Doña Marina. As soon as his friend had left he wisely appropriated Marina for himself, and she remained under his tent until the Conquest was achieved.

The moment had now almost come for the army to begin its march, but in the month before it set out three significant events occurred. The first was a straightforward plot to overthrow Cortés which he crushed with ease; two of the ringleaders were summarily executed. The second was his bold stroke in putting his ships out of commission. He did not, as the oft repeated fable relates, set fire to them; he merely had them beached and stripped of their gear, so as to tender them unseaworthy. The sailors who had manned them joined the depleted ranks of the army. Lastly he received a fresh reminder that other ambitious commanders with credentials conflicting with his own were pressing on his heels. This took the form of three ships with two hundred and seventy soldiers, under a lieutenant, of Francisco de Garay,

Governor of Jamaica. But on hearing that the country was already settled they providentially vanished over the horizon. Thus Cortés had accomplished with incredible dexterity the feat of cutting his links with Cuba without gravely upsetting his followers. Having surmounted the immediate obstacles at the Spanish end, he was free at last to penetrate inland. He took with him four hundred men, that is his original company, minus the wastage of five months and a small rear party at Vera Cruz commanded by Juan de Escalante.

August in Mexico is the height of the rainy season. For the first few days the army toiled through the deluges and steamy heat of the coastal plain. The men bore their personal weapons only; the rest, baggage, stores and artillery, was on the backs of hundreds of Zempoalan porters. Some prominent Zempoalans accompanied the expedition as advisers, together with a number of Aztec guides—or spies. The way led roughly along the modern road from Zempoala to Jalapa (now the official capital of Vera Cruz state), where the tropics give way to fresh, grassy country, and as the road winds steeply up the escarpment to the thick forests covering the mountain known as the Cofre de Perote.

Having traversed this region, a wide, chilly plateau, the army halted on the confines of the republic of Tlaxcala, half-way between the coast and Tenochtitlán. The austere upland country reminded the Spaniards of Castile. In the distance the three great snow mountains, Citlaltepetl, Ixtaccihuatl and Popocatepetl, were clearly visible. The approaches to the republic were marked by a stone boundary wall.

Cortés, who had been apprised of the traditional hostility between Aztecs and Tlaxcalans, was bent on enlisting the latter as allies. For this purpose he sent them an embassy of eminent Zempoalans, who addressed themselves on his behalf to the governors of the republic. Tlaxcala was not a monarchy on the Aztec pattern; the supreme power resided in four chieftains (*tlatoanis*) of equal status, each representing a distinct section of the people, and important decisions required unanimity. After long debate these dignitaries resolved to oppose the stranger's entry into Tlaxcalan territory. They were well aware that a dialogue had been proceeding for months between Cortés and Moctezuma, and were unwilling to incur the risk that Spaniards and Aztecs were plotting to suppress their independence. When, therefore, Cortés, receiving no answer, lost patience and passed his army through the wall, he was attacked by Tlaxcalan forces under Xicotencatl the younger (to distinguish him from his father, one of the *tlatoanis*).

At the first encounter the Spaniards easily prevailed, but with every advance the opposition became stiffer. The military issue was settled after two great battles in which the Spaniards tasted the terrors of facing a Nahua army in full panoply and bent on a desperate struggle. Many times they were engulfed and well-nigh overwhelmed by tens of thousands of disciplined warriors. They lost over fifty men and if the Tlaxcalans had challenged them for the third time they might have preferred to retreat. But the enemy had suffered appalling losses, especially from artillery fire, and having tested the Spaniards' mettle, were beginning to lose their appetite for fighting. They tried a night attack but it too was a failure. Cortés countered with destructive raids against Tlaxcalan villages and hostilities gradually petered out.

The Tlaxcalans had also reached the conclusion that it would be in their political interest to make peace. Even before fighting stopped they had noticed with alarm the presence in the Spanish camp of a new and important embassy from Tenochtitlán. They therefore assured Cortés of their future amity and begged him to enter their city. They sent him ample provisions and gifts. But Cortés was in no hurry to accept their invitation or to dismiss the Aztec envoys. It was only when the four chief magistrates presented themselves in person as suppliants that he consented to move, and even then he brought the Aztecs with him. He continued to play off the rival Nahua states against one another, enjoying their recriminations and exciting their mutual jealousy and mistrust.

At the same time, however, he was seriously troubled by signs of faint-heartedness among his soldiers. It took all his tact and power of persuasion to overcome their disinclination to take on the Aztec forces, which they knew to be more formidable than anything the Tlaxcalans could put into the field. But a good rest and a respite from fighting soon heightened their morale and by the time the army made its formal entry into Tlaxcala on 23 September confidence was more or less restored. It mounted further during the ensuing month, which Cortés spent in strengthening his relations with Tlaxcala and preparing his march on the Valley of Mexico. Messages continued to flow between his camp and Moctezuma's palace. He adamantly rejected the Emperor's pleas that he should not pursue his journey to Tenochtitlán and despatched Alvarado over the mountains on a probing mission. Alvarado actually reached the lakeside before being forbidden to proceed further. Finally Moctezuma appeared to change his mind and suggested that if the Spaniards insisted on coming to his capital, they should take the road through Cholula. Disregarding the warnings of the Tlaxcalan chiefs, who thoroughly distrusted the Cholulans as vassals of Moctezuma, Cortés agreed.

The array which left Tlaxcala on 13 October included, besides the small and steely nucleus of Spaniards, the Zempoalan contingent and a strong corps of Tlaxcalans, as well as all the porters required. To reach Cholula they needed only a day's march through flourishing, well-cultivated country. Cholula was a populous city dating from at least the Toltec era and sacred to the god Quetzalcoatl. According to the legends it had also sheltered Quetzalcoatl, the hero-king, on his expulsion from Tula. His temple adorned the huge pyramid which still dominates the landscape.

The Spaniards were received by the Cholulans with formal politeness, but they soon suspected that their hosts, egged on by Mexican emissaries, were plotting an attack on them. They noticed unmistakable signs of warlike preparations and the Cholulans' demeanour became less and less agreeable. Finally an old woman sought out Doña Marina and warned her that a trap was being laid for the strangers. Thereupon Cortés seized one of the Cholulan leaders and extracted from him a detailed account of the conspiracy. He resolved to strike hard without delay. On a prearranged signal his troops fell upon the Cholulans and slaughtered all those found under arms. But as soon as the fight was over and order restored he treated the city leniently. He forbade his Tlaxcalan friends to exact further revenge, appointed new leaders and explained to them that they now enjoyed the protection of the King of Spain. Although he has been bitterly reproached by contemporary and modern writers for carrying out a cold-blooded massacre the truth, as attested by eye-witnesses, is that he took preventive action at a particularly perilous moment, and that his victims were warriors and not an unarmed mob.

The pacification of Cholula delayed Cortés for a few days. During this time he pulled down the shrine of Quetzalcoatl and erected a large cross, visible for miles around, in its stead. He also sent a party under Diego de Ordás to climb the volcano Popocatepetl. Ordás struggled bravely to the summit, nearly 18,000 feet up among the snow and smoking cinders, and caught a faint glimpse of distant lakes and cities. It was no uncommon feat of alpinism, but what his leader found more interesting was his discovery of a good but unguarded road into the Valley of Mexico. Apparently there was no question of the Aztecs offering resistance in the high pass between the volcano and its twin mountain Ixtaccihuatl. Delighted by this news, Cortés gave the order to march. He had sent his Zempoalans back to the coast and set out with four hundred and fifty Spaniards and a thousand Tlaxcalan auxiliaries. It was truly a tiny force with which to plunge into Anahuac.

The army crossed the pass, at the chilly height of 14,500 feet, on 2 November and descended through thick forests into the Valley. They halted again at the small market town of Amecameca. On the way they encountered the most magnificent of the many embassies which had come from Moctezuma. It was preceded by a carefully propagated rumour that the Emperor himself had decided to meet Cortés at the foot of the pass and escort him to the capital. The leader of the party, a man of regal demeanour, indeed tried to sustain the imperial role. But this not very clever ruse did not work. The envoy's claim was easily discounted by Cortés and he left in discomfiture. This odd incident is difficult to explain; probably it was only the last of repeated attempts to test the Spaniards' reactions and to resolve doubts about their divine or human nature. To Cortés it looked like just another piece of Mexican trickery. At this juncture he was more than ever on his guard, and particularly since he had received a report, which he kept to himself, of the ambush and death of two of his soldiers at the hands of an Aztec governor in the coastal region named Cuauhpopoca. This official had evidently been instructed by the emperor to catch a Spaniard and send him to Tenochtitlán dead or alive. In the event it was two severed heads that reached Moctezuma; we are told that having inspected them he inclined to the opinion that the Spaniards could not be gods, but were certainly human beings with exceptional and dangerous qualities.

At Amecameca the leaders of the neighbouring communities in the Valley gathered to greet Cortés and assure him of their goodwill. They poured out the usual complaints about the arbitrary behaviour of the imperial government. It seems remarkable that such disaffection should have been rife in the Nahua heartland and so near to the capital. Doubtless it was the reflection of a protest movement which had recently involved even the docile Texcocans in armed rebellion but which could have been easily stifled in normal times. Cortés, on the point of putting his head into the lion's mouth, was much encouraged by these developments, which tallied with what had been predicted by the Tlaxcalans and Zempoalans.

It was however Cacama, the reigning King of Texcoco—a son of the luxurious Nezahualpilli and Moctezuma's nephew—who was deputed to appeal for the last time to Cortés to turn back. Accompanied by a glittering suite, he met the army just after its arrival on the southern shore of Lake Chalco. Needless to say his mission was in vain. Cortés plied him with soothing oratory and resumed his march. The Spaniards advanced in an atmosphere of palpitating excitement and filled with the premonition of great events. They kept close formation as they passed through vast throngs of Indians watching them from the roadside or clusters of canoes on the lake.

Nothing in fact occurred to hinder their peaceful progress. At the village of Mixquic they turned north along a short causeway separating Lake Chalco from Lake Xochimilco and leading to the hilly peninsula of Ixtapalapa. They marvelled at the beauty and orderliness of the smaller townships and especially of Ixtapalapa itself, where they were entertained on the last night of their journey by no less a person than Cuitlahuac, the emperor's brother. At this point the panorama of Lake Texcoco and of Tenochtitlán in its full glory burst upon their gaze. They looked for the first time on the white city mirrored proudly in the waters and its *teocallis* towering into the most limpid of skies.

On the next morning, 8 November, they took the broad causeways leading across the lake to the capital. At the junction of the Ixtapalapa and Coyoacán causeways, where the way was blocked by a stone fortress, they were met by a thousand dignitaries in rich ceremonial attire. Proceeding with this escort, they soon reached the point where the causeway became a road into the city proper. The grand climax of the day was at hand. Cortés, riding slowly forward, beheld approaching an even more gorgeous cortege of richly dressed but bare-footed notables, in whose midst Moctezuma was borne high in a litter. The bearers stopped and the Emperor alighted. Flanked by Cacama and Cuitlahuac, he walked on while Cortés in turn dismounted and came towards him. When he moved to embrace the Emperor he was gently restrained, but he was allowed to hang the necklace he was wearing round Moctezuma's neck. After an exchange of the most flattering salutations, Emperor and Captain-General proceeded on foot, Moctezuma in front with Cacama, with Cortés following hand in hand with Cuitlahuac.

The Spaniards, mute with wonder not unmixed with apprehension, were conducted to the palace of Moctezuma's father Axayacatl, which stood on the western side of the main square, opposite the new imperial residence and adjoining the great religious precinct which contained the double *teocalli* of Huitzilopochtli and Tlaloc and the other principal religious buildings. Having courteously installed his guests, Moctezuma withdrew and left them to enjoy the elaborate feast provided for them. Later he returned for a formal visit, which Cortés reciprocated on the following day. The representative of the Holy Roman Emperor was scrupulous to observe the protocol expected of him.

The Spaniards lost no time in putting their comfortable and well-equipped quarters in a state of defence. Cortés, for his part, spent the days that followed in a series of talks with the Emperor and in sight-seeing under his guidance, while Marina interpreted tirelessly. These contacts with Moctezuma gave him much food for thought and material for the meticulous reports which, among other preoccupations, he somehow found time to compose for his master Charles V. The Emperor continued to be affable, courteous and open-handed. He also appeared ready, in deference to the ancient prophecies about bearded white men from the west, to regard as his overlord the mysterious potentate in Europe to whom Cortés owed allegiance.

On the religious issue, however, he proved entirely obdurate. Although he listened politely to Cortés expounding the Christian faith, he firmly refused to be shaken in his loyalty to the gods of Anahuac. The Spaniards were much disquieted by his attitude. Lodged as they were in the vicinity of the sacred precinct, and on their visits to the principal *teocallis* of Tenochtitlan and Tlatelolco, they were confronted at every turn with the bizarre and gruesome practices of the Aztec cults. They became shudderingly familiar with the grotesque idols, the human hearts steaming in the *cuauhxicalli* (sacrificial dish), the rack lined with thousands of skulls (*tzompantli*) and the dismembered bodies destined to be devoured in some kind of detestable communion. They were impatient to put an end to such horrors, just as they longed to become undisputed masters of the country and to gain a free hand in amassing booty.

But meanwhile they were getting nowhere and were in control of nothing outside their quarters. While they stayed confined in the palace of Axayacatl, the life of the Mexican empire flowed undisturbed around them as if their irruption had been irrelevant.

They had lost the initiative and their position was thoroughly precarious. Worse still, Cortés received a message to the effect that Moctezuma's supporters were up in arms against the tiny Spanish garrison at Vera Cruz and had killed its commander, Juan de Escalante. Pondering these matters, he made up his mind that there was but one way of breaking the deadlock. He must lay hands on the Emperor's person, keep him as a hostage and use him as a puppet.

This plan was promptly executed. Cortés appeared before the Emperor with a strong escort and taxed him with the Cuauhpopoca episode. He demanded that the offending *tecuhtli* be brought to the capital for examination and punishment. To this Moctezuma raised no objection, but he blenched when Cortés went on to insist that he should transfer himself and his court across the square to his father's palace. He protested energetically but, taken by surprise and with blades at his throat, he was forced to comply. Moreover, on being assured that he would be treated with deference, he agreed to calm the very real agitation which now arose among the populace. As for Cuauhpopoca, Cortés condemned him and his chief officers to be burned alive and in public; and while the sentence was being carried out he went so far as to clap fetters on Moctezuma, an agonising humiliation which was stoically endured. To replace Escalante at Vera Cruz he sent his trusted captain Gonzalo de Sandoval.

Thus, before the year 1519 was out, Cortés had made himself the virtual ruler of Mexico. So far as externals were concerned, Moctezuma was allowed to live in the imperial state to which he was accustomed. Dignitaries and officials came as before, the pomps and rituals were observed and the traditional forms of power respected. But it was Cortés who gave the essential orders and manipulated the Emperor's authority for his own benefit and the interests of Spain. So deep was the inborn reverence of the people for their sovereign that their hostile reaction to this state of affairs was slow to mature. Moctezuma failed to call them to arms and appeared resigned to his fate. He actually connived at the arrest and imprisonment of several of his princely kinsmen, including Cacama and Cuitlahuac, who were sick of the situation and plotting rebellion. He plied the Spaniards with gold, jewels and women. Finally he was prevailed upon to summon the dignitaries of his empire and to announce to them, in tortuous and melancholy language, his acceptance of the overlordship of Charles V. Apparently his docility and submission were complete.

In these favourable conditions the Spaniards began to extend their activities. During the winter, and the early spring of 1520, expeditions were despatched in various directions to explore the country and prospect for precious metals, while in the capital treasure was accumulated at a feverish rate. The luckiest haul was a hoard found walled up inside the palace allotted to the Spaniards. The melting down of exquisite golden objects into ingots and the division of the spoil into lots for the King, the Captain-General and the soldiers, absorbed an immoderate amount of energy and created sharp jealousies. Things were going so well that Cortés, who was not the man for misjudgements or sudden impulse, thought the moment opportune for delivering a frontal attack on the Aztec religion. He personally led a party which broke into the shrines on the great temple and hurled down the blood-encrusted images. As soon as they were purged of stench and human offal an altar and image of the Virgin were set up and Mass was celebrated.

A wave of horror at this act of desecration swept instantly over the city. The priests of Huitzilopochtli sought out Moctezuma, insisting that the outrage against the gods must be punished, and the indignation of the people assuaged, by unleashing war on the strangers. To the surprise of Cortés the Emperor was shocked out of his apathy: using for the first time the most direct and unambiguous language, he summoned him to flee the city with his army. Cortés, who realised too late that he had thrown away the advantages he had gained since his seizure of the Emperor, tried to temporise; he gave Moctezuma to understand that if he would restrain his people, the Spaniards would make preparations to leave. Furthermore, he sent carpenters to Vera Cruz with orders to have three ships put in commission. Distrust between the two chief actors in the drama was now complete, but before the intentions of either could be put to the test, they were faced with a new situation. Summoned again by Moctezuma, Cortés heard to his consternation that a Spanish fleet of eighteen ships had arrived off Vera Cruz. He rightly suspected that this was not a rescue operation or a reinforcement, but an attempt to overturn his authority. He sent Andrés de Tapia hurrying to the coast to ascertain the facts. His information, and his worst fears, were soon confirmed. The purpose of the new expedition, which had been placed under the command of Panfilo de Narváez, a landowner in Cuba, was indeed to depose Cortés and enforce Velázquez' claims.

It will be recalled that before leaving Vera Cruz Cortés had despatched a ship to Spain with the object of announcing his discoveries to the King and of seeking royal approval of his actions. Contrary to his express instructions, this vessel had called at a Cuban port and Velázquez had learned, to his fury, how Cortés had usurped his authority. Having failed to intercept the ship before it resumed its voyage, he had spent the following months preparing a sufficient force to reduce Cortés to submission. Meanwhile Cortés' two commissioners, Puertocarrero and Montejo, had met with every conceivable frustration in Spain, where they found Bishop Fonseca, the King's minister for the affairs of the colonies, violently prejudiced in favour of Velázquez. He recommended that Cortés be disowned and his commissioners arrested. Nevertheless their story caused a sensation at Court, as did the treasure which they exhibited. The King received them graciously, but failed to make up his mind on the crucial question whether it was Velázquez or Cortés who was legally entitled to exercise the royal jurisdiction in Mexico. The issue was left to be decided on Mexican soil, and by force of arms.

As soon as Cortés was sure of his facts, he moved boldly and skilfully. Leaving Alvarado in command at Tenochtitlán with only eighty Spanish soldiers, but prepared if necessary to withstand a siege, he left for the coast early in May with the remainder of the army. Two detachments on missions of exploration were ordered to meet him at Cholula. During the next three weeks he slowly approached Zempoala, where Narváez, confident in his superiority but indolent in action, had set up his camp. He used the interval before confrontation to soften up his opponents by all the diplomatic means at his disposal. To the high-handed messages of Narváez he returned the suavest of replies. His captain Velázquez de León (the Governor's kinsman) and the friar Olmedo, well provided with gold and seductive arguments, circulated freely in the camp of Zempoala. So did three of Narváez' soldiers whom Sandoval, remaining admirably staunch throughout the crisis, had kidnapped and forwarded to Tenochtitlán, trussed up on the backs of Indian porters. Cortés had treated them well and now they were back among their fellows, loud in their praise for his generosity and achievements. Consequently his duel with Narváez was half won before the fight began.

Nevertheless it was a tricky affair, for Cortés was heavily outnumbered and outgunned, and lacked cavalry. But his tactics were as successful as his diplomacy. Avoiding a straightforward battle, he launched his exhausted force in a night attack. In the first rush Narváez' cannon were seized and he himself taken prisoner. The rest of his army put up no fight at all; indeed they eagerly repudiated their feckless commander and placed themselves under Cortés' orders. Thus on 29 May 1520, Cortés found himself at the head of more than a thousand Spaniards, plentifully supplied with artillery, horses and treasure, with a good fleet at his disposal and assured of the support of numberless Indian allies. Surely the conquest of Mexico was an accomplished fact.

If he had such illusions, he was at once undeceived. Hardly had he won his victory and set to work integrating his own forces with those of Narváez, whom he kept in honourable captivity, than another dramatic reversal of fortune occurred. He learned to his dismay that Alvarado, through his own folly, had placed his whole grand enterprise in jeopardy. The tiny garrison in Axayacatl's palace was besieged and reduced to deplorable straits.

The Spaniards in Tenochtitlán were suffering from nervous tension. Eighty of them were isolated among a million Aztecs, in whom they detected a growing truculence and a reluctance to provide them with regular supplies. Nor could they help speculating what nasty fate was in store for them should Cortés fail to overcome Narváez. In this atmosphere they watched the population preparing to celebrate the great festival of Tezcatlipoca, for which Alvarado had granted them permission on condition that it did not conclude with the customary sacrifices. It soon became obvious that the Aztecs, in their new mood, had no intention of complying with this stipulation and Alvarado convinced himself that warriors were being assembled under the cloak of the festival and an uprising planned. He decided to repeat Cortés' exploit at Cholula and attacked the massed celebrants as they were performing ritual dances in the temple courtyard. This time several hundred Mexicans were massacred without a real fight. The reaction, however, was prompt and savage. Two heavy attacks were launched on Axayacatl's palace and were with difficulty repelled. Moctezuma's attempts to quiet his infuriated subjects were simply ignored. Either he was in fact losing his prestige or he was in league with the attackers.

The assaults had fortunately slackened before Cortés, at the head of his formidable array, reached the shores of Lake Texcoco, but Alvarado had already been beleaguered for over a month, and it does seem strange that the Aztecs did not press home their advantage during this period. If they had done so, the garrison could hardly have survived. Possibly their leaders had calculated that while they could not hope to beat the Spaniards in the open field, they had a good chance of overwhelming them in the constricted area of the city, and were bent on destroying both garrison and main army in the same sanguinary finale. When Cortés entered the city by the northern causeway on 24 June, and took over from the chastened Alvarado, he was not opposed, but the Aztecs avoided all contact with him and withheld provisions. Moctezuma, too, was deaf to pleas and threats; he could only suggest that it might help to release a prominent prisoner to reason with the leaders of the insurrection. The choice, singularly unfortunate from the Spanish point of view, fell on Cuitlahuac. Unwittingly Cortés had removed the last obstacle to total war between Aztecs and Spaniards, for the supreme council of the empire lost no time in deposing Moctezuma and electing Cuitlahuac as his successor. This was the prelude to six days and nights of continuous battle.

The fighting was much fiercer than anything which the Spaniards had so far experienced. The Aztecs displayed fanatical determination in attack and perished in thousands by cannon, arquebus and cross-bow fire. Although they failed to swamp their opponents by sheer numbers they defeated all sallies from the fortress. The great *teocalli* changed hands twice in furious struggles. The Spanish dead and wounded mounted ominously and food had almost run out. On the third day the wretched Moctezuma was paraded on the battlements and made to appeal for peace. But he was greeted by a shower of arrows and stones and fell back severely wounded. He was physically and morally crushed, and died within three days.

After this there was only one resort left for the Spaniards, an immediate flight, and Cortés employed all his courage and ingenuity to that end. He decided to retreat by the Tlacopán (Tacuba) causeway, which was the shortest way to the mainland and has become one of the busiest thoroughfares of Mexico City. To secure the army's flight he had to seize and hold eight crossing points on the causeway from which the Mexicans had removed the bridges, and to fill the gaps with rubble. Unfortunately this task was beyond the powers of the united Spaniards and Tlaxcalans: they were not strong enough to defend all these crucial positions for a sufficient time to guarantee the army's passage. Cortés then organised a night operation, and a portable bridge was hastily assembled to cover the breaches in the causeway. A more intractable problem was posed by the treasure which had accumulated in the palace. The wise course would have been to leave it behind, but that was psychologically impossible. So Cortés scrupulously separated the royal fifth from the rest, piled it on the backs of Tlaxcalan porters and lame horses and placed it under strong guard. The soldiers were then turned loose on the rest, with the result that when the time came to move and fight, many of them were fatally hampered by loads of gold, and died victims of their own cupidity.

On the dark, wet night of 30 June, known to history as the 'noche triste', the unwieldy column began its flight. By the time it reached the second bridge, the enemy were alerted and it was beset on every side. Struggling slowly forward, it lost its cohesion and the passage of each bridgehead, among the debris and the slime, cost hundreds of lives. Spaniards and Tlaxcalans were clubbed down and hacked to pieces, trampled and drowned, or dragged away for sacrifice. The guns and most of the treasure were abandoned. Only the fortitude of Cortés in the van, and the epic exploits of Alvarado in the rear, preserved a measure of discipline and saved the lives of slightly less than half the Spaniards. Dawn found the survivors huddled together in the market-place of Tacuba. Cortés rallied them into some sort of order and led them, skirmishing all the way, round the northern shores of Lakes Zumpango and Xaltocan towards Tlaxcalan territory.

On 7 July the Aztec army, commanded by the Ciuacoatl in person, caught up with them in the vast open plain between Otumba and Apam, criss-crossed with maguey plantations. The battle that followed was crucial, for the Mexicans, in the full flush of their victory in Tenochtitlán, had a unique opportunity of overwhelming opponents deprived of firearms, weak from wounds and hunger and as usual enormously outnumbered. But the Spaniards had miraculously recovered their spirit. In open country they were unbeatable, though fighting on foot with the basic weapons of the middle ages, the sword and the spear. Like a paladin in the chivalrous romance of which the Spaniards were such avid readers. Cortés himself burst through the Indian ranks, hewed down the Ciuacoatl and captured his standard. The Aztecs melted away and the army stumbled on towards Tlaxcala, where the *tlatoanis* of the republic, unshaken in their loyalty to Cortés, gave them food and shelter. Old Xicotencatl was overjoyed to see his daughter, Alvarado's companion, return safe and sound; she and Doña Marina were among the very few women who survived the disaster.

The Aztecs did not seek to pursue the war but sent an embassy to Tlaxcala with the object of detaching the republic from the Spanish alliance. Their proposals were supported in the Council by the younger Xicotencatl, who seems to have been animated by a kind of Nahua nationalism in advance of his age and quite foreign to the feelings of his fellow-citizens. He was, however, sharply rebuffed. Nor was there any rush by the Aztecs' former subjects outside the Valley to renew their allegiance to Tenochtitlán. Cortés was quick to use this pause to build up his strength against the day when he could again invade Anahuac. The four hundred soldiers left to him had scarcely recovered from the shock of the 'noche triste' when he began to employ them on a series of small campaigns designed to seal off the country under Cuitlahuac's domination. His strategy was to isolate the Aztecs within the valley, to incite the other Indian nations against them and to cut off their sources of supply and revenue.

Various small towns on the skirts of the volcanoes were thus secured. Cortés also founded a new Spanish municipality, Segura de la Frontera, formerly known as Tepeaca, to serve as a strong point where the highway from Anahuac to the Gulf meets the road from Oaxaca and the south, a region from which he was obtaining many Indian adherents. With Sandoval firmly established at Vera Cruz, his base for a new venture against the Valley was assured. Another reassuring factor was that his defeat had not lowered his prestige among his own countrymen. They were still attracted by his personality and the glamour of the Conquest. During this period his army was constantly increased by parties dribbling in from Cuba and Jamaica as reinforcements for the abortive expeditions which had been despatched to oust him. He had no difficulty in inducing the newcomers to renounce their loyalty to Velázquez or Garay. Reserves of armaments and horses were carefully accumulated. To add to his power of manoeuvre he put in hand at Tlaxcala the construction of the thirteen small brigantines with which he was to gain control of Lake Texcoco. They were designed in sections for transport by porters and reassembly by the waters. While organising his campaign with such masterly forethought and precision, he did not neglect his duty to the King, to whom he rendered full reports of his progress and plans.

Shortly after Christmas Cortés quitted Tlaxcala with an army of six hundred Spaniards supported by large contingents of Indians. He marched directly to Texcoco over the Rio Frio pass (now the main road from Puebla to Mexico City) and found it deserted. It was an excellent site for a headquarters during the first phase of his operations, which was devoted to the reduction of outlying communities and damaging raids up to the outskirts of the city. The Tlaxcalans, eager to pay off old scores, were particularly active in these forays. Cortés hoped that the Mexicans would lose heart as the net was drawn closer and ask for terms, but he had underestimated their obstinate courage. By this time they had acquired a new emperor. Cuitlahuac, a man of great talents, had been carried off by an epidemic of smallpox, the first of a succession of European plagues which were to decimate the Indians during the sixteenth century. He was replaced by Cuauhtemoc, a son of the dread Ahuitzotl and nephew of Moctezuma.

The memory of this brave and gifted young man has exercised a singular fascination over the minds of modern Mexicans. Along with Juarez, he is the folk-hero par excellence whom no breath of criticism must be allowed to sully, the fearless champion of an outraged people against the brutal intruder. But even when the adulation of his official biographers is discounted, he epitomises the most admirable qualities of his race. No worthier leader could have been found for the Aztecs in their last valiant struggle. He combined a spirit of uncompromising resistance with a tactical skill in defence matching that of Cortés in attack.

While the brigantines were being assembled at Texcoco, under constant harassment from the Aztecs, Cortés led a strong force in a sweep to the south. He subdued or won over several towns in the sub-tropical country of Morelos before recrossing the mountains into the Valley. As he closed in towards the city the Mexicans came out to meet him and there was heavy fighting at Xochimilco and Coyoacán, a region of luxuriant lakeside gardens. Thence he marched to Tacuba and back to Texcoco, completing the northern circuit of the lakes and garrisoning the vital points. The Aztecs were by now completely blockaded. At the end of April the brigantines were launched and the siege proper began.

The Spanish army, which had grown to nine hundred men, was organised in three columns, commanded by Alvarado, Cristobal de Olid and Sandoval. Many thousands of Indian allies were attached to each, lending an aspect of civil war to the death throes of the empire. The plan was for the columns to advance along the causeways from Tacuba, Coyoacán and Ixtapalapa respectively, leaving the northern (Tepeyac) causeway temporarily unobstructed in the hope that the Aztecs might decide to evacuate

The Conquest of Mexico. 17th Century Painting. Artist unknown.

(*Ministry of Public Building and Works*)

BOLCAN DE MEXICO
N°3

(Ministry of Public Building and Works)

the city by that route. Later it too was to be blocked. Finally the sufferings of the inhabitants were horribly sharpened by the severance of their water-supply from Chapultepec.

Two and a half months of ferocious combat followed. As the attackers pressed slowly onwards they filled the gaps in the causeways with the rubble of demolished houses, and the straight avenues of the city were swept by cannon fire. The Aztecs counter-attacked continuously, reopening the breaches and landing in the rear of the columns from their fleets of canoes. But the brigantines wrought havoc among these and gradually prevailed in the naval war. Two ground assaults were delivered in June and both failed. Although groups of Spaniards penetrated into the centre of the city, they could not hold their ground and many were cut off. The second reverse was particularly grave, as sixty-two Spaniards were taken alive and sacrificed in batches. Their horrified comrades watched them cavorting grotesquely on the temple platforms as the sacred drums boomed and, prodded by the priests, they went through the motions of a ceremonial dance. When their hearts had been wrenched out, their heads were exhibited on poles, their bodies carved up and eaten (apart from religious requirements, food was short in Tenochtitlán). Not to be outdone in cannibalistic zeal, the Tlaxcalans devoured the Mexican prisoners who fell into their hands and Cortés, who longed for the agony to be ended by surrender, tried with indifferent success to save from massacre the unarmed citizens seeking to cross the besiegers' lines.

The Aztecs had scored their last success on the anniversary of the 'noche triste'. In the ensuing six weeks the Spaniards resumed their dour and methodical advance, in conditions of increasing horror. But this time the city was half destroyed and had lost half its population by the sword, hunger and disease. It rained every day and the canals were choked with muddy débris and putrefying bodies. But the surviving warriors fought on doggedly in the stench and desolation, and Cuauhtemoc rejected repeated summons to surrender. On 13 August 1521, the last bastions of the defence were stormed and Cuauhtemoc, endeavouring to escape by canoe from Tlatelolco, was intercepted by Sandoval and delivered to Cortés. In this saddest of confrontations both Indian and Spaniard behaved with classic dignity. Pointing to Cortés' dagger, the Emperor demanded death on the spot. But Cortés raised him up, lauded his courage and ordered that he and his family be taken to a place of safety.

Chapter Four   Colonial Mexico (I)

The Aftermath of the Conquest

The fall of Tenochtitlán added yet another realm, New Spain, to the dominions of the King-Emperor Charles. The name derived from a suggestion by Cortés himself, and the reality endured for three hundred years. The first century of the colony was a formative period during which the most radical transformations were carried out within a short space of time. Vast new territories were subjugated, their resources exploited and their populations swept into the Christian fold. The very appearance of the land-scape, as well as the habits and economy of the people, were modified by the introduction of the plants, animals and techniques of other continents. A new settled society of European origin quickly took root and developed traits which distinguished it not only from the society of the homeland but also from the variants of the latter which were growing up all over the Spanish overseas empire.

This society very soon acquired a specifically Mexican character. Moreover it was infinitely more vigorous than the febrile and unhealthy colonialism which had already made such a mess of Spain's Caribbean possessions. The Creole (a Creole is a person of European descent born in the Indies) civilisation which came into being within one or two generations on Mexican soil was lively and constructive. On the other hand it could not have prospered, or even existed, apart from the docile and laborious mass of Indians on whom white rule had been imposed by such stunning force. The hierarchical but well-integrated society of pre-Conquest days fell apart when the native ruling castes were destroyed and dispersed and was replaced by a system based on the frank domination of one race by another. A remnant of the native aristocracy lingered on for a few decades and exercised a traditional but limited authority in the Indian communities: it was treated with respect by the colonists, and its daughters married without prejudice into Spanish families. But it gradually ceased to be a living force, was assimilated into Creole society or faded away into the mass. In general the races lived in separation and inequality except below the roof of a church. Outside their own communities, the Indians were barred from offices and professions. The sharp distinction only became blurred when a new mixed (*mestizo*) race started to emerge in any numbers and to lay the human foundation of the Mexican people of today.

Colonial history proper begins with the establishment of the viceroyalty in 1535. The intervening period is one of confused activity and chaotic incident, a welter of intrigues, treacheries, brutalities and of painful struggle towards order and peaceful organisation. It is marked by the decline in the fortunes of Cortés, who gradually lost his power to control events and was fatally caught up in conflicts between his own ambitions, the selfish interests of the settlers and the demands of the Crown. He would have been superhuman if he could have held the balance. Nevertheless he manoeuvred with skill and decision during the early years. The immediate problems which engaged his attention were the foundation of the new Mexico City and the disposal of the booty taken in the campaign. His decision to build on the ruins of Tenochtitlán, instead of choosing a fresh site, was momentous and correct. It was entirely fitting that there should be continuity between the city of the Aztecs and that of the conquerors; besides, it was politic to build at once and where Indian craftsmen and workers were readily available. That indispensable Mexican magnate, the Ciuacoatl, was pressed into service in order to recruit the necessary labour and to induce the population to return to the environs of the city, where they were regrouped under leaders of their own race. Thus the new town was already taking shape in the year succeeding the siege. The traditional buildings of a Spanish municipality, together with churches and substantial houses of red and white stone for the foremost citizens, were traced among the wreckage of palaces and *teocallis*.

In dealing with the booty Cortés encountered the usual hazards, and when danger was removed jealousies became even more acute. The soldiers were dissatisfied with their share of the treasure and with Cortés' reservation of a fifth to himself as

Captain-General. Encouraged by agents of Velázquez and Bishop Fonseca, they insinuated that Cortés was conniving with the Indian leaders in concealing the gold withheld from them. They insisted that Cuauhtemoc and the ruler of Tacuba, whom Cortés began by treating with every courtesy, should be tortured and forced to reveal its whereabouts. Much against his will, Cortés consented to an act which has stained his reputation ever since. In the end the torture, nobly sustained, was ineffective and the booty reserved for the King never reached Spain. It was captured at sea by a French freebooter and brought in triumph to La Rochelle.

Of crucial importance for Cortés was the need to parry the attempts of his enemies at home and in the Indies to wrest from him the government of New Spain. Fonseca, his inveterate opponent, promptly sent out Cristóbal de Tapia with instructions to supersede him, but this envoy was compelled to retire baffled in the face of united opposition from the colonists. Next came the persistent Garay from Jamaica, trying to encroach on Cortés' territory by detaching from it the province of Pánuco on the Gulf coast. He too was frustrated by a clever combination of diplomacy and arms. In October 1522 Cortés received long-awaited letters from the Spanish Court confirming him in his office of Governor and Captain-General. To all appearances this was a great victory and an end to the uncertainty about his status, but the reality was not quite so golden. His authority was still limited by the presence of four royal officials charged with supervising his administration, and especially its financial aspects, on the spot, and with enforcing a carefully drafted set of instructions prepared for the purpose.

Quite obviously this was a system calculated to cause friction. For a time Cortés kept the upper hand. He threw all his energies into the organisation of the realm. During 1521-2 his subordinates were busy extending its boundaries to the west and south. The submission of the Tarascan kingdom opened the way to the Pacific, on which a fleet was soon launched. The Mixtecs, Zapotecs and the tribes of the Isthmus were likewise brought into subjection. At the same time Cortés' agents resumed the task, initiated during his first stay in Tenochtitlan, of compiling an inventory of the country's mineral and agricultural wealth. The problems of land tenure and of the treatment of the Indian countryfolk immediately involved him in the bitter controversy about the *encomienda* which was then agitating the home Government and the Indies, and was to do so for the greater part of the century.

84

The *encomienda* was the system by which selected colonists—the *encomenderos*—were permitted to exact tribute and labour from the Indians in return for teaching them the Christian religion, supplying them with dwellings, clothes and other basic necessities and protecting their elementary personal rights. On the death of the colonist the *encomienda* reverted to the Crown, which might or might not find another incumbent. The Indians, however, were not allowed to migrate. In law this institution was carefully distinguished from slavery, and the elaborate codes drawn up in Spain for its regulation insisted that the Indians on the *encomiendas* were to be regarded as free. But the early application of the system in Santo Domingo and elsewhere had produced the most flagrant contradictions between theory and practice; and after barely two decades it had resulted in virtual enslavement and galloping depopulation. Economically it had not proved its worth, and although they despaired of restraining the inhuman behaviour of the colonists, the high authorities in Spain, both laymen and ecclesiastics, had become uneasy in their Christian consciences about the fate of the native population.

The Dominican Order, to which Loaisa, the President of the Council of the Indies, and Bartolomé de Las Casas, whose ardent hostility to the *encomienda* was to earn him the title of 'Protector of the Indians', both belonged, was especially loud in its disapproval of the institution and active in its efforts to mitigate its effects. The conquest of Mexico occurred at a moment when Las Casas and his supporters were influential at Court and Charles V was seriously considering the total abolition of the *encomienda*. Furthermore, the King was by no means anxious to encourage in his overseas dominions the development of a form of that feudalism which, as a centralising Renaissance despot, he was engaged in combating in Europe. Hence the instructions which his officials laid before Cortés enjoined him categorically to forbid *encomiendas* in Mexico. The Indians were to be treated as free men and direct vassals of the Crown.

Cortés' reply to this enlightened directive was a polite but firm no. He explained respectfully to his sovereign the various good reasons why the royal policy would be impracticable. He pointed out that without *encomiendas* there could be no possibility of satisfying the colonists or of converting the Indians. He went on to propose that the *encomiendas* in Mexico should no longer be terminable by the Crown but should be granted in perpetuity. This was remarkable presumption on the part of one whose tenure of power and legal authority were still precarious. On the other hand, the directives which he issued to the local *encomenderos* notably restricted their pretentions and emphasised their responsibilities. He was acting as if he knew at heart that the royal policy was right, but incompatible with the interests of the settlers on whom the orderly development of the colony depended. Thus he proceeded coolly to distribute *encomiendas* in defiance of the King's government and of the superintending officials in Mexico, not neglecting his own interests in the process.

A typical estate would include several villages of Indians bound to an *encomendero,* but adjoining it were lands apportioned to self-governing native communities owing direct allegiance to the Crown, or to Mexican potentates such as the children of Moctezuma. These last were treated essentially like Spanish *encomenderos*. Cortés judged correctly that the Crown would reluctantly accept the logic of his arguments, and in the event the *encomienda* survived in New Spain throughout the century, though hedged round by regulations and safeguards. Nevertheless his independent attitude could not fail to cause irritation at Court and in the Council, and fresh curbs on his freedom of action were soon to be devised.

At the outset of 1524 he felt himself secure enough to send out two strong expeditions to Central America. Alvarado marched down the Pacific coast to Guatemala while Olid took the eastern route to Las Hibueras (Honduras). As they vanished into the jungles a mission of another kind was leaving Spain for a very different but momentous purpose, the spiritual conquest of Mexico. It consisted of twelve Franciscan friars who, at the urgent insistence of Cortés, had been entrusted with the conversion of New Spain. Later the Franciscans were to be joined in this task by two other orders, the Dominicans and Augustinians, no less ardent in their zeal for spreading the gospel, but it was peculiarly fitting that the first missionaries to the poor Indians should be followers of St. Francis. Among them were some very exceptional men who devoted their whole lives to the welfare of the Indians, and one of the most poignant records of early colonial history is a mural in the Franciscan convent of Huejotzingo, founded in 1525, depicting Fray Martin de Valencia, their leader, with eleven others. Cortés received them with a demonstration of deep respect; the Indian leaders whom he brought to meet them were astounded to see the gorgeously dressed conquerors fall on their knees and kiss the habits of the barefooted fathers, dusty and ragged after their long walk from Vera Cruz.

So far Cortés was holding his own, but before 1524 was out he proceeded wantonly to throw away the fruits of his statesmanship. The cause of his behaviour, which was quite out of character, was the news that Olid, engaged in the subjection of Las Hibueras, had repudiated his authority. Instead of biding his time, or sending another of his captains to bring Olid to heel, he himself gathered an army and plunged into the fetid swamps beyond the Isthmus. This ill-considered venture had fatal consequences. It achieved nothing by way of further conquest and, as it transpired, Olid had already been murdered by rivals. Cortés ruined his own health and committed an act for which he will never be forgiven by those who value Mexico's Indian heritage. As a measure of precaution he had included in his suite Cuauhtemoc, the former Kings of Texcoco and Tacuba and other native magnates. At a critical stage in his march one of these notables denounced to him a plot by Cuauhtemoc to assassinate him and his captains and to join the local Indians in their resistance to his army, with the eventual object of returning to Anahuac and there provoking a general rebellion. After examining the accused, Cortés concluded that Cuauhtemoc and the ruler of Tacuba were guilty of conspiracy and must die. They were hanged forthwith. Whether Cortés was justified in his suspicions or not, it was a sorry end to an association which had once been marked by chivalry and mutual respect.

Back in Mexico all semblance of orderly Government was disappearing. The deputies exercising power in Cortés' absence quarrelled with each other and with the colonists, and allowed the Indians to be indiscriminately exploited and maltreated. Their reports to Spain were designed to destroy the Captain-General's prestige at Court, while for local consumption it was proclaimed that he was dead. When chaos was at its worst Cortés returned as suddenly as he had departed and resumed his government amid universal acclaim. But neither his efficiency nor his popularity could efface the effects of eighteen months of maladministration for which he could hardly escape the blame. Henceforth the home government, while prepared to treat him with generosity and deference, were determined to deprive him of real power. He was allowed to retain the post of Captain-General but forfeited his administrative and judicial functions.

These were taken over, during 1526-7, by a commissioner nominated to enquire into the state of affairs in the colony and to direct its government. The experiment was not a success as two commissioners in succession died and the third, Estrada, had already shown his incapacity as one of the deputies during the disastrous eighteen months. Finally, after much hesitation, the King despatched to Mexico an *Audiencia,* that is to say a Commission composed of a President and two or more members, called *oidores,* with full powers to exercise the royal authority. Cortés was invited to return to Spain and give an account of himself. He sailed in 1528 and remained away for two years. Despite the calumnies with which his enemies had sought to poison the King's mind against him, Charles received him with the utmost kindness and loaded him with attentions and honours. His progress through his native land resembled a Roman triumph, enhanced by the showmanship with which he exhibited the curiosities and riches of New Spain. The royal favour bestowed on him the Marquisate of the Valley of Oaxaca, endowed with enormous estates in central and southern Mexico, and a lady of ducal rank for his wife. His first wife, Catalina Xuarez, had joined him at Coyoacán in 1522 but died soon after her arrival, while Doña Marina, who had borne him a son, had been tactfully passed on to a captain named Juan Jaramillo.

It is incredible that the intelligent and high-minded members of the Council of the Indies should have chosen such unworthy men for the *Audiencia* which took office in 1528. The President, Nuño de Guzmán, was a brute already notorious for his misgovernment of the province of Pánuco, while the best that can be said of the *oidores,* Matienzo and Delgadillo, is that they were greedy nonentities. Their two years' rule plunged Mexico into worse anarchy than in 1524–6. They unmercifully harried the supporters of Cortés, and even humiliated and imprisoned Alvarado, the conqueror and newly appointed Governor of Guatemala. The Indians, whom they treated with utter callousness, luckily found a champion in the first Bishop of Mexico, Juan de Zumárraga, a Franciscan friar and a Basque with all the courageous obstinacy of his race. His tireless denunciations of current abuses brought him into violent conflict with the *Audiencia,* and he narrowly escaped assassination at their hands. But a letter which he smuggled through the *Audiencia's* censorship revealed such an appalling situation that the Council of the Indies were moved to adopt a new and, as it turned out, final solution to the intractable problem of governing the colony. They recommended to the King the appointment of a Viceroy who would be the monarch's personal representative and rank with the highest dignitaries of the realm. Until the right choice could be made they deposed the *Audiencia* and replaced it with a second body similar only in name to the first.

The new President was Ramirez de Fuenleal, formerly Bishop of Santo Domingo, and one of his *oidores* was Vasco de Quiroga, who was later to win a legendary reputation for his fatherly care of the Tarascan Indians. As administrators they were competent, honest and humane, with the result that the next five years were marked by real progress. The only troubled area was the west where Nuño de Guzmán, evading justice, led a freebooting expedition. He ravaged Michoacán and Jalisco and penetrated as far as the coast in Sinaloa. His only constructive act was the foundation of Guadalajara, destined to be the most flourishing centre of Creole culture in Mexico. It was six years before the government caught up with him and ended his career of devastation and crime.

Another personality who did not fit into the new scheme of things, though for different reasons, was Cortés himself, the Marquess of the Valley, whose return coincided with the arrival of the second *Audiencia*. Cortés was to spend the next ten years in New Spain, but he neither received nor claimed a share in the government. He wisely busied himself with the development of his lands and left public affairs to the *Audiencia,* and later to the Viceroy. His relations with these powers were usually correct and sometimes cordial. Nevertheless he brushed sharply with them over the extent of his estates, which the *oidores* were anxious to restrict and did not like to see him managing as a little kingdom of his own, and over the freedom to which he thought himself entitled in organising further maritime expeditions. He was not entirely content with his princely life in his battlemented palace at Cuernavaca. The idea of Pacific exploration fascinated him and as time passed he became absorbed in dreamlike projects which could never be realised. In 1535 he himself led an abortive attempt to establish a colony on the beautiful but bleak peninsula of Lower California. But the ports which he built at Acapulco and Zacatula, and the surveys which his ships made of the coast of Tehuantepec northwards, were of lasting value.

Meanwhile Mexico flourished under the peaceful guidance of the second *Audiencia*. Its best work was accomplished in the protection of the Indians against the abuses of the *encomienda*. Nuño de Guzmán's numerous grants were revoked and the lands restored to the villagers to be worked as Crown property under a system known as the *corregimiento*. On the lower level the administration of the community was left in the hands of native officials (*regidores*), who in turn were subject to a Spanish superior, the *corregidor,* who was a salaried functionary. He was required to collect the tribute, supervise cultivation and educate the Indians in Spanish techniques and manners. He was given a constable (*alguacil*) to keep them in order and punish malefactors, and a priest to attend to their Christian instruction.

These paternalistic arrangements were of course admirable so long as the officials were honest and energetic, and the *oidores* to whom they were responsible kept a vigilant eye on their activities. The familiar abuses were apt to creep in when, as often happened, the *corregidor* succeeded in exploiting his charges for his own ends or in league with the *encomenderos* whose estates adjoined his territory, but by the standards of the sixteenth century in Europe the Crown's policy was extraordinarily enlightened. Its touch was less certain when it came to dealing with the slave trade. Indian (as opposed to Negro) slavery was officially forbidden in the colony and indeed disappeared from the countryside, where the prohibition was easy to enforce. The mines, however, were insatiable in their demands for forced labour, and the authorities were obliged to swallow their principles to the extent of allowing the miners to use as slaves wild Indians taken on the frontiers or those found already working as slaves in the native communities. It was no easy task to achieve a balance between the demands of the colonists and the rights of the Indians, but the *Audiencia* had made an honourable effort to find it when the time came to surrender its mandate to the Viceroy.

The Viceroyalty in the Sixteenth Century

Don Antonio de Mendoza, first of the long line of Viceroys of New Spain, set a high standard for his successors. He was a very grand personage indeed at Court. His illustrious descent was matched by the distinguished services which he and his ancestors had rendered to the Crown and he stood high in the King's favour. Charles could have made no better choice, for Mendoza was a devoted servant of his interests and indifferent to the selfish inclinations and petty rivalries of the settlers. He could be depended upon to overawe by the mere strength of his prestige the men of very diverse origins and capacities who composed the immature society of the colony. His integrity was unquestioned and he was equally contrasted by temperament with the raw and quarrelsome adventurers whom he had come to rule. Cool, firm and shrewd, this accomplished Renaissance statesman was eminently fitted to govern Mexico with impartial justice and in strict conformity with the royal instructions.

As the viceregal train slowly climbed the steep ladder of the road past Jalapa and emerged on the plateau, Mendoza looked upon a rapidly changing scene. Everywhere a Spanish veneer was beginning to spread over the age-old fabric of Indian Mexico. In Cortés' fortress town of Segura de la Frontera, and a little further on where, in sight of ancient Cholula, a new colonial city called Puebla de los Angeles was springing up, he was welcomed by the magistrates and officials of a typical Spanish *cabildo*. In the teeming Indian towns, however, where he was greeted by the native governors with the homage due to an Aztec emperor, he found the pre-Conquest atmosphere barely changed, except that the *teocallis* had been demolished and levelled off to provide platforms for the tall churches which the friars were building, or had already built, in Huejotzingo, Tlaxcala and the principal pueblos of the plain. Continuing his progress through Anahuac, he saw how the crops and fruit trees of Europe were bringing diversity to the monotonous expanses of maize, maguey and beans, while newly imported cattle and sheep grazed on the lands of the *encomenderos,* and Indian herdsmen tended the unfamiliar pigs and goats. At the gates of the city Mendoza was received with stately ceremony by the *Audiencia,* the municipal officers and deputations of Indian dignitaries, and took charge of his domain. His capital was still in the throes of construction, an ant heap of toiling Indians, but already capable of forming a proper setting for viceregal pomp and the lavish festivities with which Mendoza knew well how to appeal to the Creole love of ostentatious display.

In the heady air of the colony, Castilian austerity soon yielded to luxury and pleasure. Flattered by the condescension of so splendid a grandee, the citizens of Mexico proceeded to enjoy their riches and privileges with unashamed gusto. Extravagantly apparelled and bejewelled, they dissipated the profits of their mines and *encomiendas* on a glorious profusion of feasts, tournaments and masquerades. Fortunes were cheerfully gambled away, recovered and lost again. Hunting, bullfighting, the breeding and racing of fine horses, whiled away their time on their estates. In the remoter provinces the *encomenderos* indulged in fancies which would not have been countenanced in the home-

land, like the incumbent of Yanhuitlán (Oaxaca), who is represented in a codex of about 1545 as sporting a Moorish turban,
perhaps a throwback to his non-Christian ancestry. In more sober
times the Creoles were to look back on the brilliance and gaiety
of Mendoza's viceroyalty, and that of his successor Luis de
Velasco, as a golden and carefree age, confident in its infinite
opportunities for the flaunting of wealth and power.

The Viceroy's deep political experience, and the popularity
which he won by his tactful handling of the colonists, availed him
well in his efforts to mitigate a new clash between the Crown and
the *encomenderos* provoked by the publication of the so-called
New Laws of 1542. This code, inspired by the writings of
Francisco de Vitoria, the famed jurist and theologian of Salamanca, and by the ceaseless propaganda of Las Casas against the
exploitation of the Indians, decreed that no more *encomiendas*
should be created in New Spain and that the existing ones should
all lapse at the death of the holders. The colonists, who were
supported in Mexico even by the religious orders with the best
record for the protection of the Indians, objected that the security
and prosperity of New Spain rested in large measure on the
encomienda. After much wrangling and tactful interventions by the
Viceroy, the dispute petered out in a compromise by which the
Crown abstained from pressing its extreme demands. In return,
however, the *encomenderos* were shorn of their powers to coerce
unpaid labour. Gradually the Crown strengthened its authority
over them and reduced the system to an anachronism. In his
dealings with the Indian notables the Viceroy was affable and
accessible; he spent long hours in listening to their complaints
and confirming them in their rights and offices.

In these circumstances Mendoza had little trouble with the
Indians in those regions of Mexico which had been conquered by
Cortés, but he had to face a serious uprising in Jalisco, where the
savageries of Nuño de Guzmán produced a fierce reaction in the
Mixtón rebellion of 1540–41. Alvarado, most seasoned of all
Indian campaigners, headed the defending army but was defeated
in battle, trampled by a horse in the rout that followed and died
at Guadalajara, which barely withstood assault. The Viceroy
intervened to restore the situation and this was the only occasion
on which he had to take to the field in person. But Yucatán, in the
far south-east, was the scene of continuous warfare during the
period of the *Audiencias* and of the first viceroyalty. Here
Francisco de Montejo and his son, who had been given a free

hand to reduce and settle the peninsula, encountered embittered resistance from the Mayas, who kept up the struggle for over twenty years. It was a cruel and devastating war that ended in mutual exhaustion. The Mayas submitted but clung tenaciously to their language and racial identity, while the Creole society of Merida and Campeche developed its own characteristics and links with the outside world, if only for the reason that its land communications with the main centres of government in Mexico and Guatemala were slow and rugged.

In the turmoil of the sixteenth century the friars tamed the Indians far more effectively than the soldiers. They also brought the humanities to Mexico in the train of the Christian religion. The twelve Franciscans who arrived in 1524 had been preceded by three members of the same Order, all Flemings from the King-Emperor's dominions in the Low Countries. One of them was Pedro de Gante (Peter of Ghent), who happened to be an illegitimate kinsman of Charles V. Each convoy from Spain brought more of them and by the middle of the century they numbered about two hundred.

The Dominicans followed in 1526 and the Augustinians in 1533. It is an astonishing fact that the mass conversion of the Indians in the early years after the Conquest was accomplished by these few score friars, ignorant of native languages and customs and in conflict with a deep-rooted religion permeating every aspect of indigenous life. At a time when in Europe the foundations of the Church were being sapped by Lutheranism, its missionaries brought into the fold populations which, in Mexico alone, far outnumbered that of Spain. As a feat of concentrated energy it has no equal.

The apparent ease with which the Indians abandoned their gods and flocked to submit to the teaching and direction of the friars in no way detracts from the grandeur of this performance. It is true that the Indians, once their religious hierarchy had been dethroned and their own deities had lost their magic, desperately needed a spiritual substitute. Equally they soon accepted the friars as their natural defenders against the excesses of the colonists, and turned to them in their trouble. But in spite of these favourable factors the friars could not have scored such a spectacular success if they had not possessed more than a normal share of the qualities of zeal, perseverance, abnegation and charity, joined to a quite remarkable talent for organisation and insight into the character of their converts.

The Orders divided the territory of the viceroyalty into three parts for the purposes of its evangelisation. While all were active in the capital and its environs, the Franciscans took the Tlaxcala-Puebla region, Michoacán and the west, the Augustinians the north-west and the Dominicans the south. Their monasteries multiplied with amazing speed; by 1550 the Franciscans alone had set up no less than fifty houses. These establishments varied in size, but as the total number of friars in Mexico at the end of the century did not probably exceed fifteen hundred, no single monastery contained more than the minimum necessary for the immense work in hand. Indeed the cry was always for more recruits from Europe, for the profession did not much appeal to the Creoles, and Indian neophytes were by royal decision ineligible.

The buildings, true spiritual fortresses, conformed to a uniform pattern—a high barrel-vaulted church in a style which can only be described as Mexican Late Gothic and has no exact parallel in Europe, adjoined by refectory, chapter-house, library and other monastic necessities built round a small two-storied cloister, with the friars' cells on the upper floor. Flanking the church door was a so-called open chapel where mass could be celebrated before a congregation grouped in the huge forecourt of the monastery, which was enclosed by a wall and embellished with chapels at the four corners. The buildings were surrounded with workshops where the converts practised crafts and by extensive gardens where the friars cultivated the fruits and vegetables of Europe. Although the general effect of these splendid constructions, with the churches rising like tall ships above the countryside, was one of simple austerity, Indian artists were encouraged to use their imagination in the sculptural details of cloister and portal, and interior walls were covered with edifying frescoes in black and white. These great foundations, whether in decay or restored to a semblance of their former magnificence, still convey an over-powering impression of the will-power and enthusiasm of the men who created them.

The friars worked hard to fortify the Indians in their new faith. Converts were assiduously catechised before and after baptism and regular observance of the rites and disciplines of Christianity was firmly enforced. They were encouraged to celebrate Church festivals in a blaze of exotic colour, to the blended strains of native music and of the European instruments which they learned to play with alacrity, and to the accompaniment of their traditional dances. The fathers were delighted with the aptness of their pupils for everything they taught them. The only question was how far the process of their education should be carried; in other words should the élite be assimilated into the European way of life and become Spaniards in all respects save the colour of their skins? There could of course be no objection to their being instructed in religion, morals, craftsmanship, agriculture and the use of the Spanish language, and this was the aim of the school which was set up in the city by Pedro de Gante very soon after the Conquest and attracted hundreds of pupils. Similar training was given in monasteries all over the country.

But the Franciscans were not content to stop there; they thought it entirely logical that the Indians should have access to higher education. In 1536, with the approval of the Viceroy and of Bishop Zumárraga, himself a member of their Order, they founded the College of Santa Cruz at Tlatelolco, where the sons of prominent Indians were to be introduced to the whole range of studies available at a Spanish university in that age of transition from mediaeval to Renaissance culture. From the first their curriculum included Latin, philosophy and theology, and the founders intended that the graduates should primarily be destined for the priesthood. But the experiment proved too revolutionary for the times. It foundered upon the distrust of the colonists and the prejudice of King Philip II, who sternly vetoed the candidacy of Indians for orders. The College decayed into an elementary school and vanished by the end of the century.

The vigour of the Church's activities in early colonial times was largely due to the forceful personalities of its Bishops. In Michoacán the learned *oidor*, Vasco de Quiroga, virtually took over the government of the province, where he laboured for years to repair the injuries inflicted on it by the frightful atrocities of Nuño de Guzmán. He found it a desert and left it a scene of Arcadian prosperity. 'Tata' Vasco is still held in affectionate veneration by the Tarascans. In Chiapas, Las Casas had a similar problem on his hands; an unbending enemy of oppression, he showed himself as effective in preventing abuses on the spot as in denouncing them at Court.

Zumárraga, who had so successfully trounced the first *Audiencia*, is chiefly remembered for having established the cult of the Virgin of Guadalupe and for having allegedly caused the wholesale destruction of pre-Conquest manuscripts and works of art in general. The story of the Virgin's appearance to an Indian peasant,

Juan Diego, on the hill of Tepeyac, and of the miraculous imprint of her picture on his cloak, has become part of the Mexican national legend and inspired the heroes of the Independence and the Revolution. Every good Mexican wears a medal of Our Lady of Guadalupe next to his skin. Zumárraga's role, however, was confined to the cautious sponsorship of the miracle with the papal authorities. Not unnaturally it aided the work of conversion. As for the charge of vandalism, it does nothing to detract from the Bishop's fine record as educator, evangelist and friend of the Indians. Deeply cultivated himself, he promoted the setting-up of a printing press in the capital and the foundation, which was achieved three years after his death in 1548, of the Royal and Pontifical University of Mexico. But in his episcopal activity he was an implacable foe of heathenism and heresy. He had the current ruler of Texcoco burned at the stake for fostering secret pagan practices (not that the Aztec religion, essentially a solar cult, was suited to flourish by night and underground); he broke up the idols and destroyed any pictographs that struck him as serving the devil's cause. For he was not a modern museum director but a sixteenth century churchman and Inquisitor in New Spain. Even more contradictory, to our manner of thinking, was the behaviour of his colleague Bishop de Landa of Yucatán, who was a furious burner of Mayan picture writings but also wrote a classic description of the Mayan culture of his diocese.

Other men, no less distinguished for their missionary and pastoral activity, were moved by curiosity and love of learning to find out all they could about the vanishing Indian world and record it before it was too late. These friar scholars produced a succession of fascinating books, among which the *General History of the Indians of New Spain*, by Bernardino de Sahagún, stands supreme. Only second to it in interest is the *History of the Indians* by Toribio de Benavente, one of the twelve original Franciscans, who adopted the surname of Motolinia ('poor man' in Nahuatl). The friars not only studied the pictographs but encouraged their converts to write down, in Nahuatl or Spanish, their own accounts of the life and traditions of their ancestors and of the natural history of Mexico. We owe it to their efforts that so much source material of the pre-Conquest period was saved and reproduced.

Thanks to the first two Viceroys, Mendoza and Velasco, and to the friars, Spain gave her best to Mexico as a civilising power in the middle years of the century. Within the settled areas of the pre-Columbian cultures there reigned peace and a new prosperity engendered by the fusion of Europe with the new world. North of the old frontier of the Aztec empire, in the boundless territories sparsely inhabited by nomadic tribes, it was a period of movement and restless experiment. The more adventurous spirits of the colony were haunted by the idea that these regions contained fabulous kingdoms fated to dissolve at the conqueror's touch: in their heated imaginations new Eldorados loomed beyond each wilderness and mountain range. Such mirages lured the explorers into strenuous but fruitless ventures into the sierras of Arizona and New Mexico, the prairies of Kansas and the marshes of Mississippi.

The fever was started by one Cabeza de Vaca, a straggler from an unsuccessful attempt by Narváez, Cortés' old opponent, to occupy Florida, and a rogue of the first order, though a brave and resourceful one. Cast up on the shores of Texas with three companions, he walked across the continent, following roughly the course of the present Mexican-United States border, and after eight years' wandering turned up among his compatriots on the Pacific coast. He found plenty of gullible listeners to the tales he spun about a land called Cibola, which supposedly contained seven cities, each rivalling Tenochtitlán in beauty and wealth. Even the cautious Mendoza was sufficiently attracted by his story to send a Franciscan to investigate. The friar, Marcos de Niza, disappeared into the north, taking with him one of Cabeza de Vaca's trio, a Moor named Esteban. Of this incongruous pair, only the friar survived to return, but whether from dishonesty or credulity, he confirmed the fable about Cibola.

Thereupon the Viceroy equipped a large expedition and appointed Vásquez de Coronado, Governor of Nueva Galicia (as Jalisco and the West were then called) to lead it. This time the legend was exploded. Coronado and his men trekked with obstinate persistence into the heart of North America and back again, finding nothing to compensate them for the privations and grievous losses of the march.

Nevertheless the quest for Cibola had two important results. It staked the claim of the Spanish Crown to sovereignty over the infinite expanse of territory beyond the Rio Grande, and it led to the gradual penetration by ranchers and miners of the empty regions which now comprise the border states of the Mexican Republic, each of the dimensions of a sizeable European country. Here the Creole pioneers were free to carve out huge estates for themselves without interference by the viceregal authorities or remoter bureaucrats in Spain. Not that the area was pacified until comparatively modern times, for until the last quarter of the nineteenth century Comanches and Apaches were still raiding the mining settlements and haciendas.

But if the myth of Cibola never became a reality, the mountain fastnesses of central Mexico yielded riches of a more substantial kind. The early conquerors' thirst for gold could never be satisfied, and when the original treasures had been melted down it became embarrassingly clear that supplies of that metal were limited. On the other hand the newly discovered silver mines exceeded expectations. During the fifties and sixties one sensational bonanza succeeded another. The richest strata were those of Zacatecas and Guanajuato, San Luis Potosí and Pachuca. In these places the hills were honeycombed with narrow galleries where thousands of Indians laboured in the grimmest conditions to extract the ore, while endless mule trains converged on the Valley of Mexico with the produce of the mines, braving the hazards of Indian arrows or the assaults of professional bandits. The royal share of the inexhaustible silver flow proceeded on its way to Vera Cruz, there to be launched on its perilous voyage to Spain, exposed to Atlantic gales and the ferocious depredations of heretical pirates.

Mendoza inherited Cortés' penchant for maritime exploration. Under his government vessels built in the Pacific ports were sailing to Peru and Panama, plotting the shores of California and Oregon and scouring the wastes of the ocean. Later, in 1564, Juan de Legazpi's expedition left Acapulco to establish Spanish rule in the Philippines; Manila was founded and the trade route opened to China and Japan, thus adding an oriental colouring to the bright variety of the Mexican scene. The silks and spices, the fragrant and exquisite products of Ternate and Tidore, were transhipped at Acapulco from the Manila galleons. If it had not been for the inhibitions of Spanish commercial policy, Mexico would soon have been in a fair way to fulfil the role she may assume in the present century, that of a link and staging post on the inter-continental routes, where the influences of Europe merge, on the soil where the first American civilisation flourished, with these flowing from the further East and the South Seas. But unlike the New Englanders, the Creoles were not fated to become seamen and traders on a large scale; their temperament inclined them to stick to the land and any maritime ambitions they may have entertained were thwarted by the interdict of the Spanish government on economic competition between the colonies and the homeland.

Their geographical position and their long coast-line did not bring them the benefits they deserved. All too often the sea, instead of gaining them a livelihood, attracted to them the dreadful attentions of English, French and Dutch freebooters. Of these the English were the most noxious and persistent. As early as 1568 Hawkins and Drake battled in the bay of Vera Cruz itself with the fleet bringing the Viceroy, Enriquez de Almanza, from Spain. The rough handling which the English suffered there, and subsequently at the mouth of the river Pánuco, they ascribed to Spanish treachery, and as the years went by they strove to exact their revenge. For a time the mere suspicion that Drake—El Draque—was at large paralysed navigation on the Pacific side. But in the sixteenth century Spain was powerful at sea and her fleets, manned by Biscayan and Portuguese sailors second to none in daring and experience, were still capable of protecting the shores of New Spain and the passage of the treasure ships across the Atlantic.

When Almanza reached Mexico City after his brush with Hawkins, he found it in a grievous state. The second Viceroy, Luis de Velasco, had died at his post in 1564. Under his predecessor and himself, New Spain had enjoyed thirty years of firm and benevolent government. In an era of vigorous expansion and flamboyant appetites, Velasco had been particularly successful in keeping the *encomenderos* under control and defending the interests of the Indians, for whom he had a deep affection. He had presided over the development of the colony in aristocratic magnificence and with quiet efficiency. While he lived his authority was respected. Under the surface, however, serious trouble was brewing between the new generation of Creoles and the government. The higher administration, the *Audiencia* and the viceregal entourage, were staffed almost exclusively by Spaniards without a permanent stake in the country, and the young Creoles were growing to resent the curbs and slights, genuine or fancied, which they had to endure from these people. They were coming to regard European-born lawyers and officials with a mixture of distrust and contempt, not unmingled with fear.

Moreover, they thought they had acquired a natural leader in Martin Cortés, the second Marquess of the Valley, who had arrived in 1563 to claim his father's possessions and was behaving with showy arrogance. What began with wild talk among idle and frustrated young men turned into a full-blown conspiracy, the aim of which was to create a Creole Kingdom with Cortés as its sovereign. But if the conspirators' plans were serious, they were also amateurish and had the enterprise ever been launched it would probably have failed to overcome the innate loyalty to the Crown of most of the white inhabitants of New Spain.

In any case the plotters, a band of excitable and rather fatuous persons, were not in the least suited to take over the administration. Martín Cortés, for all his bravado, was a weakling with none of his father's qualities, while the two Avila brothers, who were pushed into the leadership of the malcontents and gave their name to the conspiracy, did not have the courage to carry out their design. Early in 1566 they took fright and decided to drop the whole affair, but they had gone too far to guarantee their own safety. The *Audiencia*, administering the government in the interregnum between Viceroys, had been alerted and struck heavily to forestall a last-minute blow. The Avilas were arrested, hurriedly tried and beheaded, and the rash but cowardly Cortés might have shared their fate if he had not been rescued by the arrival of the new Viceroy, Peralta. Being a sensible and humane nobleman in the style of Mendoza and Velasco, he decided that justice had gone far enough. He halted further trials and released numerous Creoles jailed by the *oidores*.

When, however, the *Audiencia's* reports reached King Philip, he disavowed and recalled his own representative, Peralta, whom he replaced by special judges with extended powers. These creatures set up a reign of terror in the capital; throughout 1567 it was the scene of endless arrests, tortures and executions. Martín Cortés was lucky to be sent back to Spain, there to await the pleasure of King Philip, whom he had once served as a gay courtier and knight. He survived, but he was never allowed to reclaim his Mexican patrimony, which passed to his descendants. His half-brother and namesake, the son of Doña Marina, behaved under torment with the same stoical bravery as Cuauhtemoc on an earlier and more famous occasion.

The strange feature of this long drawn out and horrible business is that the Creoles were cowed by judicial ferocity, when the royal authorities could have been swept aside by the resolute action of a few hundred armed colonists. But such was the Crown's prestige that no sword was drawn in open rebellion. As soon as the King realised that he had made a mistake, and that his judges were running wild, he revoked their powers and their president, Muñoz, was packed off to Spain in disgrace. The racks and the scaffolds were dismantled. But irremediable damage had already been done to the relations between Spaniards and Creoles. From then on a hard line was to be drawn between the latter and the *gachupines* (the slang Mexican name for metropolitan Spaniards), and there was no love lost between the two groups.

Nevertheless the severity of the royal judges put a stop for more than two hundred years to any serious challenge from the Creoles to the government. There was plenty of grumbling and satire, but no effective protest against arbitrary rule, even during the long decay of the Habsburg monarchy in the seventeenth century. It needed the stimulus of the French Revolution, and the impact of the Napoleonic invasion of Spain, to jolt the Creole conscience out of its age-long condition of prosperous indolence.

Shortly after these events another metropolitan institution, the Inquisition, was set up in Mexico by royal decree. Until 1570 the work of the Holy Office had been delegated to the Archbishop of Mexico, and had mostly been concerned with the suppression of heathen practices. The Church was not, however, so much worried by the danger of the Indians relapsing into idolatry as by external threats to the integrity of the Catholic faith. Although stringent regulations had been framed for excluding from the New World all immigrants from the peninsula who could not prove their status as 'Old Christians', a great many unreliable persons were in fact slipping through the net. In the eyes of the authorities the least desirable of the new arrivals were converted Jews, or the descendants of such *conversos,* who were making their way to the Indies in defiance of the prohibitions. Some of these were sincere Christians, but more crypto-Jews who openly professed Christianity but practised the religions of Moses in secret.

Such people were attracted to Mexico by the prospect of a less cramped existence and of social and economic betterment, but also by the hope that their hidden religious life would escape detection in the more open atmosphere of New Spain. And, as the Spanish authorities were well aware, they were great pro-selytisers. Given the chance, what damage might they not inflict on the faith, in the still unformed society of Mexico, where a population of mixed origins—*mestizos,* negroes and mulattos, the offspring of bizarre racial mixtures—was multiplying between the white upper crust and the Indian masses? It was against the religious deviations of the Old World, Judaism, Protestantism, and in a few cases Mohammedanism, that the operations of the Holy Office were chiefly directed, as well as against sorcerers, blasphemers and notoriously immoral individuals. Like the great Spanish cities, Mexico became the scene of many a solemn and sinister *auto-da-fé*. But although the tribunal was lavish in its punishments, the number of victims actually burned or garrotted was very small by the European standards of the age. Indeed, as Salvador de Madariaga has pointed out, only sixty to a hundred executions are known to have been inflicted in the whole of the Indies during the entire period of colonial rule.

The *cause célèbre* of the sixteenth century in Mexico was the trial of Luis Rodriguez de Carvajal in 1596. It is interesting not only because it reveals the Inquisition at work but because it provides a closely documented record of the life led in Mexico by a group of *conversos* occupied in the promotion of their fortunes but even more keenly attached to the observance of Jewish practices. The tragedy is played against the inscrutable Indian background and to the accompaniment of restless military and economic activity.

The Carvajals were a family of *conversos* of Spanish and Portu-guese descent. Luis de Carvajal, maternal uncle of the Inquisitor's victim, was a tough and resourceful man of business who came to Mexico in 1566 and settled in the Pánuco region, not far from the modern Tampico. It was he who inflicted the second defeat on Hawkins's squadron. In 1579 he obtained from the Crown a licence to subjugate the area to the north-west known as Nuevo León, and was authorised to recruit a hundred settler families in Spain. Oddly enough, these were exempted from the obligation of proving that they were 'Old Christians'. It was therefore hardly surprising that they should have included a high proportion of persons of Jewish origin. Among them was a group of Carvajal's own relatives. He himself was a straightforward Catholic and less interested in matters of doctrine than in making money and subduing Indians, and one of his sister's children was actually a Dominican friar. The others, however, were fanatical crypto-Jews and the young Luis Rodriguez de Carvajal was the most fanatical of them all. His uncle, who had received permission to designate the person of his choice to succeed him eventually as Governor of Nuevo León, had intended to select Luis, a lively and intelligent young man. But Luis showed no aptitude as a frontiersman, and the Governor reluctantly abandoned his plans for his advancement. So Luis, with his parents and the remaining members of his family, transferred himself to Mexico City. Here they were quickly absorbed into the numerous Jewish colony, which they found thriving on commerce and the mines and quietly practising Judaism under the Inquisition's nose.

If they had shown the same discretion as most of their co-religionists, they might well have remained unharmed. It was Luis who, in his proselytising zeal, brought ruin upon them all. He was duly denounced to the Holy Office and in 1590 the whole family were arrested. The old mother was dreadfully tortured. At the *auto-da-fé* that followed they abjured their Judaism and were sentenced to various forms of confinement and supervision. Although they had barely escaped with their lives, Luis, on regaining a measure of liberty incorrigibly resumed his proselytising habits. Inevitably he was again denounced and re-arrested. This time he refused to recant. He fervently proclaimed his faith in the God of Israel and his rejection of Christ. As the hour of his final condemnation approached, he poured out his soul in mystical invocations to Adonai. On 8 December 1596, another grand *auto-da-fé* was mounted on the square of San Hipolito, in the presence of the Viceroy, the *Audiencia* and a huge concourse of people. Luis, his mother and his sisters went to the stake. It was only by a last moment act of repentance (we shall never know if it was feigned or sincere) that he gained the privilege of dying by the garrotte instead of in the flames. Other members of his family shared his fate, but two younger brothers fled from Mexico and eventually found refuge on the faraway Mediterranean, one in Italy and the other in the dominions of the Grand Turk. As for the proud Governor of Nuevo León, he fell from favour and died in penury.

The sad dramas, minutely described in contemporary writings, of the Avilas and Carvajals, are the highlights of the second half of the century, but they were exceptional, not typical, events in the unfolding history of the colony. Long before 1600, New Spain had forgotten the turbulent years of discovery and conquest; it had turned towards the peaceful assertion of its own identity and the development of its peculiar culture.

The Seventeenth and Eighteenth Centuries

The realm of New Spain rose to maturity, and developed its own Mexican consciousness, at the time when old Spain, the mother country of the Creoles, was living through the most glorious years of what is known as its golden century. In 1600 Spain was the strongest military power on the European mainland. At sea, her squadrons disputed the mastery of the Mediterranean with the Turks and exchanged blow for blow with the English and others when they tried to prey on her oceanic empire. At the same time the brilliance of her writers and artists was unsurpassed. It was the age of Cervantes, Calderón, Lope de Vega, El Greco and Velázquez.

The Spanish achievement was mirrored in the civilisation to which it gave birth in America. There is no parallel between the modest stirring of the early French Canadians and British North Americans and the grand style affected from the first by the Viceroyalties of Mexico and Peru. It is true that the Spaniards were earlier off the mark as colonisers and that in the Aztec and Inca lands the riches were there for the taking. More important, however, was the Creole's sense of pride and honour which demanded that his standards should in no way be judged inferior to those of metropolitan Spain. This spirit of emulation took many forms and was not confined to the dull flaunting of material wealth against a background of squalid oppression, as all too readily assumed. In fact Mexico City achieved in the age of Philip II and his successors of the House of Austria a level of prosperity and culture which compared very favourably with the ancient cities of Europe and put them in many respects in the shade. The Mexican capital was famed for its order and cleanliness and for the spacious regular planning of its beautiful buildings. It was as if the civic talents of the Aztecs purposely provided a setting in which the architectural genius of the Renaissance Spain might display itself to its full value.

Throughout the period the city flowered in an atmosphere of restless change. Its early monuments did not last long and gave way to ever more ambitious development. The first cathedral, for instance, was demolished in 1573 and the construction of the present splendid church lasted for most of the following century. The same rhythm prevailed in the other principal centres— Puebla, Guadalajara, Querétaro, Valladolid (Morelia)—and a score of dignified little cities, in no respect falling behind the European creations of the baroque and rococo eras. They can all boast a similar history of enlargement and embellishment on a grandiose scale. Churches and monasteries, town halls and private palaces, colleges, hospitals and aqueducts bear the same stamp of confident grandeur. There was nothing provincial about the stage on which the elaborately attired, and often eccentrically mannered, citizens of the colony disported themselves. Nor were their achievements unworthy of their surroundings.

We luckily possess a series of accounts of Mexico by contemporary writers. Some are uncritically flattering, or too extravagant and rhetorical for our taste. Spanish visitors to Mexico are apt to satirise the manners of the Creoles, while the latter are at pains to proclaim their own virtues, and to complain that the descendants of the conquerors have not been given their due by their unappreciative cousins across the Atlantic. But what is common to all these early writers is the lively interest and sometimes passionate admiration which Mexico has aroused in them. They are fascinated by the colour and sweeping vitality of Mexican life as well as by its mysterious profusion and apparently inexhaustible potentialities. The same spirit of wonder pervades the official reports of Viceroys and clerical dignitaries to their superiors in Europe. Their stilted formulas cannot disguise their absorption with the strangeness of the new world, where the most astonishing transformations are being worked out in a natural environment much vaster than anything conceivable in Europe, and in an equally unfamiliar human climate. They seem to despair of the eloquence of their descriptions and pleadings ever quite matching the realities which they are trying to describe: those who have not shared their experience of America will never fully comprehend.

The first contemporary account of what colonial Mexico City looked like was composed as early as 1554 by one Cervantes de Salazar, in the form of Latin dialogues. Cervantes was a lamentable pedant, and his work is dreadfully dull when compared with the earthy narratives of the Conquest from the pen of Bernal Diaz and others, who were fortunately not scholars, and with the picture of Indian life drawn by friars, who were scholars but not pedants. Nevertheless it is by no means devoid of interest.

Cervantes takes his readers on a tour of the town with the personages in the dialogue. He makes them chat about its attractions and manages to produce, in spite of the inhibitions of language, a lively and exact account of what was going on in the palace, the courts of justice, the plaza and the markets. He describes the grave lawyers and disputatious students, the bustling craftsmen and shopkeepers plying their trades as they would in Seville or Toledo, and the market round the corner where the Indians squatted in their immemorial attitude behind little heaps of herbs and fruits. Outside the city, Cervantes points to the fine houses embowered in gardens, and to the thriving estates and well-stocked hunting preserves of the Valley. Subsequent Spanish visitors in the seventies and eighties praise in verse and prose the ease, elegance and abundance of colonial life, so refreshing after the cramped atmosphere of home. They dwell on the courteous manners of the Creoles, the purity of their Castilian speech and the beauty of their women and children. But it was the horses that moved them to the most spontaneous outbursts of enthusiasm. Many pages are devoted to these marvellous animals, the splendour of their trappings and the grace of their riders. There was something in the soil and air of Mexico peculiarly conducive to the breeding of blood horses and the cultivation of the skills and virtues of the perfect cavalier.

All these subjects are combined by Bernardo de Balbuena in an epic poem published in 1603 and appropriately entitled *Grandeza de Mexico*. Though born in Spain, he heads the line of great Mexican writers of the golden century. Educated at the Royal and Pontifical university, he made his career as a churchman in the Indies, rising to be Bishop of Puerto Rico. But Mexico was his first love, and his poem is a sustained eulogy of the land where he was brought up. Even when allowance has been made for the rhetoric and conceits typical of the literature of the period, there was nothing artificial or inflated in his theme. Both materially and intellectually Mexico was great and it was right that he should proclaim this fact with all the polished eloquence at his command. He was a leading member of the creative minority which called the tune in the Viceroyalty, breathed life into the university and printing presses, patronised the theatre (for which Creoles were already composing comedies) and imported from Europe shiploads of classics and contemporary books.

So far as the colonial élite was concerned, the legend of intellectual backwardness and obscurantism in Spain's overseas empire is ludicrously incorrect. There is evidence of well-stocked private libraries and the monastic foundations amassed enormous quantities of books. It is a real tragedy that these were dispersed and destroyed in the troubled century following Mexican independence. Before we leave Balbuena, it is interesting to hear him indulging in the political vision of Mexico as an imperial capital, in which the widely separated dominions of the House of Austria could establish a stable centre of authority and influence.

In much the same way as the civilisation of the classical age depended on slavery, Creole affluence and culture were supported by the labour of innumerable Indians. The treatment of these underdogs was by no means uniform; it varied from kindly paternalism to extreme brutality. In the mines conditions were at best harsh, and at worst quite intolerable. In the countryside millions of villagers went about their traditional occupations undisturbed and, in the remoter areas, hardly conscious of the presence of the dominant race. They obeyed Indian authorities who were in turn responsible to a royal *corregidor*. If the latter and his minions behaved well, and did not exceed their powers, so much the better for the Indians, who paid their tribute but were otherwise left in peace.

Doubtless there were many communities in the sierras and forests which never saw a white man, apart from the occasional trader or missionary friar. On the monastic lands the Indians were treated with benevolence, though the discipline could sometimes be severe. Private ownership of estates had been temporarily limited by the decline of the *encomienda*. In the neighbourhood of the capital the Indians were subject to various forms of compulsory labour, as indeed they had been in Aztec times. They could be conscripted by the authorities for public works, and even to clear the harvests on the colonists' farms. Nevertheless these burdens were carefully regulated. The new and alarming factor was that there were no longer enough Indians to go round, especially in the central region. The country was suffering from depopulation.

Epidemics of smallpox, and other European diseases previously unknown in Mexico, spread havoc throughout the sixteenth century. Lack of reliable statistics makes the extent of the decline hard to determine, but it is safe to assume that the population of the Valley was halved during the period. Possibly the loss was much greater. Particularly disastrous outbreaks occurred in the forties and seventies, and it took a hundred years for the Indians to develop a degree of immunity against these plagues. The lowest point was reached about 1650, after which a steady rise is registered until the end of the colonial era. But the viceregal government could no longer afford to be prodigal in its use of human resources. They were faced with a reduction of revenue from tribute and by an acute shortage of labour.

Agriculture, which had been diversified and enriched by the Spaniards, did not suffer as much as might have been expected, but much land went out of cultivation. Maguey plantations tended to replace maize on the dry uplands. The colonists liked to grow wheat, but as the Indians obstinately continued to prefer maize *tortillas* to bread as their staple diet, the authorities became increasingly worried about the maintenance of the maize supply. Depopulation also favoured the emergence of a new Creole landowning class, the owners of *haciendas*. As the villages shrank and much of their land was abandoned, private owners moved in. They built up large estates, worked by hired peons, on which commercially profitable methods replaced the Indian communal system. The *hacienda* developed into a self-sufficient rural unit farming tens of thousands of acres. It could be inherited or freely disposed of. The *hacendado* thus enjoyed all the advantages which the *encomendero* had never succeeded in wresting from the government, and vast stretches of land consequently passed into the possession of comparatively few families. It was a process which the authorities no longer had the power or the inclination to resist. The huge fortress-like *hacienda* building, surrounded by all manner of stables, barns, workshops and other agricultural dependencies, became a distinctive feature of the Mexican landscape and flourished exceedingly until the twentieth century. And as an institution the *hacienda* is still not entirely extinct.

Another problem which baffled the Viceroys of the time, and was endlessly wasteful of men and money, was the recurrent flooding of the city and adjacent parts of the Valley. It was not only that the heavy stone colonial houses rested on flimsy foundations and had the inconvenient habit of subsiding into the marsh soil. In the seventeenth century the city was regularly awash in the rainy season, and its health and amenities were gravely prejudiced. The Aztec system of protective dikes had been allowed to fall into disrepair.

At the same time the colonists, with typical Mediterranean insouciance, had been cutting down the woods on the lower slopes of the mountains. Erosion was beginning to silt up the lakes and the destruction of forest cover accelerated the flow of seasonal water into the Valley. The level of the lakes rose ominously. After serious floods in 1604 Luis de Velasco (son of the former Viceroy of that name) decided that the trouble had gone too far to be checked by the mere rebuilding of dikes. On the advice of the engineer Martinez, he caused a tunnel four miles long to be bored through the mountains on the north-western edge of the Valley. This was designed to carry off the waters of Lake Zumpango, which was collecting the greatest volume of overspill. Thousands of Indians were taken off the land to toil in the darkness and mud. Many of them succumbed but the task was finished in eleven months, an extraordinary performance in terms of human effort.

The engineer's conception was excellent. Unfortunately it was defeated by unsound methods of construction. The earth walls of the tunnel, imperfectly strengthened by timber and stone, continually caved in; the canals leading to its mouth became choked with mud and it was not wide enough to cope with a sudden and simultaneous rise in Lakes Zumpango, Xaltocan and Texcoco. For twenty years great gangs of workmen were employed in patching it, but it grew less and less effective. The authorities were tempted to abandon the project altogether and revert to a programme of dike construction. But before a new Nezahualcoyotl could be found the catastrophe which had been long impending struck the city. In 1629 it was completely inundated and normal activities were paralysed.

This time the flood failed to recede even in the dry season. In fact streets and squares remained under several feet of water for four years. Houses sagged and collapsed. Transport was confined to canoes, disease was rife and commerce disrupted. Many of the inhabitants fled to dry land and the permanent transfer of the capital to a higher site was seriously canvassed. Luckily the crisis was eased by a succession of less rainy years. Martinez was restored to favour and it was resolved to convert his tunnel into an open cutting thirteen miles long and two hundred feet deep. For the next ten years the main energies of the viceroyalty were consumed in the excavation of this gigantic artificial canyon, the size of which may be appreciated by anyone who chooses to rumble through it in the train. Even then the job was not completed; indeed work on the project continued intermittently until late in the eighteenth century. The *Tajo de Nochistongo,* as it was called, did not solve the perennial problem of the *Desague,* or drainage of the Valley, which is still the nightmare of the Federal District's engineers and accountants. It did, however, save the city of Cortés from being engulfed in the mire, at enormous cost to the viceregal treasury and grievous waste of manpower. The insatiable demands of the *Desague* stripped the countryside within a radius of fifty miles.

The reputation of Spanish America at this time has long suffered from wilful misrepresentation. The popular legend that it was sunk in lethargy, obscurantism and general backwardness dies hard in the Anglo-Saxon world. The facts are of course otherwise. Compared with the Europe of the Thirty Years War, Spanish America was a haven of peace and plenty. It is quite wrong to conclude that because its history lacked sensational events the scene was one of ignoble stagnation. New Spain was indeed lucky to escape the horrors of war, except when a coastal town was brutally assaulted by foreign buccaneers. But if life was tranquil and secure by the standards of other continents, it was the reverse of dull, a panorama of colourful and bustling activity. It offered a striking contrast to the old world grimly racked by wars of religion and dynastic feuds.

There is ample evidence to disprove the old gloomy view. Take, for example, the accurate as well as picturesque account of colonial ways found in the writings of Thomas Gage. Gage was an Englishman who travelled widely through Mexico and Guatemala in the thirties of the seventeenth century. Being a Dominican friar, he was in a unique position to form a correct judgement, for all doors were open to him. Later he was to shed his habit, abjure his faith and devote his talents to furthering Cromwell's plans for conquests on the Spanish Main. He was not an altogether attractive character, and it was in his interest, when addressing himself to English readers, to decry rather than praise Spanish colonial institutions. Nevertheless he was an honest observer with a witty style and a real gift for exact description. He was intelligent and highly inquisitive. The very fact that when he wrote down his experiences he was professionally, so to speak, ill-disposed towards the Spaniards enhances the value of his record. Except when it is purposely tendentious it has the ring of truth, and bears remarkably favourable witness to the condition of Mexico.

Gage was naturally enchanted by the stateliness and brilliance of the capital. It was, he says, one of the richest cities of the world; it was also the cleanest (notwithstanding the floods). His panegyric is no less sincere than Balbuena's, and sounds more convincing because it is expressed in simple English.

He was fascinated by the panache of Mexican life, by the finery worn by women of all classes and the 'gallantry' of the horses. But his admiration was by no means confined to what he saw in the principal towns. He ranged freely over the countryside in southern Mexico, a region where Dominican monasteries were numerous. His descriptions of Indian townships are especially interesting, because he repeatedly stresses their prosperity and the freedom in which their inhabitants were left to run their own affairs. His picture is of a contented people and of leaders living in dignified comfort. It was a far cry from the mines and the Nochistongo cutting. Having an eye for economic detail, Gage was impressed by the profusion and variety of crops and fruits and by the thriving state of commerce and manufactures. He extols, for example, the textiles of Puebla, an industry which has prospered down to modern times. It is clear that in his day the increasing taxation, and the regulations protecting Spanish products against colonial competition, were not seriously inhibiting internal or external trade. The shops of Mexico City were well stocked with goods from Europe and the Far East which had succeeded in entering the country through lawful or other channels. Prohibitions framed in Madrid were ignored or evaded by everyone from the Viceroy downwards, and contra-band was the most profitable industry of all. In an age when the principle of state protection was undisputed, and the expansion of maritime trade was limited for physical reasons, this was the normal march of affairs. No contemporary would have regarded Mexico as a sluggard in trade.

Stable conditions and material well-being favoured the development of Creole culture. Throughout the seventeenth century Mexico hummed with intellectual activity and the world of letters was adorned by a variety of accomplished and original figures. Juan Ruiz de Alarcón, later recognised as one of Spain's greatest dramatists, was born in Mexico, graduated at its University and began his career as a playwright in the country of his birth. The nun Sor Juana Ines de la Cruz wrote lyric poetry of unsurpassed purity and elegance, remarkable for depth of feeling and intensity of devotion. As a young girl, and before she took the veil, she created a sensation at the viceregal court by her beauty and learning, and when she retired into a convent her cell became the focus and inspiration of literary and scientific studies. She died at the age of thirty-four.

Mexican history was the province of the religious orders. The turn of the century saw the publication of a series of important books in the tradition of Sahagún and Motolinia, such as the *Historia Ecclesiastica de los Indias* by Fray Jeronimo Mendieta, the *Monarquia Indiana* by Fray Juan de Torquemada and the *Historia Natural y Moral de las Indias* by Father José de Acosta. These writers are united by a deep interest in the Indian past, in native languages and customs and in the natural history of the New World. While their basic theme is the introduction of Christianity into the Americas, they are also animated by an independent spirit of scientific enquiry. Acosta was a member of the Society of Jesus, which was tending to supersede Franciscans and Dominicans in the fields of education and missionary activity. The friars, as Gage maliciously points out, were losing their original zeal and apostolic simplicity: they had lapsed into comfortable ways and lived off the fat of the land. The Jesuits, however, were indefatigable and ambitious. Their colleges provided the best education in the colony. It was at Tepotzotlán, their splendid foundation on the road to Querétaro, that the famous polymath Carlos de Siguenza y Gongora was trained for the priesthood. Siguenza was a prodigy of erudition, an intellectual all-rounder of amazing versatility. He excelled as poet, philosopher, astronomer and cosmographer, and occupied the chair of Mathematics at the University. His reputation for scientific controversy and experiment reached across the Atlantic. He was in fact a worthy contemporary of Leibnitz and Newton, and the epitome of the cultural achievements of New Spain in the baroque age. One of his major interests was the study of pre-Columbian antiquities, and he composed a history, which has unfortunately perished, based on the earlier works of two hispanicised Indians of royal descent, Alvarado Tezozomoc and Fernando de Alva Ixtlilxochitl.

Siguenza was also concerned with the practical problem of strengthening the maritime defences of the Spanish Indies against French encroachments. In these matters he acted as adviser to the

Viceroy, the Conde de Galve; on whose orders he accompanied a fleet despatched from Vera Cruz in 1692 to reassert Spanish sovereignty in the Gulf of Mexico and strengthen the outposts of the colony as far north as Pensacola. In a memoir drawn up in the same year he described a violent riot by the Indians of Mexico City, which caused great damage by fire and pillage. The Viceroy was in danger of his life and a general massacre of Creoles and Spaniards narrowly averted. The old scholar's record of these events is a masterpiece of journalism. He himself sallied forth heroically to rescue the city's archives from the flames. This uprising, which was provoked by a shortage of maize, subsided as quickly as it had blazed up, but it gave the authorities and the white population a nasty scare. Fortunately events of this kind were rare in Mexico, which was much less troubled than other parts of the Spanish Empire by unrest among the Indians or faction-fights between the Creoles.

It is remarkable that such tranquillity should have prevailed from decade to decade in a country where the rule of a small racial minority did not depend on repression by armed force. Authority rested on the consent of the governed, or at least on a high measure of contentment. Apart from the natural docility of the Indians and an unusual absence of the anarchic individualism which so often breaks out among people of Spanish descent, this happy state of affairs was due to the fundamental good sense and humanity of the viceregal régime. The Spanish colonial institutions of the time may appear stuffy and antiquated to us, but they were on the whole well suited to the land in which they were implanted. Of the sixty-one Viceroys who succeeded one another in a majestic procession for three centuries, the majority were easy-going and tolerably efficient aristocrats. Some were men of proved administrative capacity who devoted their working life to service in the Indies; thus it was not uncommon for a Viceroy of New Spain to be transferred to Peru. Only a few were incompetent or even harmlessly fatuous.

This is not to say that no cases of corrupt and arbitrary conduct occurred from time to time. One of the best known and most ludicrous incidents concerned the Marqués de Gelbes, who cornered the market in maize and when the Archbishop intervened on behalf of the suffering population, arrested him at the altar and hustled him off to Spain, thus bringing down on himself a sentence of excommunication. But semi-farcical scandals of this time barely ruffled the surface of colonial life.

During the long reign of the weak-minded Charles II, the last Habsburg king (1665–1700), Spain, exhausted by two centuries of intense effort, was tottering towards political and economic ruin. Yet the beggarly condition of the mother country was not reflected in the colony, which remained prosperous and secure. Nor did the decline of Spanish power inspire any movement towards Creole independence during this inglorious period. There was absolutely no sign of disloyalty to the Crown. On the other hand the differences between the European and the American born Spaniards were becoming slowly accentuated. After two centuries the Creoles no longer spoke, behaved or thought exactly like the new arrivals from Castille and Andalucia. The immigrants, whether they had come to settle permanently or intended to make their fortunes and return to Spain, bore the distinctive marks of the *gachupin* and constituted a separate element in the white population.

Although the Spaniards were few in number as compared with the Creoles and the evergrowing mass of *mestizos,* who themselves formed a bridge between Creoles and Indians, they had established themselves in positions of privilege and advantage. In the first place, they occupied a high proportion of government posts, great and small. If the office-holder had been appointed directly from Spain, the Creoles took it for granted that he had been unfairly preferred, while if he owed his appointment to the Viceroy's patronage, it was assumed that he had succeeded through prejudice or corruption. Indeed the sale of offices seems to have been a common practice in the lax years of the later seventeenth century.

Secondly, the Spaniards were extremely active in business, for which they had greater aptitude than the Creoles. Where money was to be made, there the industrious *gachupines* gravitated. Many acquired rich mines and plantations, while the lesser fry flourished as tradespeople, or served as overseers, book-keepers and the like on the *haciendas*. More competitive than the Creoles, they looked down on the *mestizos* and bullied the Indians. Rightly or wrongly, they were regarded as tight-fisted, arrogant and exclusive. They were certainly clannish and pushing.

The Creoles considered that they were no less fitted than the Spaniards for high position in the colony. They felt themselves at least equal in nobility and intelligence, and were able to point to outstanding examples of Mexicans who had held offices of importance in the peninsula, or had won intellectual distinction.

They did not expect that the Viceroys should be chosen from their ranks, but it did irk them not to receive an equitable proportion of the secondary posts in the *Audiencia* and the municipalities, to say nothing of minor clerkships.

Generally speaking, it was easier for them to rise in the Church than in State service. There were plenty of Creole bishops, and in 1679 an Indian priest, Nicolas del Puerto, actually occupied the see of Oaxaca. But his was an exceptional case, like that of the American-born Viceroy the Marqués de Casa Fuerte. In the absence of equal opportunity, animosity between the two rival groups of whites was bound to increase. It was, however, slow to develop, since they both belonged to the same racial and social caste and were consequently united by common interest. Moreover, apart from their loyalty to the Crown, the Creoles were part of the fabric of Hispanic civilisation. And in the reign of Charles II, when Spain was sunk in poverty and sloth, they could justly claim to be the more vigorous representatives of that civilisation. Mexico surpassed Spain in the wealth and beauty of its physical resources, and it bred, in the Creole view, the finest type of Spaniard.

Mexico was little disturbed by the long war of the Spanish Succession which resulted in the replacement of the Habsburgs by the Bourbons. Nevertheless the radical change of outlook which followed the adoption by the Court of Madrid of French modes of thought and methods of government quickened the tempo of colonial life and prepared the way for the introduction of new ideas. New Spain increasingly felt the repercussions of events in Europe. In the preceding period it had virtually governed itself, subject to the remote direction of the Council of the Indies. By the new dispensation the Council's more important functions were transferred to a Secretary of State for the Indies, an administrator on the French model who kept a much sharper watch over colonial affairs.

New Spain was now regarded as a province to be administered according to the principles of centralism and uniformity, rather than as a self-sufficient realm united with other kingdoms, in the peninsula and overseas, in common allegiance to the Crown. The existing structure of colonial institutions was at first left intact, and it was not until the reign of Charles III (1759–88) that Mexico really felt the influence of enlightened despotism. During this period, however, the wind of reform blew strongly. The King had an acute if eccentric mind which, before succeeding to the throne of Spain, he had successfully exercised in ruling Parma and Naples. He knew how to choose efficient administrators, and one of his best choices was José Bernardo Galvez, who in 1765 carried out a thorough survey of Mexico in the capacity of *visitador,* or inspector-general of the viceroyalty. Later, as Secretary of State, he put into effect the recommendations which he had framed in the course of his mission. By his direction local government was completely reorganised and entrusted to twelve regional Intendants, who took over the powers of the time-honoured apparatus of *corregidores, alcaldes mayores* and other provincial and municipal officials.

This faithful imitation of the French system produced excellent results. The intendants cleared up the prevailing financial mess and worked hard to improve the lot of the Indians. According to the great Prussian traveller, Alexander von Humboldt, this was their most notable achievement, but it was not one which necessarily commended itself to the Creoles, for whom bureaucratic centralism had little attraction. Of more obvious benefit to them was the relatively liberal policy for overseas trade which Galvez applied to New Spain towards the end of Charles' reign. Many new ports in Spain, Mexico and other parts of the empire were opened to commerce. The old maze of duties and tariffs gave way to a more rational system. As a result the colony's exports increased fourfold in ten years. Colonial Mexico, already a mature society, responded to the new stimulus from outside by a final brilliant flowering.

Throughout the eighteenth century the varying fortunes of war between the European powers with interests in America produced constant territorial changes. It so happened that between 1763 and the beginning of the struggle for Latin American independence Spanish North America attained its widest extent. The Spanish flag flew over New Orleans. The wastes of Texas, New Mexico and Arizona were dotted with tiny settlements and missions, and a determined effort was made to strengthen Spanish claims to effective possession of California.

Here again the friars, headed by the most saintly and daring of all missionaries, Fray Junipero Serra, were patiently advancing the borders of civilisation, slowly taming the wild Indians and preparing the way for the trader, the miner and the *hacendado.* San Francisco, founded in 1778, was about the northward limit of the Spanish colonial presence on land, but from the seventies to the nineties repeated expeditions by sea were fitted out by the Viceroys in Mexico City. They crept steadily up the coast towards what is now British Columbia. From that remote zone, where Vancouver and Cook had already touched, and where the Russians, pressing down from Alaska, were engaged in the fur trade, the Spaniards from Mexico eventually withdrew—the government in Madrid was not disposed for a conflict with Great Britain on so distant a territorial issue—but not before they had completed the most valuable scientific researches.

The enquiring spirit of that philosophic age was as active in New Spain as in the old continent. (Cuadra, the Admiral who led two of the maritime expeditions to the north-west, was a member of an old Creole family whose *hacienda* house still nestles in the wooded mountains behind Taxco, a region rich in silver-bearing ores.) Nevertheless it should not be imagined that a revolutionary situation existed among the Creoles of Mexico before the foundations of Spanish authority had been sapped by the Napoleonic wars. Indeed Mexico seems to have been less susceptible to subversive ideas than other parts of Spanish America. It was not that the works of the French philosophers— Voltaire, Rousseau and the Encyclopaedists—were not read in New Spain. On the contrary, they circulated freely among educated people in spite of the prohibitions of the Church and the lukewarm disapproval of the State. But the radicalism of their ideas, which called in question the value of all traditional beliefs, including that of the superiority of the whites over the subject races, was hardly calculated to appeal to the conservative-minded Creoles. The expulsion of the Jesuits from New Spain in 1767, which was enforced in the most high-handed manner at the behest of Charles II and his progressively inclined advisers, was profoundly unpopular among all classes of Mexicans, who correctly foresaw the ruin of their educational standards.

The triumph of the American colonists over the British Government, and the consequent emancipation of the North American counterparts of the Creoles from transatlantic control, posed a more serious threat to the integrity of the Spanish empire. Throughout the Indies the obvious conclusion was drawn that sooner or later Spanish America would follow the example of the thirteen colonies. At the same time the Creoles' resentment against the privileges enjoyed in their country by European Spaniards, and their vague aspirations to be rid of restrictions imposed by the home government on their freedom of action, were working in favour of secession. A few small groups of drawing-room conspirators angled unsuccessfully abroad for support for their very immature independence plans. They were not however, representative of Creole sentiment in Mexico, where the news from North America was far more likely to evoke simple satisfaction at the discomfiture of the old foe, England, than to spark off treasonable activity against Spain. As for French revolutionists, their excesses inspired horror rather than enthusiasm. There was no urge for violent change in political institutions or in the shape of society.

Thus, in the absence of incentives strong enough to overturn, or at least discredit, the old régime, colonial Mexico basked in its Indian summer of prosperity and good order. In the chaotic years which followed the achievement of national independence, the older generation ruefully remembered the wise government of the Viceroys Bucareli (1771–9) and Revillagigedo (1780–94). The arts and sciences were actively fostered by the authorities and various notable institutions founded for their development. Such were the School of Mines, the Mint and the Academy of Fine Arts (San Carlos), all of which have survived in one form or another into our own times.

Humboldt, who travelled through Spanish America at the turn of the century, praised them exhaustively, and as a scientific observer of a liberal and progressive turn of mind he was peculiarly fitted to appreciate their achievements. He declares outright that Mexico surpassed all other centres in North and South America in scientific accomplishments and bears enthusiastic witness to the intellectual curiosity and ability of Mexican youth. Although no writers of genius emerged to challenge those of the preceding century, the age was singularly rich in architecture, architectural sculpture and the minor decorative arts. By then the Churrigueresque style, which had run rampant over New Spain in the middle years of the century had reached its zenith and was giving way to classical influences derived from France. But in a short space of time it had completely transformed the aspect of the cities, and even of the villages, by the ornate magnificence of its monuments. Large and small, these churches vie with each other in the intricacy and exuberance of their decoration, and in cities like Puebla the secular buildings are almost as extravagantly bedecked. The scale and extent of this outburst of creative activity are astonishing; in its concentrated energy it recalls Gothic France or Renaissance Italy. Although financed by the wealth of the mines and of the Church's estates, it was in its artistic aspect a spontaneous expression of the national vitality. All over the country armies of Indian craftsmen were occupied in this tremendous effort, directed by architects whose names are largely unknown, but whose works have triumphantly survived.

Unfortunately the trend towards an academic classicism brought the Churrigueresque movement to an abrupt end. The new arbiter of taste was the Spaniard Manuel Tolsa, who dominated the Academy of San Carlos. He built fine palaces and churches and cast in bronze the imposing equestrian statue of Charles IV, nicknamed the *Caballito*—or Little Horse—which formerly graced the Zócalo of Mexico City and now stands in an equally commanding site on the Paseo de la Reforma. He was a gifted architect, but the austerity of his style was quite foreign to the Mexican spirit and froze its luxuriant imagination to death. However the greatest of all Mexican artists of the time, Eduardo Tresguerras, who excelled as architect, painter and sculptor, pursued his highly individual line unaffected by foreign fashions. His splendid churches adorn the little cities of the Bajío, the broad valley stretching westwards from Querétaro. In the seventeenth century Mexico had produced its own very flourishing school of baroque painting (described with a wealth of detail by Siguenza y Gongora), and this tradition was continued and perfected in the Churrigueresque age, notably by Cabrera, an Indian from Oaxaca. But when these outstanding figures had disappeared, the arts decayed in Mexico for many years to come. Any possibility of their early revival perished in the impoverishment and insecurity of the next half century.

Humboldt's account of Mexico in 1800 is contemporary and objective. It is also derived entirely from personal experience. He presented Mexico as judged by the standards of an honest, critical European with no prejudices to air. Without exaggerating the good or concealing the bad, he demolishes the misconception which has so stubbornly prevailed of a country groaning in misery under the colonial yoke. What he describes is a land full of vigour and promise, where the population, production, trade and revenue are rising and where the underdog is often better off than his opposite number in the old world. He comments, for instance, that there is no forced labour in the mines, where good wages may be earned, and that the lot of the Indian peasant is generally superior to that of the Eastern European serf. His assertions are supported by a formidable deployment of facts and figures. It is well to use his spectacles when taking a last look at Mexico on the verge of the upheaval which led to independence.

The colonial scene undeniably exhibited glaring defects, injustices and absurdities, but they were certainly no worse than those prevailing in countries which affected to despise the primitive conditions of the Indies. The government, authoritarian but easy-going, would have been perfectly bearable without the *gachupines* who so largely staffed it. If the Church had grown lethargic, this was hardly a matter of popular concern, much less of scandal. The upper class might be lazy and pretentious, but it cut a fine figure and was no less civilised than in any average Christian country of the time. Merchants and shopkeepers were making money and had little to worry about. The condition of the Indian villagers had improved during the later years of the viceroyalty, and the swarms of beggars, or *léperos,* who infested Mexico City were no more brutish than the gin-soaked mobs of the Gordon riots.

Yet, among patriotic Creoles ambitious for office, intellectuals moved by the tidings from revolutionary France and the whole restless, shifting class of *mestizos,* discontent was stirring. Under the pressure of catastrophic changes in Europe, the small cracks in the majestic façade of the viceroyalty were soon to widen into dangerous fissures.

Chapter Six   Independence

After the death of Charles III in 1788, the situation in Spain degenerated rapidly. His successor, Charles IV, was a dullard dominated by his unscrupulous favourite, Godoy, who was no adequate substitute for the able reforming ministers of the previous reign. Neither King nor minister were of the calibre to cope with the diplomatic and military complications of the French Revolution and the resultant wars. After a brief spell of opposition to republican France, Godoy allowed himself to be swept into its orbit. Notwithstanding his master's abhorrence of the régime which had put to death his kinsman, Louis XVI, and the dangerous impact of French political ideas on the stability of the Spanish empire, Godoy was determined to restore the traditional alliance which had united the two Bourbon monarchies in a policy of hostility to Great Britain. In the days of the so-called Family Compact, Spain had pulled her weight and had been treated as an equal partner. But in her association with the republic she was reduced to a satellite with no will of her own, and with no mission but to further French ambitions. Her powerful fleet and the resources of her overseas territories were at the disposal of the Directory in Paris. Later, when Bonaparte rose to power, he established a sinister personal ascendancy over Godoy and Spain was dragged even more ignominiously in the French wake.

From this condition of subservience she derived no profit at all. British command of the sea crippled her trade and endangered her communications with the colonies. Her fleet was shattered at Trafalgar. While Napoleon extended his grip over continental Europe, she seethed with frustration and wounded pride. Even Godoy made a feeble effort to reverse his disastrous policy. But events were moving too fast. A French army was already operating against the British in Portugal and Napoleon judged the moment right to seize the whole peninsula. In 1808 he sent his troops into Spain. The wretched Spanish royal family was tricked and bullied into renouncing its rights in favour of the Bonapartes. Charles IV and his heir, Ferdinand, were successively forced to abdicate and interned in France, while in one of those dynastic switches to which Napoleon was addicted his brother, Joseph, was made to exchange the throne of Naples for that of Spain.

At this point Napoleon's progress was checked by the reaction of the long-suffering Spanish people. Although Madrid was held for King Joseph, the whole country sprang to arms. Juntas established at Seville and Oviedo assumed authority in the name of King Ferdinand. The struggle for liberation had begun and was to last until Napoleon's downfall. Meanwhile, however, Spain ceased to rank as a great power. The awe-inspiring prestige which had upheld her sovereignty in the Americas for nigh on three hundred years was grievously shaken, and the royal authorities there were left to fend for themselves without effective support from home.

In New Spain the rot started with the dismissal of Revillagigedo, last of the great viceroys, in 1794. During the next sixteen years the foundations of authority crumbled slowly. On the surface all was calm, but the humiliations of the French alliance were keenly felt and the subventions exacted from Mexico to help finance Godoy's unpopular policies were much resented. The idea of Mexican independence began timidly to be aired in small, politically-minded coteries. After 1804, when the struggle between Great Britain and France entered a critical phase, it became known that the British Government was studying plans for the over-throw of the Spanish empire with the assistance of Creole malcontents. At one moment a force, to be commanded by no less a person than Sir Arthur Wellesley, was actually earmarked for a descent on Mexico and it is intriguing to speculate whether the sepoy general would have been more successful in eliminating Spanish rule from Anahuac than his colleagues who so signally failed to fulfil a similar mission in the River Plate (1806–7). The dizzy turmoil of events in Spain, however, put an end to these projects. British efforts were concentrated on the prosecution of the war in the peninsula, in co-operation with the national Juntas. The Spanish Americans were left to thrash out their problems with the vestiges of Spanish government subsisting on their own soil.

The Viceroy of New Spain in 1808 was Iturrigaray. He owed his appointment to Godoy and, like his patron, he had acquired a bad name for corruption. His aim, if he had one, was to hang on to his place as long as possible, or at any rate while the war lasted. As Godoy's man he could expect no sympathy from the Juntas. Consequently he was obliged to conciliate the Creoles, who disliked him for his past behaviour but might be disposed to keep him as a figure-head or use him as a convenient political instrument.

Creole sentiment at once declared itself as passionately anti-French and loyal in its allegiance to the exiled King Ferdinand VII. But it was decidedly cool towards the Juntas, which were regarded merely as improvised organs of government dependent on foreign support and lacking the mystical prestige of the monarchy. The Mexicans were unable to accept them as automatically succeeding to the King's authority over his realm of New Spain. They argued that if it were found necessary to set up in Mexico a body corresponding to a Spanish Junta, it should be composed of Mexicans, who could be relied upon faithfully to interpret and execute the presumed wishes of the Sovereign in respect of his Mexican dominions. In other words, the new situation demanded the replacement by a Creole administration, loyal to the King, of the existing government directed by *gachupines*. Those who liked to use the language of Rousseau talked of interpreting the sovereign will of Mexican people. What they really desired was the rule of a native white minority released from the trammels of Spanish legalists and bureaucrats.

If the Creoles had been more resolute and better organised, this is what they might easily have achieved. But the men of birth and property who formed the most powerful element among them were too hesitant to move quickly and decisively. New Spain failed to produce a Bolívar or a San Martín, an aristocratic leader of Creole stock ruthlessly determined to repudiate the Crown, crush its armies on the battlefield and set up an oligarchical régime with republican forms. Respect for the monarchy was too deeply ingrained in the Mexicans for them to follow the South American example. Their movement towards independence and eventual adoption of a republic was a tentative and even reluctant process. In its earliest stage it was summarily halted by the *gachupines,* supported by a few regiments of royal troops.

While Iturrigaray and the Creole leaders were still groping for a solution, the Spaniards struck. On 15 September (a fateful date in Mexican history), they arrested the Viceroy and rushed him off to Vera Cruz in much the same way as Cortés himself might have acted. The Spanish-dominated *Audiencia* replaced him with an elderly gentleman named Garibay, who soon yielded his office to the Archbishop, Lizana. No Creole counter-stroke occurred; the country seemed cowed and a few manifestations of protest were easily suppressed.

For the next two years the *gachupines* remained firmly in control, receiving their instructions from the regency which had by this time established itself in the part of Spain liberated from the French. Evidently there was little enthusiasm among the propertied Creoles for starting a rebellion which might involve serious fighting; they recoiled before the risk of disorder, bloodshed and civil war. When trouble eventually broke out it took quite a different form from that of a palace revolution or *coup d'état* at the centre. The first real challenge to the *gachupin* government was launched by an obscure priest in a little country town, with the backing of a band of conspirators drawn from the middle ranks of society.

The cradle of the revolt was the region between Querétaro and Guanajuato, where the Indians were mostly of Tarascan and Otomi stock. It was at that time eminently a country of big *haciendas* worked by landless peasants, as well as of mining communities of an independent and unruly spirit. The many small towns were prosperous centres of Creole culture, abounding in treasures of colonial art and architecture, and their flourishing economy had attracted a large *gachupin* element. In the cities of Querétaro, standing at the junction of the roads from Mexico City, Guadalajara and San Luis Potosí, a club had been founded, in the guise of a literary society, for the discussion of political and society affairs. Scores of similar groups were meeting all over the country without causing any particular concern to the authorities, but the patriots of Querétaro happened to be unusually active. The leading spirit was Ignacio Allende, a young officer in a Creole regiment and citizen of San Miguel, a little town in the hinterland. Not far from San Miguel lies Dolores, whose parish priest, Miguel Hidalgo y Costilla, had been induced by Allende to join the Querétaro circle, and had become one of its keenest members.

Hidalgo was an originally minded man of striking appearance, tall and gaunt, with prophetic features which mirrored his strong convictions and impulsive character. He had attended, as student and teacher, the college of San Nicolas at Valladolid (now

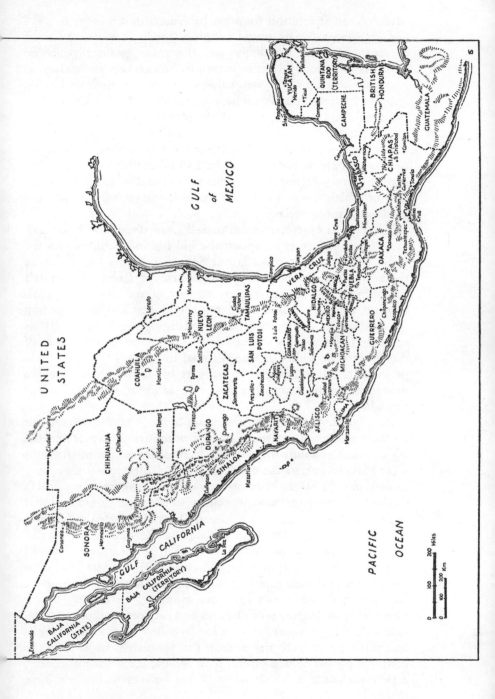

Morelia), an institution founded by Vasco de Quiroga in 1536 and celebrated for its sound learning (today it boasts the most ancient university buildings and the most politically-minded students in Mexico). Deeply versed in French as well as classical and Spanish culture, he sympathised strongly with liberal ideas, and for that reason had won little advancement in the Church. At the age of fifty-seven he was still the humble priest of Dolores, an unimportant townlet. Here he occupied himself with teaching useful crafts and agricultural methods to the Indians, with whom he was deservedly popular, but he had fallen foul of the government for encouraging them to plant vines and olives, the cultivation of which was not officially permitted in Mexico outside the gardens of monasteries.

The club at Querétaro soon passed from discussion to conspiracy. Their plan was to launch the bid for independence on the occasion of the December fair at San Juan de los Lagos, where there was sure to be a large concourse of Creoles. Allende's programme was simple, the overthrow of the *gachupin* administration, the convocation of a national congress and the formation of a Mexican government acknowledging Ferdinand VII as sovereign. These aims were of course no different from those of the movement which had been foiled in Mexico City two years previously. Allende hoped to subvert his fellow-soldiers in the provincial garrisons, gather a Creole army and march on the capital.

As might have been expected, news of his intentions leaked out through his numerous soundings of potential adherents and the government was duly forewarned. In mid-September instructions were issued to arrest the chiefs of the conspiracy, but they were in turn alerted by the wife of the *corregidor* of Querétaro, Josefa Ortiz de Dominguez, who was privy to the plot. Convinced that their cause was doomed, Allende and his patriots fled to Dolores and conferred hurriedly with Hidalgo in the midnight hours of 15 September. The priest pointed out that their only hope of success lay in striking at once, although their preparations were incomplete and their supporters dispersed. He then took matters into his own hands. On the next morning, 16 September, he summoned the populace of Dolores and the surrounding countryside to the town square by the loud pealing of the church bells and exhorted them to rise against the Spaniards. In inciting the common people he was careful to avoid the term 'independence', a political concept which most of his hearers would not have understood, but roundly accused the *gachupines* of conspiring to betray Mexico, their King and the Catholic faith to Napoleon and the irreligious French. In the name of Ferdinand VII, he called upon all good Mexicans to expel the traitors and interlopers.

Hidalgo's hearers were fascinated by the almost Messianic eloquence of his appeal. Its very simplicity, combined with a blatant distortion of the facts, assured its success. He immediately found himself at the head of an elated mob of Indians and *mestizos,* avid for bloodshed and plunder. This was hardly the kind of insurrection that Allende and his friends had bargained for.

Whatever their misgivings, the conspirators stuck together and their forces, though ill-armed and disorderly, swelled daily. The insurgents moved first on Allende's birthplace, San Miguel, passing by way of Atotonilco, a pilgrimage shrine of peculiar sanctity among the Indians. There they picked up the banner of the Virgin of Guadalupe which served as their standard throughout the coming campaign. Having appropriated this supernatural sanction, they proceeded thoroughly to sack both San Miguel and Celeya, spreading terror among townspeople and *hacendados*. Although their war cry was 'Death to the *Gachupines*', they soon ceased to differentiate between Spaniards and Creoles when loot was for the taking. The revolt was assuming the character of a social upheaval, a totally strange occurrence in the long history of New Spain. Within two weeks Hidalgo's forces were numbered in tens of thousands, an ill-armed rabble leavened only by one or two battalions from the army which Allende had won over. But Hidalgo, in the full flush of his early triumphs, would not allow Allende to exercise military command. Proclaiming himself Captain-General of America, he marched on Guanajuato, seat of the local intendancy.

The Spanish intendant, Riano, rightly judged that he could not protect Mexico's principal mining city against the huge rebel mob. He therefore withdrew his troops into the Alhondiga de Granaditas, a tall thick-walled warehouse standing like a castle in the centre of the town, and prepared to withstand a siege, rejecting Hidalgo's summons to surrender. The assault was delivered on 28 September. For a while the improvised fortress, packed with refugees and silver bullion, held firm, but after the intendant had been shot dead a young Indian miner nicknamed 'El Pipila' took advantage of the momentary confusion among the defenders. Protecting his head and shoulders with a slab of flooring stone, he staggered across the bullet-swept street to the shelter of the massive wooden doorway of the building and managed to set it on fire. The entrance was then stormed and the garrison overrun. Any Spaniards who survived were imprisoned in the same *Alhondiga,* only to be executed some months later on the approach of the avenging royal army. The whole town was subjected to an orgy of massacre and pillage which Hidalgo and his subordinates, genuinely horrified by these outrages, were powerless to prevent. Swallowing their scruples, they advanced on Valladolid, where the authorities were too frightened to put up any resistance. This time the insurgents refrained from the worst excesses.

Hidalgo's next objective was Mexico City. During a short pause in the town where he felt most at home he laboured to create some semblance of order among the untrained masses of his followers, and to equip them with the necessary minimum of cannon and muskets. Meanwhile he received heartening news from other provincial centres. The northern towns—Zacatecas, San Luis Potosí, Saltillo—enthusiastically acclaimed the revolution and his agents were busily stirring up unrest in the west and south. The government, thoroughly alarmed but apparently underestimating the threat to the capital, elected to send its main force, under the capable and experienced General Calleja, to reduce San Luis Potosí. He was still absent when Hidalgo led his eighty thousand men through the difficult forest country of eastern Michoacán toward the Valley of Mexico—no mean feat of organisation even for a better disciplined force. His army passed without hindrance through Toluca and the Lerma marshes and climbed the steep road through the last natural obstacle, the Sierra de las Cruces.

The scanty force which the government had scraped together, seven thousand men under the command of General Trujillo, was drawn up to block the pass, and a fierce battle was fought without either side gaining a definite advantage. The revolutionaries were too numerous to be repelled or dispersed, but they failed to swamp their opponents, who retreated in good order towards the city, claiming a victory. The Viceroy, Venegas, who had taken up his post the day before Hidalgo acted at Dolores, was not deceived; he knew that the capital lay open to attack after Trujillo's remaining troops had abandoned their line of defence on the heights. The citizens, who were well aware what they had to expect in the almost certain event of Hidalgo's horde getting out of hand, shared his dismay. But to the general amazement nothing happened. Instead of rolling down from the hills in an irresistible, exultant flood, the rebels were trailing despondently back to Toluca, dwindling as they went.

The reasons for this fatal irresolution have never been convincingly explained, and the *gachupines* could only attribute their salvation to the intervention of the Virgen de los Remedios, patroness of the Spaniards in Mexico and rival of the Virgin of Guadalupe, whom the Viceroy had solemnly invoked. It was certainly strange that the iron-willed Hidalgo should suddenly falter on the brink of success. He may have decided that he could not face the moral and political responsibility for the sack of Mexico City. He may also have been preoccupied by the problem of dealing with Calleja, who was approaching by forced marches, and confused by the conflicting arguments of his military advisers. Allende was strongly in favour of going forward, and for Hidalgo the temptation to install himself without delay in the viceregal palace was indeed seductive. He perhaps felt, however, that it would be more prudent to engage Calleja away from the capital and its demoralising influence on his own forces. Even so, it was a disastrous error to turn back. From that day he lost the initiative and sealed his fate.

The returning rebel army was overtaken by Calleja at Aculco, not far from Toluca, and roughly handled. Hidalgo got away to Valladolid and Allende, whose differences with his chief had become acute, to Guanajuato. There was still a faint chance of a revolution succeeding if a rival government could be set up in the broad lands of northern and western Mexico which had already risen in response to Hidalgo's call. With this object in view Hidalgo fixed his headquarters at Guadalajara and tried to organise a regular administration. But it was too late for so anarchic a movement to reverse its direction and resort to conventional methods. By then it had forfeited the sympathy of moderate Creoles and many liberals who had joined it before its fortunes began to fade were making their peace with the government in Mexico City. Hidalgo's position in Guadalajara, capital of the conservative west, was both false and precarious, though he was at first treated with cautious deference by the local dignitaries.

Moreover, the war was being waged with increasing cruelty on both sides. Executions of *gachupines* were avenged fourfold on the rebel partisans captured by Calleja's troops, and the passage of the armies left a trail of atrocities and devastation. After a long era of settled peace, Mexico was experiencing a foretaste of the callous brutality which was to become so dreary a feature of the revolutions, civil wars and social convulsions of the next century. In this atmosphere of savage resentments it was beyond Hidalgo's capacity to stabilise his movement and work for reconciliation.

It was also too late to restore his military prestige. Allende, who had failed to hold Guanajuato against Calleja, first retired to Zacatecas; then, in January, he loyally rejoined the main rebel army for the crucial battle, which took place at the bridge of Calderón over the river Lerma, to the east side of Guadalajara. Again discipline prevailed over numbers, and this time Calleja won a decisive victory. As the insurgents escaped northwards, Allende at last assumed military control, but was unable to avert collapse. In the vague hope of finding support in the United States, he abandoned Zacatecas and Saltillo, making for Texas and safety. As the forlorn remnant crept through the deserts of Coahuila, it was intercepted by a force commanded by one Elizondo, a Creole officer who had quarrelled with Allende and chose this moment to change sides. All the principal leaders of the revolution were caught unawares and delivered into the hands of the government. In subsequent Mexican history such betrayals were not uncommon, but none was so shameful as Elizondo's.

The last act of the tragedy was played out during the summer of 1811. The prisoners were taken to the remote city of Chihuahua for judgement and execution. Hidalgo had to wait three months before his time came, on 30 July, to face the firing squad. He bore his long confinement with dignity and fortitude. What preyed on his mind during the last weeks was not so much the collapse of his enterprise, or even the very real remorse which he felt for having brought death and suffering to so many innocent people, but the fact that the Church which he had served in deep faith, and in charity towards the humble, repudiated and cast him out. Before he was handed over to his executioners he had to undergo the crowning humiliation of degradation from the priesthood.

To all appearances Hidalgo's revolution had proved a total fiasco. Personally he had failed both as soldier and as statesman; he had neither won a battle nor framed a constitution. From start to finish his movement had suffered from a haphazard lack of purpose and from a lack of clear thinking behind the exciting slogans. It had aroused the worst human instincts and left a disastrous trail of ruin and slaughter.

Nevertheless this depressing record does not destroy Hidalgo's deep historical significance. His countrymen are right in revering him as the father of the Mexican nation and as the source and symbol of its independence. His act of decision on the night of 15 September, by infecting the common people with the urge to revolt, damaged the colonial system without hope of repair. Independence would inevitably have come sooner or later, but it needed a Hidalgo to strike the first blow. The courage, simplicity and generosity of his character powerfully support his legend. In his concern for the welfare of the people he was well ahead of his times, and he may rightly be considered the precursor of the whole social movement of the 1911 revolution, on which the political philosophy of modern Mexico rests.

The struggle for independence did not cease with the death of Hidalgo and his associates, but it changed its form and method. There were no further formless mass movements. Instead, compact groups of trained guerrilla fighters, occasionally coalescing into small armies but splitting and reforming as the fortune of war dictated, began to harry the government's forces and for ten years defied attempts to crush them. These guerrillas were led by patient and resourceful chiefs and their operations were launched from virtually inaccessible bases in the sierras. The regular troops opposed to them were equally well led, especially while Calleja remained in charge, first as Commander-in-Chief and subsequently as Viceroy, but although they won many local successes it was beyond their power to stamp out for good and all the fires of revolt which flickered so stubbornly in the mountain fastnesses. The rebels were disconcertingly elusive, dodging rapidly from one province to another, spreading confusion and insecurity in the style of liberation movements of the twentieth century. Their first military aim was to destroy Spanish authority over the rugged regions of the south, which had hardly been affected by Hidalgo's insurrection and which the ponderously moving forces of repression would find it impossible to pacify. The present states of Michoacán, Guerrero, Vera Cruz, Puebla and Oaxaca were the scene of the exploits of a score of determined guerrilla champions, of whom José María Morelos was by far the most capable. He gave the rebellion a fresh impulse and inspired its depressed partisans with new hope.

Like Hidalgo, Morelos was a village priest—in a very remote rustic community—and he had been a pupil of Hidalgo in the College of San Nicolas. There the resemblance between the two men ends. All national uprisings breed guerrilla priests, but these were greatly dissimilar in appearance as well as in character and attainments. The tall fiery Creole was succeeded by a stocky bull-dog of a man, an astute, combative and tenacious *mestizo*. Morelos also was an idealist, but a strictly practical one, with his feet firmly planted on the ground. From the moment when he was despatched by Hidalgo on a long mission to rouse the south, he showed an uncommon gift for organisation and a fine political flair. Unlike Hidalgo, he got on well with his subordinates and attracted competent men to his side. Above all, he developed into a military tactician of no mean stature. In the four year duel which he fought with Calleja, he proved a wily and formidable opponent. In short he was a splendid partisan leader.

In the second half of 1811, while the royal army was mopping up in the north, Morelos was busy setting up a strong rebel command in the country which now forms the state of Guerrero, taking its name from Vicente Guerrero, one of his most active lieutenants. Here the terrain is forbidding in the extreme, a military nightmare and a perfect sanctuary for guerrillas. It surges upwards from the narrow coastal strip to the central plateau in successive ranges of jagged mountains. The serrated ridges are divided by ravines of dizzy profundity and fearsome steepness. Thick pine forests alternate with stretches of spiky scrub, bristling with giant cactuses which look as if they had been transplanted from some weird planet. Along the only road through these wastes wound the laden mule caravans from Acapulco, then cut off from Mexico City and blockaded by the insurgents. The western end of the territory abutted on the Cuautla plain, where Morelos' men were holding the rich sugar planters to ransom and raiding uncomfortably near to the central valley.

Before coming to grips with Morelos Calleja turned to subdue a remnant of Hidalgo's army which had entrenched itself in the wooded heights of Zitácuaro, the first village of the Tarascans on the road from Mexico City to Valladolid. In this stronghold Ignacio Rayón, a member of Hidalgo's short-lived administration at Guadalajara, hoped to hold out indefinitely while maintaining his links with sympathisers in the capital. After dispersing this force without difficulty, the Spanish army moved southwards in February 1812 and came up against Morelos at Cuautla, where the rebels, instead of vanishing into the mountains, decided to confront the enemy and fight it out.

There followed three months of fierce and indecisive encounters. For the first time Calleja's professional army failed to win a clear-cut victory. Repulsed in their attempt to storm the town, the Spaniards invested it closely, but Morelos, after a successful sortie, slipped away towards Puebla. He was severely mauled, but as events soon showed, he emerged with the strategic advantage on his side. The mere fact that the dreaded Calleja had not caught his man, but had been compelled to retire baffled to Mexico City, gave a tremendous impulse to the revolutionary cause. Morelos regrouped his forces at Tehuacán and steadily extended his conquests throughout 1812 and 1813. Orizaba, Oaxaca and finally Acapulco fell into his hands. At the height of their power the rebels dominated the eastern sierras as far north as the Huaxteca, together with the whole of the mountain mass stretching south and south-westwards between Vera Cruz and the Pacific. The government's communications with the Gulf were imperilled and its revenues curtailed. After so many months of unbroken military success, Morelos turned to the task of political and social organisation.

In September 1813 he called a conference at Chilpancingo, a small highland town on the route to Acapulco, of delegates from the area under rebel control, and expounded to them his plans for an independent Mexico. These envisaged the establishment of a republic, universal suffrage for all citizens without distinction of race, the abolition of privilege and the breaking up of the great estates belonging to private landowners and the Church. A programme of this kind would have been considered advanced in Europe; by Creole standards it was shockingly and impracticably radical. Nothing could have been more certain to alarm the partisans of the traditional order, who still constituted a strong majority among the Creoles, including many who wished to see the end of Spanish rule. The delegates, however, dissenters and revolutionaries to a man, heartily endorsed Morelos' ideas, which were in fact embodied in a constitution drafted at Apatzingán (Michoacán) in the following year. Designed as Mexico's first parliamentary charter, it was never tested in practice and was swept aside in the rush of events. It survived, however, not only as a historical curiosity but as a model for reformist statesmen in later years.

The conservative reaction against Morelos and his dangerous ideology was accentuated by the widespread revulsion against a ruinous war. It also coincided with another swing of the military pendulum. While Morelos was enjoying his brief period of triumph Calleja had taken over from Venegas as Viceroy and was in turn regrouping for the next campaign. A superb organiser, he mobilised the remaining resources of the colony against the insurgents and by the end of 1813 had regained the initiative. In endeavouring to seize Valladolid, the main rebel army under Morelos himself was shattered in two decisive battles, and Calleja's generals proceeded methodically to retake all the main towns lost by the government in the preceding year. Once again the revolutionaries were on the run and split up into unco-ordinated and sometimes mutually hostile groups.

One of these comprised the members of the congress of Chilpancingo, to whom Morelos loyally attached himself, although, by a singularly empty as well as ungracious gesture, they had removed him from the supreme command as responsible for the current disasters. While on the way to Tehuacán, where they had hoped to find a safe haven, they were surprised by government troops and only escaped because Morelos, in creating a diversion, allowed himself to fall into enemy hands. Like Hidalgo, he was subjected to degradation from the priesthood. His execution took place on 22 December 1815, at San Cristóbal Ecatepec, a village on the present industrial fringe of Mexico City. The house where he was confined, now a national monument, stands by the ornamental bridge marking the end of the ancient causeway separating Lakes Texcoco and Xaltocán. For nearly two years he had been a fugitive or a prisoner. It was a real tragedy that his eminently constructive talents could never be employed on the tasks of peace.

In 1816 Calleja was recalled to Spain, having carried the process of forcible pacification about as far as it would go. The rebellion was not wholly extinguished, and would indeed never die out until independence was won, but the King's authority had been firmly reasserted over the infinitely greater part of his huge Mexican domains. In order to bring the remaining rebels back into the fold, the new Viceroy, Apodaca, tried out a more conciliatory policy, and met with considerable success. Many leading guerrilleros took the opportunity of making peace with the government. The only effective leaders still at large were the unbeatable Guerrero in the mountains behind Acapulco, and the equally obstinate Felix Fernandez in the hinterland of Vera Cruz. Calleja, the mainstay of Spanish rule during five years of remorse-less struggle, was not an attractive character, and has earned a bad name for cruelty. Nevertheless, to give him his due, it may be doubted whether the excesses committed under his authority surpassed, or even equalled, the contemporary horrors of the Napoleonic era and its aftermath in Europe.

With the issue of independence still undecided, Mexico was feeling the effects of political fluctuations in Spain, where liberalism and reaction were contending in the stirring atmosphere of liberation from the French. While this was being accomplished the Spanish Estates (Cortes), including delegates from Mexico, met at Cadiz and produced an extremely liberal constitution which was designed to apply to overseas as well as metropolitan Spain. In 1812 the Viceroy was instructed to put it into effect. It was a very unpalatable order indeed, for apart from the fact that Morelos' movement happened to have reached its apogee, this new development had a thoroughly confusing effect on the Creole mind.

For the liberals, the offer of representative government was of course as welcome as it was unexpected; nevertheless those with secessionist tendencies were not happy about the confirmation of links with Spain which was bound up with the grant of free institutions. As for the conservatives, they were profoundly disturbed by the democratic threat to their privileged position. Municipal elections held under the new charter favoured the partisans of independence. Threatened by political chaos within the territory still under his control, as well as by the progress of the insurgents, the Viceroy (Venegas) suspended the constitution until more peaceful times, and his action was approved by the Cortes in Spain. When King Ferdinand, having recovered his throne, proceeded to annul the constitution, the Mexican conservatives were much relieved. The country as a whole waited, in a state of exhaustion and uneasy calm, for the next turn of events.

This came in 1820, when the liberal revolution of Riego in Spain compelled Ferdinand to return to the 1812 constitution. Again the Viceroy (Apodaca) was directed to apply it in Mexico, and again the Creole establishment was filled with apprehension. Its leaders, both clerics and laymen, began to discuss plans to stop the rot. Meeting at the convent of La Profesa, only five minutes walk from the viceregal palace, they considered the chances of mounting a reactionary *coup d'état* against Apodaca on the lines of that which had removed Iturrigaray twelve years previously. They believed that if this could be successfully carried out, it would achieve independence without jacobinism or social revolution. A prominent member of this group, Dr Martin Monteagudo, aware that the conspiracy would require military backing, persuaded his friends to enlist the help of Agustín de

Iturbide, a brilliant young officer of strong conservative sympathies who had distinguished himself in the anti-revolutionary campaigns. He had personally led the attack which had routed Morelos at Valladolid and was notorious for the zeal with which he had persecuted the defeated rebels. At the moment he was without employment, having been ousted from the service for extorting protection money from mine-owners whose convoys it was his duty to escort. Nevertheless he retained good military connexions and was duly brought into the secret. Unknown to the conspirators, he cherished far-reaching ambitions.

At the end of 1820 the Viceroy, equally unwitting, restored Iturbide to favour and commissioned him to extirpate Guerrero. This gave him the opportunity which, though the gamble was a risky one, he could not afford to miss. After suffering a sharp repulse at Guerrero's hands, he boldly approached the rebel diehard and proposed a deal. It was that they should join forces and proclaim Mexican independence under a simple formula unencumbered by legal or ideological subtleties. Despite Guerrero's initial reluctance to co-operate, Iturbide went ahead and on 24 February 1821, announced his famous Plan of Iguala (a town between Taxco and Chilpancingo), which was at last to provide a solution acceptable to all shades of Creole opinion.

The plan consisted of a broad political programme based on three general principles known as the Three Guarantees. Mexico was to be an independent kingdom, ruled by Ferdinand VII or another suitable European prince; Roman Catholicism was to be the only recognised religion and to retain all its privileges; and all Mexican citizens were to be free and equal regardless of their racial origin. The plan also envisaged that until the monarch was chosen sovereignty would be vested in a junta, or council of government, while elections would be held for a constituent assembly. But the key to its success was the provision ensuring that there would be no interference with property rights, which was calculated to appeal to all persons of consequence.

The misgivings of the few radicals who still hankered after the social ideals of Hidalgo and Morelos were drowned by the general chorus of acclaim which greeted the plan. During the spring and summer of 1821 the country was swept by a wave of unanimous enthusiasm. The surviving leaders of the rebellion were suddenly united with the Creole generals who had fought for ten years to suppress it. Iturbide's progress at the head of the *Trigarante,* or Army of the Three Guarantees, was triumphant and virtually unopposed, since Apodaca's forces had been reduced to a few Spanish units barely capable of garrisoning Mexico City and Vera Cruz. The rest of the country had seceded. Seeing that his position was untenable, the Viceroy resigned. He was anyhow due to be relieved by the nominee of the liberal government of the Peninsula, Juan O'Donoju.

When the last Viceroy landed at Vera Cruz in July 1821, he found that independence was an accomplished fact. The only role left to him was to arrange a formal handover of power. For this purpose he was escorted to Córdoba, the nearest important city in national hands, where the negotiations with Iturbide took place. They resulted in the signature of an agreement by which the Viceroy, in the name of the Spanish government, accepted the Plan of Iguala and conceded Mexican sovereignty. He succeeded, however, in obtaining for all *gachupines* who preferred to quit Mexico the right to take their capital with them, a privilege which was to cost the new state extremely dear. It was also stipulated that Mexico should pay for the repatriation of Spanish troops.

This done, O'Donoju was invited to preside in Mexico City over the ceremonial transfer of authority. On 27 September Iturbide led his *trigarantine* army into the gaily decorated and deliriously rejoicing capital, and the new Mexican tricolour, red, white and green, was hoisted over the viceregal palace. The bloodless revolution had taken exactly seven months to overturn Spanish rule, and so far Iturbide had not put a foot wrong. He was bursting with confidence and ambition. Unfortunately he soon proved incapable of carrying out his responsibilities, and the story of his swift decline and fall forms a sad epilogue to the colonial period.

Certainly the task which confronted him was one which might easily have baffled a ruler of much wider experience and deeper sagacity, for Mexico was singularly unprepared for starting its career as an independent nation. Its whole structure needed to be rebuilt. It lacked a sovereign, a constitution, a government and a parliament. The traditional institutions of colonial rule, which had served their purpose so well for three centuries, had vanished almost overnight, leaving no core of trained officials competent to administer a vast, loosely knit dominion sprawling for over two thousand miles from Central America to the Rockies and prairies.

After a decade of intermittent warfare and banditry, the economy and finances were in utter disorder. Trade, both external and internal, was at a standstill, and the commercial community was being progressively weakened as the Spaniards departed, taking their money with them. Mexico's principal port, Vera Cruz, was blocked by the continued Spanish occupation of the fortress island of San Juan de Ulua, which was indefinitely prolonged when King Ferdinand, having once again rid himself of his liberal ministers, refused to recognise the Treaty of Cordoba. The treasury, starved of its normal revenues and particularly of the proceeds of the mining industry, which had been completely wrecked, was further crippled by the obligation to support the extravagant *trigarantine* army. In these conditions what the country required was a careful programme of retrenchment and reconstruction. What it got was an orgy of intrigue and personalist politics.

To do Iturbide justice, he did make some attempt, as head of the regency council and provisional government, to prod the constituent congress into taking its duties seriously. But the members of this assembly, who were mostly drawn from the conservative and propertied class, frittered away their time in sterile debates and pointless recriminations. Before long they were directly assailing the temporary head of state. In the background plenty of plots were being hatched. The liberals, led by Miguel Ramos Arizpe, a former Mexican delegate to the Spanish Cortes in 1812, planned to declare a republic; some conservatives were scheming to restore Spanish rule, and Iturbide, exasperated by the political manoeuvring which was sapping his influence and by threats to cut his army down to size, was preparing to make himself not only dictator but emperor.

On 18 May 1822, he gave the signal for action. The coup was carefully stage-managed with the help of the garrison and mob of the capital, for whom Iturbide was still the popular idol. Whipped up by his agents, the crowd which jammed the street outside his ornate eighteenth century palace acclaimed him as Agustín I, Emperor of Mexico. He responded with a proper show of reluctance, but was soon persuaded to accept the crown on condition that the people's offer was confirmed by congress. The deputies, hurried into session and thoroughly intimidated, prudently acquiesced, though fifteen bold spirits voted the other way. Two months later Iturbide was solemnly crowned in the cathedral, surrounded by imperial trappings hastily improvised for the occasion.

The sham Bonapartist experiment which followed was pathetic and ludicrous. Iturbide never had the ghost of a chance of carrying it off. It made neither political nor economic sense, but depended on spurious glamour and the doubtful support of an army which could not be paid or fed. The notables, who had never really liked Iturbide and envied him his success, were not placated by the titles and honours in which the imperial court abounded, or even by the creation of a Knightly Order of Guadalupe. Funds could only be raised through expropriations or the printing of paper money, which brought galloping inflation. When congress recovered its nerve and criticised the Emperor more vigorously than before, he reduced it to a rump of forty-five members whom he expected to be subservient to his wishes. Even they, however, behaved intractably, while the military chiefs prepared to hasten his overthrow.

This was achieved in due course by a curious combination between a number of former guerrillero stalwarts and a new figure, Antonio Lopez de Santa Anna, whose baneful influence was to overhang Mexican politics for the next thirty years and more. Santa Anna had served in the royal army and, like most of his fellow-officers, had joined Iturbide. Later he fell out with his chief and made contact with a group of dissident generals which included Felix Fernandez (now sporting the patriotic pseudonym of Guadalupe Victoria), Iturbide's old foe Vicente Guerrero and Nicolas Bravo, who had also been one of Morelos' most devoted adherents. These firebrands declared for a republic and broke into open revolt. After some indecisive clashes with Iturbide's forces they issued a political proclamation called the Plan of Casa Mata, which was used as a rallying point for the growing opposition to the emperor. Deserted by his army, Iturbide struggled on until March 1823, when he announced to congress his desire to abdicate. He was promptly condemned to banishment for life and left Mexico in May aboard a British warship.

He was not fated to reach old age in exile. Before the year was out he found a pretext for trying his luck again in Mexico. While living in London he learned, or pretended to have learned, of a Spanish project for the reconquest of Mexico, and persuaded himself that if he returned to his native country he would be permitted to enrol himself among its defenders. It was a desperate gamble, and he does not even seem to have been aware that the government had issued an order for his execution if he were ever found on Mexican soil. When he landed near Tampico he was arrested and shot out of hand. It was a melancholy end for this brave but unlucky opportunist whose talents did not match his audacity.

The first three decades of the Republic are not an epoch of which Mexicans are proud. Although rich in incident and abounding in picturesque characters, the story is of internal decline and of humiliation in Mexico's dealings with foreign powers. The nation was badly served by its Creole rulers, whatever their political persuasion might be. There was no continuity or purposeful direction of policy, and changes in government were almost invariably brought about by unconstitutional methods. Elections were superseded by the military *pronunciamento,* a technique invented by Iturbide and developed into a fine art by Santa Anna. The generals, a gaudy and parasitic class who were all too apt to usurp the presidency, behaved with total irresponsibility and a cynical disregard of their country's true interests. The civilian leaders who somewhat uncomfortably shared office with them were often men of ability and integrity, but failed to operate a parliamentary system of which the ordinary citizens had no experience and for which they felt no zeal. The intellectuals who professed lofty political ideals were powerless to apply them in the prevailing climate of inefficiency, corruption and violence. The economy was crippled by lack of revenue, perpetual deficits and a heavy weight of inherited debt. No intelligent use was made of the human and material resources at the nation's disposal.

Society remained thoroughly conservative and resistant to change. Thus colonial forms and manners were mostly retained, but the severance of Mexico from Spain drained away the best elements among the upper class. The old families which had graced the viceregal court, as well as the country towns, left Mexico in substantial numbers. Mexico City, which until the end of the colonial period had invited comparison with the most sophisticated capitals of Europe, relapsed into a dull provincialism. There was a depressing stagnation in culture and the general standards of civilised life. The great landowners continued to lead a lavish and patriarchal existence on their *haciendas,* but many estates had been ravaged in the revolutionary campaigns and had become heavily mortgaged, especially to the Church.

The latter emerged from the recent troubles with its prestige and properties relatively intact. It had also preserved its immunities; the clergy paid no taxes and could only be tried in their own courts. The hierarchy had lent its full support to the Spanish régime against the insurgents, and when the Creole majority declared for independence this was promptly transferred to the conservative nationalists. The alliance thus established repulsed all attacks on the Church's position until it was finally breached by the reform movement of the fifties.

Although clericalism was regularly denounced by radicals and freemasons as the fortress of reaction and the dead hand which paralysed all political and economic progress, such was the innate strength of religion among the masses that respect and devotion for the Church were only gradually eroded. By tradition the Church was the protector of the people against exploitation by powerful laymen and this reputation, which had been fully earned in its day, was slow to die. The generals might be tempted to plunder its treasures, and liberal economists dream of putting its accumulated capital to productive use, but in practice it was too solid a structure to demolish in the short term. Secure in its riches and in the privileges which had been confirmed by the republican constitution, it seemed to overshadow the bankrupt and ineffectual State.

Nevertheless the Church had not escaped the decay from which all Mexican institutions were suffering at the time. In its surfeit of material possessions it had lost the spiritual force which had sustained it in its role as evangelist and civiliser. For many years its dynamism had devolved on unconventional individuals of the Hidalgo type, on priests and friars who had neglected their calling to fling themselves into revolutionary politics. The monastic orders had largely abandoned their pastoral work, deserted their up-country convents and congregated in the larger cities, where they formed an idle, if harmless, proletariat dependent on the revenues of their *haciendas* and the generosity of the devout. But even in Mexico City some of these establishments were dying for lack of recruitment. Madame Calderón de la Barca, the Scottish wife of the first Spanish Minister to independent Mexico, records that in 1840 only seven Carmelite monks remained to occupy the huge monastery of San Fernando adjacent to her husband's Legation. As their numbers dwindled the clergy no longer produced prelates and scholars of the quality that had adorned Mexican life in the previous centuries. Whatever energies they might still possess were deployed in the selfish defence of privilege.

Among the few liberal ecclesiastics who helped to found the new republic was Ramos Arizpe, who, though his career was absorbed in politics, remained within the Church and ended up as a canon of Puebla cathedral. After the fall of Iturbide, he inspired the drafting of the constitution, which the congress at last adopted in 1824. It was of federalist design and largely modelled on the constitution of the United States. Mexico was divided into states, each with its own elected governor and legislature, and a small number of federal territories directly administered by the central government. Apart from the absence of religious liberty (for the liberal drafters saw nothing strange in guaranteeing the exclusive rights of Roman Catholicism as laid down in the Plan of Iguala), the constitution contained all the classical features of an advanced democracy, which were of course entirely unsuited to the immature and largely uneducated Mexican electorate. It could hardly be expected to work properly in a country which from time immemorial had been despotically, if paternally, governed from the centre.

The new régime, however, made an optimistic start. The state legislatures, acting as an electoral college, chose Guadalupe Victoria and Nicolas Bravo as president and vice-president. These revolutionary worthies had impeccable records as patriots and leaders, and were linked in the popular mind with the memory of Hidalgo and Morelos. They were excellent figureheads for a liberal administration, but as statesmen they possessed no positive qualities. The best that could be said of Victoria, that 'honest, plain, down-looking, common sort of citizen', as Madame Calderón de la Barca was later to describe him, was that he managed to complete his presidential term, a feat which came to be regarded as exceptional in the anarchy of the thirties and forties, when presidents were raised and deposed with bewildering inconsequence. Nicolas Bravo, for his part, was a spent force, and his sympathies were beginning to incline towards the conservatives.

The liberals in power were themselves roughly divided into two groups, the *moderados* who supported the federalist system but were lukewarm about social changes, and the so-called *puros* who represented a more radical tendency. The latters' foremost spokesman was Valentín Gomez Farías, a political leader of outstanding intellectual distinction and honesty of aim, who battled ceaselessly in the cause of reform and lived to see it triumph in the middle fifties. He was supported by other able and clever men, such as José Luis Mora and Lorenzo de Zavala, but neither the heads of the government nor their associates were equal to the task of rescuing Mexico from the economic predicament which fatally impaired its stability.

The republic had been obliged to underwrite the greater part of the debts incurred by preceding governments. It was also faced with an insoluble budgetary crisis. Income from all sources amounted to only half of the outgoings, of which an immoderate proportion was wasted on the army. Since the government did not dare to question the generals' demands, and Church funds could not be drawn upon, there was no alternative but to resort to further borrowing. For internal purposes loans were contracted with Mexican financiers and secured by mortgages on national assets, a procedure which enriched the private capitalists but further impoverished the State.

For outside sources of finance Mexico turned to Great Britain. It happened to be the moment when the British Government was actively pursuing George Canning's policy of cultivating close political and commercial relations with the newly liberated Latin American countries, and Mexican overtures were therefore favourably received in the City of London. They were warmly sponsored by H. G. Ward, the energetic British Chargé d'Affaires, who, like many of his diplomatic successors, was fascinated by Mexico. He and his wife travelled everywhere and knew everybody. Largely as the result of his advocacy, two loans totalling six and a half million pounds sterling were floated with British bankers at a high rate of interest. No blame for this transaction need be attached to either borrowers or lenders. The Mexican Government was hard pressed and in no position to select its creditors, and the bankers were quite right to secure the best terms that could be negotiated. There seemed to be no reason to fear that Mexico, known to the world as an immensely rich country, would not soon recover its economic balance when internal peace had been restored. Yet the indebtedness to Great Britain became the first of a series of claims which were to exhaust the young republic and poison its dealings with foreign countries throughout the century.

British interest in independent Mexico was not however confined to money-lending. It embraced at the same time the efforts which were being made to revive the sorely stricken mining industry. Several British companies were formed to take advantage of the Mexican Government's appeals to foreign investors to participate in new ventures on favourable terms. In fact there was a frenzied rush of speculation in London. Very large sums were expended in equipping the ancient mines of Pachuca, originally opened up in the sixteenth century, with the machinery of the industrial revolution.

These enterprises had had their ups and down in colonial times. So long as the tunnels could be kept free of water, they made spectacular profits for their Creole owners. For instance the colossal fortune which the famous mine of Real del Monte obtained for the family of Romero de Terreros, Counts of Regla, enabled them to offer a large loan to the Spanish Government, to fit out two ships of the line at their own expense and to endow the colony with many philanthropic institutions. But in 1824, when a British concern took over, Real del Monte had been ruined by neglect and flooding. For some years after its renovation all went well and the financial returns were excellent. Mexican shares continued to boom on the London Stock Exchange. Then a decline set in. The trouble about mining in Mexico was that though the prizes could be enormous, they were impermanent. The run of luck could be nullified from one day to another if the veins of silver-bearing ore gave out or by reason of technical difficulties. By 1850 Real del Monte had been forced into liquidation, and a similar fate overtook other British ventures in the district.

Nevertheless the British connexion with Pachuca, where hundreds of Cornish mining families settled at this period, was long maintained. Many of their descendants are still there. Visitors to this region of queer spiky mountains wreathed in fog, and pierced with the endless shafts and galleries of mines which still produce silver and a little gold as well, are confronted at every turn with unmistakably British features, and Cornish pasties are served with the highballs at the state Governor's receptions.

Such infusions of foreign capital, though temporarily promising, failed to regenerate the Mexican economy, which was soon to be further strained by political convulsions. In 1827 Nicolas Bravo

144

staged an abortive revolt in the conservative interest, but was at once rounded up and expelled from the country. His bad example ushered in nearly twenty years of *pronunciamentos* and bitter party feuding. The rivalry between liberals and conservatives burst into open conflict over the presidential election of 1828 for the succession to Guadalupe Victoria. The liberal candidate, backed by the *puros,* was Vicente Guerrero, whose prestige as a revolutionary hero equalled Victoria's, and who had lately been instrumental in crushing his old comrade in arms, Bravo. He was, however, narrowly defeated in the election by Gomez Pedraza, Minister of War in the previous government, a *moderado* who had attracted conservative support.

The latter's victory provoked the intervention of Santa Anna, who proceeded to 'pronounce' in favour of Guerrero, thus posing, in spite of his own reactionary proclivities, as the embattled protector of liberalism. This unnatural alliance touched off a popular uprising in the capital, where the radical Lorenzo de Zavala led the local troops and the city mob against Gomez Pedraza. In the fighting that followed the central Parián market, where many foreign traders had their establishments, was sacked and burnt, and further substantial claims were logged up against the Mexican State. The struggle ended in a shortlived triumph for the liberals. Gomez Pedraza fled the country and Guerrero assumed the presidency. As a sop to the conservatives he took one of their leaders, General Anastasio Bustamante, as his vice-president.

As head of state Guerrero proved torpid and ineffective. The chief event of his two-year presidency was a hopeless bid by the Spanish monarchy to reassert itself in Mexico. Encouraged by reports of civil commotion in the former colony, King Ferdinand despatched a small force which occupied Tampico in the summer of 1829. As a base for reconquest it was utterly unsuitable, disease-stricken and too far removed from the centres of power and population. Decimated by yellow fever, the Spaniards failed to move a step into the interior and tamely capitulated to Santa Anna, whom the president had placed in command of the defending army. This event gratuitously enhanced Santa Anna's military reputation which, despite the part which he had played in the overthrow of Iturbide and Gomez Pedraza, had not so far impressed his compatriots. Once established as a hero, he bided his time for the moment, while the conservatives manoeuvred to get rid of Guerrero.

Bustamante, to whom this task was entrusted, had ability and some strength of character, but the real chief of the conservative faction was Lucas Alamán, a man of altogether superior calibre. This many-sided personality—deputy to the Spanish Cortes, Minister of Foreign Affairs, promoter of mining interests and above all a brilliant historian—was for long years the mainstay of the reactionary cause. A convinced monarchist with a romantic attachment to the colonial past, he was never truly reconciled to the republic and heartily distrusted liberal institutions. He combined high culture with a rigid and fanatical authoritarianism in politics. Without aspiring to personal power, he usually directed the operations of his party from the background.

His first chance came in 1830, when Bustamante expelled Guerrero from Mexico City and usurped the presidency without any pretence of legality. Under Alamán's guidance, he restored Mexico's administration and finances to some semblance of order, but at the cost of imposing an intolerably harsh and arbitrary rule. The liberals were viciously persecuted, and the wretched Guerrero paid with his life for his spinelessness in office. Alamán was determined that Mexico must be governed by the same methods as those by which Metternich was simultaneously clamping down on liberalism in Europe. In his estimation the claims of freedom and justice had to be sacrificed to efficiency and reverence for vanished traditions. But his prescription was too unpalatable for Mexicans in general and it was small wonder that after two years of repression the pendulum again swung violently in the opposite direction. Again it was Santa Anna who brought back the liberals to power, and this time it was Bustamante who was chased into exile.

At the beginning of 1832 Santa Anna himself was chosen president with the *puro* doctrinaire Gomez Farías as his coadjutor. But to the universal astonishment he refused to allow his election to be confirmed. After a triumphal reception in Mexico City he disconcerted his followers by retiring to his *hacienda,* Manga de Clavo. Here he settled down to watch political developments and to await his next opportunity to intervene.

Manga de Clavo, now a barely discernible ruin, was a beautiful estate lying in the lush tropical country which skirts the Vera Cruz–Jalapa road, not far from the ruins of ancient Zempoala. It was Santa Anna's favourite retreat, from which he sallied forth at intervals to overturn a government or initiate a campaign. Although his influence on his country's affairs was almost wholly bad, he was by no means a negligible or uninteresting personality. In demeanour he appeared modest, and in the words of Madame Calderón, who visited him in December 1839, 'a gentlemanly, good-looking, quietly dressed rather melancholy-looking person. Knowing nothing of his past history, one would have said a philosopher, living in dignified retirement.' He certainly knew how to turn on the charm for the benefit of strangers. Not that he deceived this particular visitor, who summed him up as 'perhaps one of the worst men in the world—ambitious of power, greedy of money—and unprincipled—having feathered his nest at the expense of the republic—and awaiting in a dignified retreat only till the moment comes for putting himself at the head of another revolution'.

This harsh judgement was well deserved, even at a time when Santa Anna's strange career had many more years to run. Yet he was not devoid of a peculiar kind of patriotism. The only trouble was that this sentiment was overlaid with personal conceit and an irresistible urge to pose as the saviour of his country without accepting any of the serious responsibilities of that role. He was a political tactician of extreme cunning and strong nerves, with an uncanny flair for selecting the right moment to strike; his timing was rarely at fault. It was when he had attained and was exercising power that his worst qualities were revealed. Then the veil of his simple and unassuming manners fell away, and he paraded his love of luxurious living and of the appurtenances of dictatorship, gaudy uniforms, bedizened coaches and the best fighting cocks that Mexico could produce (he was inordinately addicted to that sport). The shrewdness with which he had hitherto manipulated affairs of state from behind the scenes would then evaporate, and he would appear as a vulgar and corrupt tyrant who had lost all sense of proportion. He was in any case too indolent and sensitive to opposition ever to govern well. Nevertheless frequent changes of fortune and setbacks of the most abrupt nature did not deter him from embarking on fresh political and military ventures, for he was extraordinarily pertinacious. As a soldier he was not to be despised. He was a good organiser, an indefatigable raiser of armies and quite an able strategist. Moreover, he often managed to camouflage his defeats by an adroit handling of public relations, in which he was an adept. Although no coward, his energy was apt to peter out before the battle ended and he would inexplicably fail to follow up the tactical superiority which he had worked hard to gain. His popularity as a national figure, which survived many humiliating experiences, obliged the leaders of both political tendencies to pay him court, an advantage which he would exploit with cynical skill.

Gomez Farías was not long left to his own devices. In office he behaved with the same tactless and uncompromising rigour as the conservatives whom he succeeded. His policy took the form of a reckless frontal assault on the Church and the army. In an excess of enthusiasm the new liberal congress adopted a series of sweeping measures. It voted that education should be secularised and taken out of the hands of the 'Royal and Pontifical' University; that the collection of church tithes should no longer be compulsory; that monks and nuns should be allowed release from their vows; and that certain church properties and funds should be confiscated. Following the precedent of the Kings of Spain, the State assumed control of ecclesiastical appointment. Further legislation reduced the size and budget of the army and removed its officers' privileges.

This programme provoked a violently hostile reaction. It naturally outraged the Vatican and also offended Spain, the birthplace of many of the Mexican episcopate. At home it was considered by Creole opinion in general as shockingly subversive of religion and morality, as well as unconstitutional, since in 1833 the liberals themselves, echoing one of the fundamental guarantees of the Plan of Iguala, had appeared to accept that Roman Catholicism should be immune from political attack. Gomez Farias, tenaciously defending his reforms, was not aided by a severe epidemic of cholera, which was popularly ascribed to divine anger with the government's impiety.

When the turmoil was at its worst, Santa Anna again stepped in. In April 1834 he repeated his performance of two years previously, with the sole difference that the victims of his interference were now the liberals, whose interests he had formerly upheld with a fair degree of consistency. For the next six months he wielded dictatorial power with drastic severity. Congress was sent packing, the liberal reforms were repealed and their sponsors persecuted as they had been by Bustamante. Luckier than Guerrero, Gomez Farías escaped with his life but had to flee into exile. Having conducted his purge, Santa Anna installed a conservative congress and a conservative vice-president, Barragán, and again preferred to withdraw to Manga de Clavo. A year later he was jerked out of his enigmatic retirement by the hazards of a campaign against the Texas frontiersmen.

In the early days of Mexican independence relations with the United States were correct but uneasy. The two giant republics of North America possessed a common frontier but in practice they were separated by huge tracts of desert, mountain and virgin lands sparsely occupied by fierce Indians, untamed and aggressive horsemen who raided deeply into the territory of both countries. These obstacles, and the lack of direct contact between Mexicans and Anglo-Saxons, reduced the dangers of friction. Nevertheless the Mexican government kept a wary eye on American expansionism. Shortly before independence was proclaimed the United States had swallowed Louisiana and Florida, both of which had belonged to the Spanish Crown, and Texas, fertile but undeveloped, might logically be considered as the next objective. Indeed the first American diplomatic representative in Mexico, Joel Poinsett, did not hesitate to propose its acquisition by purchase. Not unnaturally he found the Mexicans unresponsive.

Poinsett, a lively character from South Carolina, felt the same appreciative interest in Mexico as his British colleague, Ward. It was he who gave his name to the poinsettia, which the Mexicans call *flor de nochebuena*. But in his public life he was far too much inclined to advertise his political sympathies with the liberals. He figured prominently in the 'Yorkist' lodge of freemasons, well known as a nest of anti-clerical reformers. These connexions, and his lack of impartiality, hampered his official usefulness and fostered a latent suspicion of American intentions. Moreover, although Mexico had done the United States the compliment of copying their federal constitution, there was at this stage little mutual attraction between the two peoples. The Mexicans gravitated towards Spanish or French culture, and preferred to turn to Great Britain for their financial and commercial necessities. Thus Poinsett's overtures were rebuffed, and Texas remained for a few more years an enormous appendage of the Mexican state of Coahuila.

Realising rightly that an empty Texas could never be held against a further American advance, the Mexican government looked round for possible colonists. Unfortunately these were not available in Mexico itself. It would have been futile to think of transporting Indian peasants to the frontier regions, for the means of carrying out such an operation did not exist. Even in the twentieth century the resettlement of villagers from the over-populated plateau in the fertile lowlands has met with indifferent success. Nor was it practicable to seek immigrants from Europe.

Consequently, when Stephen Austin and other Americans presented themselves to the authorities in Mexico City with offers to colonise Texas with Americans under Mexican sovereignty, the government could hardly fail to accept them. If it had refused, the Anglo-Saxons would have moved in anyway.

As it turned out, each American settlement became a Trojan Horse. Although Austin did his best to make the arrangement work, the settlers, a rough and ready lot, were impatient of Mexican jurisdiction. They had not trekked many hundreds of miles in order to exchange the constraints which had irked them in their native states for conformity to laws and customs which they neither understood nor respected. They knew nothing of the Spanish language or Latin ways, and were in short unassimilable. In a few years their numbers had grown to tens of thousands, with the addition of negro slaves introduced by immigrants from the southern states. They simply ignored an anti-slavery decree issued by the Guerrero administration. The Mexican government found that its officials were losing control, and when the conservatives under Bustamante came into power in 1830, they forbade the further entry of immigrants from the United States. Troops were sent in to patrol the frontier and stop immigration and smuggling.

These measures were furiously resented and successfully defied, and for two years the situation drifted towards anarchy. By 1832 the liberals, who had hitherto appeared less hostile to Texan aspirations, had regained office, and in an effort to forestall a crisis, the Texan leaders deputed Austin to convey their demands to Gomez Farías. They were that Texas should be declared a separate state within federal Mexico and that all restrictions on immigration should be removed. But Austin found that the liberals' attitude had hardened; the Texan claims were rejected out of hand and he himself was arrested.

The stage was now set for a trial of armed strength. The first force which Santa Anna despatched to reassert Mexican authority was defeated by the settlers in several days of bitter street-fighting at San Antonio, and he was obliged to take the field in person. The campaign that followed has become part of Texan and American folk-lore. In February 1836, when Santa Anna reached San Antonio, he encountered no opposition except from a small garrison, commanded by one William Travis, which had fortified itself behind the stout walls of a former mission house called the Alamo. After a long and heroic resistance this building was stormed and its defenders perished to a man. Santa Anna continued his march towards the Louisiana border, mopping up all organised opposition.

Meanwhile, five days before the Alamo disaster, the Texans had convoked their own national assembly and drawn up a declaration of independence. One David Burnet was chosen as provisional president of the new republic and surprisingly enough, his vice-president was the Mexican radical politician Lorenzo de Zavala, an exile from Santa Anna's dictatorship who thought he had discovered in the Texans his ideal of a free people. The scanty Texan forces, unprofessional but fine fighting material, found a natural leader in the eccentric adventurer Sam Houston. They retreated slowly eastwards, covering the flight of the government and of the whole population of American origin. On 21 April 1836, Santa Anna overtook the Texans at Lynchburg Ferry, pinning them with their backs against the San Jacinto river. Here was an excellent opportunity to finish them off, but Santa Anna spoiled it by over-confidence and failure to guard against surprise attack. When Houston's men unexpectedly swept over the Mexican position to the war-cry of 'Remember the Alamo', they caught their enemy unprepared. The battle was over in twenty minutes, during which the Mexican army was virtually destroyed, with six hundred killed and seven hundred taken prisoner. Santa Anna himself was ignominiously dragged out of hiding and held as a hostage for future negotiations. This smashing victory decided for good and all that Texas was lost to Mexico.

The Mexican government was not to be reconciled to the secession of Texas. When Santa Anna, in order to procure his own release, signed a convention committing it to recognise the new republic, he was immediately disavowed. The Americans kept him for a while, and President Andrew Jackson summoned him to Washington. Eventually, however, they returned him to Mexico and further dignified seclusion at Manga de Clavo. His misfortunes had not diminished his self-esteem, but the conservatives, while not impeaching him for his blunders, elected to govern without him. They made no attempt to reconquer Texas. Intermittent skirmishing between the two countries continued until Texas was annexed by the United States in 1845. These encounters usually took the form of destructive raids across the frontier, in which the Texans were the aggressors but the Mexicans gained the upper hand. Small forces which successively invaded what is now New Mexico and Tamaulipas were easily rounded up, and Madame Calderón de la Barca, that unfailing chronicler of Mexican life in the early forties, records a visit to a convent in the capital where a Colonel Cooke and his men, somewhat the worse for wear after a march of two thousand miles from Santa Fe, were confined in wretched conditions.

In its vendetta with Mexico the Lone Star Republic had more success in harassing Mexico from the sea. From 1839 onwards it sent its small navy to support Yucatán, which was indulging in a secessionist movement of its own in protest against the abrogation of the Mexican federalist constitution by the conservative régime. These vessels were more of a nuisance than a danger, but it was alarming enough that the Yucatecos, who prided themselves on their distinctive culture and maintained their own links with the outside world, might also win their independence. It was also galling that leading European powers like Great Britain and France should have recognised Texas.

Bustamante was made president for the second time in 1837 and survived in office for four years. The country, however, was unhappy with the new centralist constitution, financial difficulties were insuperable and Mexico suffered another humiliation in its foreign relations. In December 1837 the French government, incensed by Mexico's failure to meet claims arising from the destruction of French property during the revolution of 1828, presented a peremptory demand for the payment of six hundred thousand pesos. One of these claims, which was concerned with damage to a pastrycook's shop in the suburbs of Tacubaya, gave its name to the hostilities, the 'Pastry War', which followed the rejection of the French ultimatum. King Louis Philippe's fleet blockaded Vera Cruz for many months, and when further negotiations came to nothing, bombarded and captured the fortress of San Juan de Ulua, which had only been evacuated by the Spaniards in 1825.

This episode, a grave affront to Mexican pride, again focussed attention on Santa Anna, who responded to it with a typical rodomontade. On receiving an appeal from the Veracruzanos for help in defending their city, he hurried up from Manga de Clavo just in time to be involved in a French incursion on the mainland. A confused action took place in which Santa Anna had his leg taken off by a naval cannon ball. Thus he partly regained his reputation as a national hero, while Bustamante, who was finally forced to accept a settlement favourable to the French, correspondingly lost prestige. His government finally collapsed under the pressure of two *pronunciamentos*.

The first of these coups, launched by Gomez Farías and General Urrea in the name of federalism, took the government by surprise. The president was seized while still in bed and the national palace turned into a rebel stronghold. Madame Calderón gives an exciting description of how the fighting began, with the tocsin pealing and 'the Indians hurrying back to their villages in double-quick trot'. The government troops fortified themselves in the *Ciudadela,* or garrison headquarters, on the edge of the capital, and for eleven days Mexico City echoed with bombardments, fusillades and salvoes of bombastic proclamations. In the end the centralists prevailed. Bustamante, who kept his head admirably throughout the crisis, escaped from his captors and joined his subordinates in the *Ciudadela,* while most of the military chiefs in the provinces promised him their support. Among them were old Guadalupe Victoria and of course Santa Anna, who was profuse in his professions of loyalty and offers to mediate ('it must be confessed,' comments Madame Calderón, 'that His Excellency is rather a dangerous umpire').

Continuing to behave with good sense and generosity, Bustamante then parleyed with the rebels and obtained their submission in return for safe-conducts. A year later, however, he was deposed by an unscrupulous combination of the same military leaders, including his own chief-of-staff, General Valencia. Without the slightest ideological cover for their action, Santa Anna at Vera Cruz, General Paredes at Guadalajara and Valencia in the city itself all 'pronounced' simultaneously.

This revolution, which started on 30 August, was a long-drawn affair. The roles being reversed, Bustamante entrenched himself in the palace and swapped broadsides with Valencia in the *Ciudadela*. The lines of the contending forces were drawn through the centre of the capital, whose lovely colonial façades crumbled under the relentless cannonading. Many innocent people were killed without knowing what this meaningless conflict was about. The insurgent generals, having united their forces, drew up a document entitled *Las Bases de Tacubaya,* which placed effective power in the hands of Santa Anna. Bustamante, after a fruitless attempt to save himself by announcing his conversion to federalism, capitulated on 6 October. It looked as if Mexico had reached the nadir of political ineptitude and cynical militarism.

Nevertheless the succeeding years were still more disastrous.

Santa Anna's second dictatorship, which lasted until 1844, was marked by reckless prodigality in the finances and a programme of self-glorification carried to ridiculous lengths, as when the leg which he had lost at Vera Cruz was disinterred and solemnly reburied in Mexico City with full military honours. The proceeds of the increased taxation and forced loans which Santa Anna squeezed out of reluctant compatriots were squandered on the army, and there was a continuous orgy of parades, fiestas and other useless extravagances. When the country tired of these circuses, and funds began to run low, Paredes again 'pronounced' and soon had the dictator on the run. In the capital Gomez Pedraza and the moderate liberals took over the government and raised yet another general, Herrera, to the presidency. Meanwhile Santa Anna was wandering forlornly in the sierras of Vera Cruz. Bereft of his grandeur, he was eventually cornered in a remote Indian village and expelled to Cuba.

Herrera was faced with the hopeless problem of treating with Washington about the future of Texas. What Mexico really dreaded was that its annexation by the United States would lead to further grabbing of territory, and Herrera was only prevented by regard for the national honour from recognising its independent existence. The American government, for its part, had refrained from annexation because political opinion in New England opposed the addition to the Union of yet another slave-owning state. But in 1845 the President of the United States was James Polk, who suffered from no inhibitions about slavery and longed to extend his country's boundaries. He had fixed his ambitions on California no less than on Texas. Also he was obsessed by the fear that, unless the United States pushed forward, Great Britain would be tempted to establish a new sphere of influence on the American continent, thus blocking American expansion from Oregon in the north-west to Texas in the south-east. In exerting pressure on Mexico he had a convenient excuse in the shape of heavy property claims on which the Mexican government, despite its obligations under an arbitration agreement, was in default. He thought wrongly that Mexico would be sure to agree to far-reaching territorial concessions in return for the settlement of this tiresome debt.

It was perhaps a pardonable misjudgement for someone unacquainted with the Mexican temper. Although Herrera genuinely wished to be conciliatory, his freedom of negotiation was fatally hampered by the sensitiveness of Mexican public opinion. When he at last declared himself ready to accept Texan independence, in return for American guarantees against annexation, it was too late. Texas was annexed and Mexico broke off diplomatic relations. Once American troops had moved in and advanced to the line of the Rio Grande, war was inevitable. Herrera fell and was replaced by Paredes, an honest but intransigent warrior with a weakness for the bottle. In April 1846, American forces under General Zachary Taylor squared up to a Mexican army commanded by General Arista; a cavalry skirmish occurred in which some American troopers were made prisoner; and President Polk, with suspicious eagerness, persuaded Congress to declare war. Thereupon American columns invaded both northern Mexico and the western territories.

The west, being indefensible, was easily occupied, but Mexico was not beaten into submission for nearly two years. The war was no walk-over for the Americans. Its campaigns were waged at a leisurely pace by comparatively small armies; the Mexicans rarely exceeded twenty thousand and the Americans ten thousand men. The latter, a mixture of regulars and volunteers, were handicapped by the climate, their susceptibility to local diseases and the length of their lines of communication. But they were better disciplined and equipped than their opponents, and their gunners and engineers were greatly superior. The Mexican conscript armies performed prodigies of valour and self-sacrifice in face of their enemies' technical advantages. The generalship was not brilliant on either side, and the war was sustained and finally won by the hard-slogging qualities of the troops. It was complicated on the Mexican side by no less than three political upheavals. Under the stress of defeat Paredes was ousted by Gomez Farías and the liberals, who (as so often happened) were displaced by Santa Anna, and peace was concluded by a government of *moderados*.

Taylor, a courageous but dawdling commander, defeated Arista at Matamoros, captured Monterrey, the capital of Nuevo Leon, and moved cautiously forward to Saltillo in the neighbouring state of Coahuila. There he settled down for many months, as if there was no question of urgency and no coherent strategic plan. During this prolonged lull in the fighting a strange deal was being arranged behind the scenes. Gomez Farías had come to the conclusion that the country needed Santa Anna. Notwithstanding the injuries which the dictator had inflicted on the liberals in the past, he was the only general capable of stemming the American invasion. Gomez Farías therefore swallowed his aversion for

Santa Anna and got in touch with him, proposing that he should not only take charge of the national resistance but should even resume the presidency.

The offer was accepted with alacrity, but in order to reach Mexico from Cuba Santa Anna had to pass through the American blockade. This difficulty was solved by a trick which seems almost too simple to have succeeded. Entering into correspondence with President Polk, Santa Anna undertook that if he were allowed to return to Mexico he would arrange to terminate the war, after a suitable interval, on terms favourable to the United States. Polk, beguiled by these assurances, gave the necessary orders to the fleet in the Gulf of Mexico, and in the late summer Santa Anna disembarked at his native Vera Cruz.

He soon set to work to assemble an army with which he could confront Taylor. It was past the new year before he was ready, but the Americans had still not budged from Saltillo. Marching northwards from San Luis Potosí, he found them occupying a strong position in a mountain pass near the *hacienda* of Buena Vista. Although they had waited so long to get to grips with the Mexicans, Santa Anna's assault achieved a complete tactical surprise. Moreover, he succeeded in outflanking the American position by seizing a piece of difficult ground which Taylor had omitted to defend. The Mexicans, attacking with the utmost bravery through devastating artillery fire, stormed one entrenchment after another and captured two American colours. By nightfall they were up against the last line of their enemies' defences. But their losses were so severe that Santa Anna, whose conduct of the battle had so far been impeccable, suffered one of those failures of nerve to which he was prone and decided not to renew the attack on the following day. Leaving his camp-fires burning, he disengaged under cover of darkness and retreated towards San Luis Potosí. The Americans were too exhausted to pursue, and so far as the northern front was concerned, the battle of Buena Vista ended in a stalemate. Both commanders claimed the victory and were duly acknowledged as heroes in their own countries. This enabled Santa Anna to discard Gomez Farías, who had been making himself unpopular by exacting heavy war contributions from the clergy, while Taylor won sufficient glory to ensure his eventual election to the presidency of the United States.

The military issue had to be decided elsewhere. Polk still hoped that Santa Anna would fulfil his promise to start negotiations as soon as he judged that the Mexicans were sufficiently disillusioned by defeat, but since there was no sign of this happening he decided to strike at Mexico City by the shortest route from the coast. On 7 March 1847, an expeditionary force of ten thousand men was landed at Vera Cruz, after a fierce preliminary bombardment by the fleet. Its commander, General Winfield Scott, was a cautious professional soldier who well understood the risks of penetrating into the populous heartland of Mexico with so modest a force. He therefore advanced with deliberate slowness and circumspection, and it was five months, twice the time taken by Hernán Cortés to traverse the same route, before he reached the Valley of Mexico.

In April his march was barred by Santa Anna, who had entrenched himself in a supposedly impregnable position at Cerro Gordo, where the road from the coast climbs steeply into the hills below the towering Cofre de Perote. But skilful use of his artillery enabled Scott to blast a way through the fortifications and inflict a resounding defeat on the Mexican army. By 14 May he was in Puebla, where he confidently expected to hear from Santa Anna that the Mexican government was suing for peace. All he got was a request for ten thousand dollars to help soften up the diehard opposition. The Americans grudgingly paid, and Santa Anna used the money to prepare the defence of Mexico City. Far from intimidating the Mexicans, the enemy's approach created a new sense of unity among the quarrelling factions and hardened their will to resist. Santa Anna, despite his recent débâcle and the universal distrust which his character inspired, was still accepted as the only competent commander-in-chief. He was certainly showing admirable energy in the crisis.

The Mexicans offered no resistance in the mountain passes leading to the Valley and Scott, continuing in the footsteps of Cortés, chose the rough road between the volcanoes. On 9 August he reached Chalco. It was the height of the rainy season and the swollen waters of Lake Texcoco impeded a frontal attack on the city from the east. Accordingly Scott turned his army to the south of Lake Chalco and then northwards along the foothills of the Ajusco range. A series of stubborn encounters took place among the suburban villages between the mountains and the valley floor. At Contreras, and again at Churubusco (the Huitzilopochco of the Aztecs) the Americans barely won through. Their numbers were so small that one serious reverse would have sufficed to overwhelm them. While both armies fought with obstinate courage, American discipline contrasted with the fractious behaviour of Santa Anna's lieutenants, who ignored his orders in the worst emergencies. A strange and tragic fate, however, befell a battalion of Roman Catholic Irishmen who defected en masse to the Mexican side; they were captured and a great many of them summarily executed. The Mexicans retired slowly, contesting every inch of the ground. Their last stand was made on the hill of Chapultepec, where the cadets of the military college, proudly commemorated ever since as the 'Niños Heroes', put up a brave but futile defence. The city capitulated on 14 September, the day before the celebration of Hidalgo's *Grito de Dolores,* Mexico's national holiday.

There was further sporadic fighting during the winter, while a provisional Mexican government established at Querétaro parleyed with the Americans in Mexico City. Scott's triumph might still have been frustrated by a popular uprising in the capital, or by a systematic guerrilla campaign against his communications, but the country as a whole had no zeal for prolonging the struggle. Santa Anna, the only vigorous advocate of continued resistance, was disowned by the political leaders, and was lucky to slip back into exile without being punished by the Americans for so flagrantly misleading them. Once he was out of the way, the negotiations between Scott and Peña y Peña, president of the Mexican Supreme Court, were concluded in March 1848 by the Treaty of Guadalupe Hidalgo, under which Mexico surrendered over half of its territory in exchange for fifteen million dollars and the cancellation of American claims.

It was a fearful price to pay for defeat in a quarrel resulting from historical developments over which Mexico had no control. But even if the fighting qualities of its soldiers had not been nullified by the short-comings of the political system and the personal defects of their leaders, it is hard to conceive how the nominal sovereignty of Mexico over the lost territories could have been indefinitely upheld in an age of imperialist expansion. The new frontier was altogether more natural and realistic. However that may be, what really counted with the Mexicans was not so much the transfer of vast unpopulated provinces from one flag to another as the sense of outrage to their national dignity and self-respect. Time has not yet obliterated this resentment: it was the beginning of the keen horror of foreign aggression which is embedded in the Mexican psychology. At the same time the ordeal through which the country had passed stiffened its will to withstand the further assaults which were to be made on its integrity later in the century.

The next five years were unusually calm. There were no sudden changes of régime and the two presidents who ruled during this period, Herrera and Arista, did their conscientious best to nurse Mexico back to health, relying on a majority of *moderados* in Congress. Under the federalist constitution of 1824, which had been reintroduced during the war, some of the States enjoyed sound government, and the administration was partly successful in clearing up the financial chaos. But the burden of past years was crippling, and the very honesty and comparative efficiency of those in power aroused the jealousy of the army, whose budget was sharply reduced, and opposition from the selfish or unruly elements which had thriven on the breakdown of law and order under the strain of the war. The whole north was infested with raiding Indians and in the more settled areas banditry, the curse of independent Mexico, had never been more rife.

Mexicans had become inured to this plague and submitted with fatalism to its ugliest manifestations. If necessary they barricaded themselves for weeks at a time in their *haciendas* against parties of marauders, and travellers banded together under the protection of strong escorts. Foreigners who suffered injuries to their persons and property were louder in their complaints, but the authorities were unable to save even diplomats proceeding to Vera Cruz by stage coach from robbery and murder. In 1842, D. T. Egerton, the talented English artist resident in the capital, who so brilliantly caught the feeling of Santa Anna's Mexico in his all too rare paintings, was butchered when taking a stroll with his mistress in the suburb of Tacubaya, and his case was remarkable because the murderers were exceptionally brought to justice. For the young generation of Mexican patriots who were growing up in the fifties the perpetual anarchy and near-bankruptcy of their country were as intolerable as its recent humiliation in war. They were shortly to turn their indignant protests into action, but before they could do so Santa Anna had to have his last fling.

In January 1853 Arista threw in his hand under pressure from the generals, and it was the turn of the conservatives to govern. It is a shaming reflection on their dearth of ideas that the only solution which their mentor, Lucas Alamán, could propose was to bring back the discredited ex-dictator from his retreat in Venezuela. But his belief in the virtues of a strong man was unshaken, and he persuaded his supporters to offer Santa Anna office for one year, pending the search for a foreign prince who would revive monarchy in Mexico. Needless to say, the invitation was not refused. Soon after Santa Anna was installed Alamán died, and in the absence of any moderating influence he embarked on a spending spree which surpassed all his previous extravagances and exhausted the resources of the treasury within twelve months. The search for a prince was quietly dropped and Santa Anna, now sporting the title of His Most Supreme Highness, proved that his genius for making his own position untenable had not altered with the passage of years. When the explosion came it not only blew him out of the country for good, but initiated an era of new men, new ideals and a fresh impulse towards national regeneration.

The Parroquia of Dolores Hidalgo (Guanajuato)   (*Mexican Tourist Council*)

The front of the Cathedral, Mexico City

(*J. Allan Cash*)

Chapter Eight

Reform and Empire 1855-67

The movement which overthrew Santa Anna was launched by Juan Alvarez, a rough old *mestizo* who had been one of Morelos' captains. He had kept the revolutionary tradition alive ever since in the State of Guerrero, where his word was law. He was the archetype of the regional political boss, a breed which has always flourished in the Mexican republic as a counter-balance to the central authority. Gathering round him a small group of dissidents, none of whom was a national figure, he issued the Plan of Ayutla (an obscure village in the western sierra) which simply demanded a change of president and the preparation of a new constitution. Guerrero rose in rebellion, and its guerrillas defied the army's attempts to dislodge them.

The outbreak had wide repercussions. It occurred at an opportune moment when the young liberals who were slowly coming to the fore in Mexican political life were looking for a rallying point. These men were profoundly dissatisfied with the condition of their country. They had to recognise that Mexico could hardly be considered part of the progressive world of the nineteenth century: it stagnated unhappily within the decayed fabric of the vanished viceroyalty, while the factions which bickered among the ruins could provide neither tranquillity nor well-being for their fellow citizens. Democracy had failed to take root, and the frequent experiments in dictatorship had worked out disastrously. The highflown rhetoric of the politicians too often covered up their anarchic and selfish individualism. It is true that the old-fashioned radicals of the school of Gomez Farías had striven indomitably to break the dreary alternation of weak civilian government and military interlopers, but during their short periods of office they had tried to push their reforms too fast and too far for the inclinations of the Creole minority which still called the tune. By 1850, however, the shape of Mexican society was changing. The *mestizos,* who were well on the way to forming the most numerous and active element in the population, now aspired to political power and a pure Indian, Benito Juarez, had already governed Oaxaca. In 1854 he was, with other Mexican liberals, watching events from exile in New Orleans. Thus the new reformers were men of diverse social and racial origins. Their intellectual formation was fundamentally French, and the primary target of their reformist enthusiasm was the Church, whose power was still regarded as the real obstacle to national progress.

The collapse of Santa Anna was staved off for a while by the sale to the United States of a long strip of territory on the borders of Sonora and Arizona. The so-called Gadsden Purchase netted ten million dollars and enabled the dictator to pay his army until mid-1855, but he could not prevent the rebellion from developing into a national uprising. The northern states came out strongly in support of Alvarez and as the dissidence crept southwards Santa Anna, who always knew when the game was up, deemed it useless to resist. After one or two half-hearted attempts to overawe his opponents by a display of military force, he abandoned Mexico City and on reaching Perote, on the well-worn escape route to Vera Cruz, announced that he was handing back his powers to the people. This done, he quietly embarked for Venezuela. Before entering the capital the liberals convened a congress at Cuerna-vaca which elected Alvarez to the presidency, and in November they took over the government.

Alvarez himself was barely literate and plainly unqualified for the job, but his ministry was full of talent. It included Juarez as Minister of Justice and Miguel Lerdo de Tejada at the Treasury, and drew its intellectual inspiration from Melchor Ocampo, a scholar of great distinction and advanced radical tendencies, who had been a successful governor of Michoacán in the mid-forties. Its driving force, however, was furnished by Ignacio Comonfort, a former chief of the customs office at Acapulco, who had served as Alvarez' right-hand man in the Ayutla rebellion. It was he who succeeded to the presidency in December, when Alvarez wisely surrendered his office, and was entrusted with enforcing the initial programme of reform.

The measures adopted were of a stringency that left the

conservatives aghast. First, the Ley Juarez did away with the privileges of the clergy and of the army. It was followed by the Ley Lerdo, a piece of legislation calculated to shake the whole structure of society. Its declared purpose was to raise money by forcing the Church to dispose of its estates to private buyers, while the state collected a heavy sales tax on each transaction. The government hoped that the Church would thus automatically lose its economic and political power and that it would itself win the loyalty of the new class of landowners which would be created by the division of the clerical or monastic properties. The law was also framed to cover all corporate bodies, including the *ejidos* or communal lands of the Indian peasants, the ownership of which had been respected throughout colonial times and the early decades of independence. Here again it was hoped to bring a new class of grateful smallholders into being.

But no sooner had the law been applied than its results, both financial and social, deceived the planners' expectations. The revenue accruing to the state was disappointingly meagre and the Church estates, instead of being split up among peasant proprietors, fell into the hands of speculators, both Mexican and foreign. These exploited the peons who worked on them with a harshness of which the Church had never been guilty. Some properties were quietly annexed by neighbouring *hacendados* or politically influential persons. The peasants were also deprived of the educational and charitable benefits dispensed by the clergy and the monastic orders. Worst of all, countless Indian villagers were dispossessed of their *ejido* lands and reduced to a condition resembling serfdom. Thus the shock administered to the conservative religious conscience was accompanied by wide discontent among the masses in the countryside.

While the government hastened the drafting of a fresh constitution, the reactionaries mustered their forces for the crucial struggle and the Church deployed all its moral and material resources. Revolts broke out at Puebla, a stronghold of Creole clericalism, and among the Indian populations of the central core of Mexico. Comonfort, though barely holding his position, acted sternly against the recalcitrants. There was a spate of arrests, banishments and confiscations and as a salutary warning against clerical intrigue, the great convent of San Francisco, a landmark of historic sanctity in the centre of Mexico City, was dissolved and all its buildings, except the church, pulled down. It was a foretaste of what was to happen all over Mexico in the succeeding years. In an atmosphere of grim tension, the new federalist constitution was submitted for approval in February 1857.

The charter which emerged from the deliberations of the liberal lawyers was a creditable piece of work. Indeed it remained in force for the next sixty years, although it was no better suited to Mexican realities than its predecessor of 1824. The constituents tried hard to strike a balance between the need for a strong central authority and the firm guarantees required for protection against dictatorship. They made no attempt, however, to defend the economically weak against exploitation. These issues were eclipsed by the impassioned controversy about religion. The incorporation in the constitution of the provisions of the Ley Juarez and the Ley Lerdo not only infuriated the conservatives but stirred up grave doubts in the consciences of the liberal majority. Even those who were foremost in denouncing clerical abuses were Catholics at heart and members of traditionally devout families. They had no inclination to attack religion as such. Consequently, when the deputies were required to swear personal loyalty to the constitution and to append their signatures to it, many balked and absented themselves from the ceremonial occasion on which the elderly paladin of the *puros,* Gomez Farías, was the first to take the oath. The bishops, acting under the full authority of the Holy See, threatened with excommunication all those who subscribed publicly to the constitution or trafficked in Church property.

In this confusion of allegiances the extremists on both sides set the pace. Comonfort, who was confirmed as president by the first elections held under the 1857 constitution, was a sincere Christian who wished to see the Mexican Church curbed but not crushed. He was thoroughly alarmed by the prospect of the division of the people into two irreconcilable camps, but his appeals for moderation were disregarded by his own party as well as by the clericals. He disappointed his supporters by his refusal to deport the Archbishop of Mexico and by his open dislike of the restraints imposed by the constitution on the presidential powers. By the end of the year he had lost his grip on the situation and was taken by surprise when General Felix Zuloaga, 'pronouncing' at Tacubaya, called on him to dissolve congress and repeal the constitution. Victim of his own hesitations, he oscillated wildly between acceptance and repudiation of Zuloaga's demands. His last act was to order the release of Juarez, who had been seized and imprisoned by the general's troops. In January he fled the country, leaving it to be ravaged by an atrocious civil war.

There were now two rival claimants to the presidency, Zuloaga in Mexico City and Juarez seeking a base from which to reassert liberal supremacy. He was hounded from Querétaro to Guadalajara, where he nearly lost his life, and from Guadalajara to the Pacific port of Manzanillo. Thence, by way of the isthmus of Panama, he returned by painful stages to Mexican soil at Vera Cruz. The former fief of Santa Anna thus became the headquarters of the legal government. It was hardly an ideal centre of the direction of the war, but it afforded security against attack from the land and, what was more important, a window on the outside world. There the liberals collected such scanty customs dues as could be raised in the prevailing confusion, and received supplies from abroad, especially from the United States.

The War of the Reform was waged for three years with a bitter intensity quite untypical of the sporadic guerrilla fighting with which Mexico was so familiar, or of the encounters between 'pronouncing' generals. As is habitual in wars of ideas, the bravery of the combatants was equalled by their cruelty. Prisoners and hostages were summarily executed and the irregulars who skirmished in the wake of the armies indulged in indiscriminate massacre and pillage.

The actual campaigns are hard to follow. They resembled destructive brush fires which spring from one mountainside to another and burst out afresh as soon as they are extinguished. No part of the country escaped devastation. At first the two sides were well matched in numbers, but the conservatives had the more skilful generals. During 1858 a brilliant trio, Miramón, Marquez and Mejía, the first two Creoles and the third an Indian, held the principal cities and had the liberals on the run, although the Valley of Mexico was not immune from guerrilla raids. But Miramón, who superseded Zuloaga in the presidency early in 1859, failed to take Vera Cruz, while Santos Degollado, the lawyer from Morelia whom Juarez had appointed his commander-in-chief, refused to be discouraged by repeated reverses. In April he staged an attack on the capital and penetrated as far as Chapultepec, but his army was smashed and dispersed by Marquez. In this war there were no regular fronts and few planned operations. Advance and retreat, victory and rout, alternated with bewildering speed and unpredictability.

Where the liberals excelled was in the quality of their chief and of the men who surrounded him. Melchor Ocampo, Santos

Degollado, the two Lerdos de Tejada, Miguel and Sebastian, Manuel Doblado, the poets Guillermo Prieto and Ignacio Ramirez, were a team infinitely superior in character and talent to any of the conservative leaders, who could offer no remedy for the nation's ills but blind attachment to the past.

This body of exceptional leaders unquestionably acknowledged the primacy of Benito Juarez, the little middle-aged Indian from Oaxaca. The president's origins were so humble that it is almost incredible that he should ever have won through to high office. He was born in 1806 at Guelatao, a tiny village perched on a ledge of the Sierra de Oaxaca, amid scenery of incomparable grandeur. In his peasant childhood he spoke only Zapotec. Later he was taken into a Creole household at Oaxaca as a domestic servant and his master, attracted by his industry and intelligence, arranged for him to be educated by the friars, in the hope that he might enter the priesthood. But he preferred the law to the church, married the daughter of his benefactor and prospered in his profession. An ardent partisan of liberalism, he was sent to congress by his native State and governed it from 1847 to 1852, at a time when Mexico enjoyed a sensible and moderate administration.

Under Santa Anna's dictatorship he was exiled to New Orleans, where his ideological fervour was stimulated by his fellow refugee Ocampo. When the rebellion of Ayutla broke out he hurried home and was soon rewarded by a place in the government. On the fall of Comonfort he was accepted as the natural champion of liberalism in adversity.

To the sheer honesty of his patriotism, his unswerving devotion to his political ideals and his intense diligence as an administrator, was joined a complete incorruptibility of mind and character which amazed his contemporaries. In a crisis he was supremely courageous and imperturbable; it was unthinkable that he should ever despair of the republic. His way of life was austere and unassuming to the point of primness, but the simple puritanism of his manners does not appear to have caused irritation. His defect as a statesman was a dour and unbending legalism which, although stemming from the highest motives, sometimes verged on the inhuman. Where issues of principle were at stake, there was no room for compromise in his cold logical mind.

In 1859 the arch-enemy was still clericalism. In the teeth of the Ley Lerdo, the Church was spending its resources freely to finance the conservative armies, and when the government's fortunes had been depressed by Marquez's victory, Juarez concluded that the only way of stopping this flow of funds to the enemies of the State was to cripple the Church by further legislation. He therefore decreed the expropriation without compensation of all remaining Church property and ordered the dissolution of the monasteries. This meant that the clergy were left with nothing but edifices in which to say Mass. Everything else was to be forfeit—lands, buildings and the accumulated treasures of three centuries. The government's commands were all too faithfully executed, and the confiscations were accompanied by an orgy of looting and vandalism.

The damage to Mexico's historic and cultural heritage was incalculable. It was not only that gold and silver vanished into the melting pot; precious books and manuscripts perished in tens of thousands when the monastic libraries were ransacked or burnt. The immediate purpose of the operation, however, was fulfilled. The Church, which had formerly owned between a third and a quarter of the country's real wealth, was a disestablished beggar and the liberal coffers were at least temporarily restocked.

This advantage soon gave the Juarists a decisive superiority in numbers. During 1860 they redoubled their pressure. Miramón was heavily defeated at Silao and Marquez near Guadalajara. As a result the conservatives lost control of western and central Mexico and were flung back on the capital. On 22 December the liberal general Gonzalez Ortega, who had replaced the plodding Santos Degollado, overwhelmed Miramón on the plains of Calpulapam, between Texcoco and Tlaxcala, and on the first day of the new year he marched into Mexico City. Ten days after his triumphal entry Juarez drove in from Vera Cruz in his little black travelling carriage.

The country was more thoroughly wrecked and exhausted than after the struggle for independence or the war with the United States. In the hope of restoring some measure of internal concord, Juarez announced an amnesty, but this was not welcomed by his more radical supporters. Among the latter was Melchor Ocampo, who resigned from the government and retired to his native Michoacán. There he was kidnapped and murdered by Marquez, who was still lurking in the mountains with a force of guerrillas. Shortly afterwards Santos Degollado suffered the same fate.

Meanwhile the financial situation was desperate. The proceeds of the expropriated ecclesiastical properties had already been dissipated and the ordinary sources of revenue had been reduced to a trickle. Nearly eighty per cent of the Customs duties were earmarked for meeting indebtedness to foreign powers and individuals, whose claims had vastly increased in the chaotic conditions of the war. There were no other assets available for satisfying the exasperated creditors, much less for keeping the machinery of state in motion. Juarez was obliged to notify foreign governments, that although he had every intention of eventually paying legitimate claims, there must be a moratorium of two years. Inevitably he was becoming embroiled in the exigencies and ambitions of several powerful nations. Fortunately for him, these found it hard to make up their minds about the measures needed to bring Mexico to reason.

Of the countries concerned, the United States was at the moment the least dangerous, as its energies were about to be absorbed by its own civil war. Nevertheless American pressure on Mexico had not been relaxed since 1848. The Democratic Party in particular had not been satisfied by the immense accretions of territory resulting from the Treaty of Guadalupe Hidalgo. It believed that it was the 'manifest destiny' of the United States to extend American influence, if not sovereignty, as far south as Panama. Apart from the temptation to repeat the use of violence against a weak neighbour, there was always the possibility that, following the precedent of the Gadsden Purchase, a Mexican government might consent to further cessions of territory in return for cash. Gadsden himself (the United States Minister to Mexico) was so active in proposing transactions of this kind that he embarrassed his own government and had to be recalled. But the demands were kept up during the presidency of Comonfort, when Gadsden's successor was authorised to offer various millions of dollars for Lower California, Sonora and Chihuahua. He met with no success, and an independent filibustering expedition which tried to grab Sonora was easily foiled.

After Zuloaga had also resisted American blandishments it was the turn of Juarez to be approached. In August 1858 a special American envoy, McLane, visited Vera Cruz with instructions to press the previous offer for Lower California. He opened negotiations with Ocampo, whom he found adamantly opposed to any deal involving the surrender of Mexican territory. The talks were, however, continued and resulted in the signature of an agreement whereby the liberal government obtained the valuable gift of recognition by the United States, as well as certain financial advantages. In return the United States was granted a perpetual right of way across the isthmus of Tehuantepec. Although the treaty was thrown out by the American Senate, the recognition of Juarez as head of the legitimate government of Mexico was not disavowed. Hence Ocampo had won a notable diplomatic success, which paved the way for eventual American support for Mexico against European intervention. It was to be the last service which he was able to render his country.

There remained three European powers with grievances against Mexico. Spain, Great Britain and France all had good cause to complain of its failure to honour debts, or to pay compensation for outrages against the persons of their nationals. On several occasions during the Reform period Spain and Mexico had come to the brink of war, and the Spanish government was known to favour the idea of joint armed intervention. In 1861 Juarez brusquely expelled the Spanish Minister.

British patience had been even more sorely tried. In 1850 the British bondholders had agreed to reduce the rate of interest payable on the loans raised at the time of independence, and to remit part of the arrears; but the arrangement also stipulated that twenty per cent of the Customs duties should be reserved for the service of the British debt. It worked out well until Santa Anna returned to power, when Mexico again went into default, and during the war both factions resorted to barefaced robbery. In 1859 Marquez waylaid a convoy of silver, the property of British mineowners, to the value of six hundred thousand dollars: a year later Santos Degollado appropriated another worth a million. The British Legation at Mexico City had not recovered from the shock of these exploits when Miramón broke into its premises and removed from the strong-room a further sum of six hundred thousand dollars which had been collected by the bondholders' agents.

In the face of these provocations the British Chargé d'Affaires, who personally sympathised with the liberals, withdrew from the capital. Nevertheless when Juarez, after winning the war, promised reparation for these incidents, he was promptly accorded recognition by Great Britain. There was no enthusiasm for intervention in London, though the pros and cons had been weighed by two successive Foreign Secretaries. In fact two petitions from prominent Mexican conservatives begging Queen Victoria to sponsor such action had been politely turned down.

A different spirit prevailed in Paris. The Emperor Napoleon III had long been interested in Latin American affairs. In the forties, while interned by King Louis Philippe in the dreary castle of Ham, his imagination had been caught by a project for driving an interoceanic canal across Nicaragua, and he had assiduously canvassed it from the seclusion of his not very secure prison. After his escape to London in 1847 he had written a paper extolling the commercial attractions of the scheme and stressing the political desirability of building up a strong state in Central America which could act as a barrier to American expansionism. He suggested that the European powers would be well advised to help Mexico rise to greatness as the kernel of a new empire stretching from Panama to the Rio Grande. When he became emperor he continued to toy with this idea and in 1856 he conveyed to the unresponsive British government a hint that the Duc d'Aumale, a son of the dethroned Louis Philippe, might be the right man to place on the throne of Mexico.

But in the late fifties France was in no position to engage in transatlantic adventures, either alone or in conjunction with other countries. Even if Napoleon had not been fully occupied with the Crimean and Italian wars, no such expedition could have been successfully launched in the teeth of certain opposition from the United States. In 1861, however, France was at peace in Europe and the Americans were fighting each other. Therefore the way was clear for bringing into effect the plans which had been maturing in the emperor's mind. Throughout the year his ministers took the lead in promoting consultations between the European governments.

Meanwhile the French representative in Mexico, Saligny, was trying to bully Juarez into accepting responsibility for a peculiarly monstrous claim. It transpired that Miramón, in his frenzied search for funds, had accepted a loan of seven hundred and fifty thousand dollars from a Swiss banker, Jecker, who had subsequently changed his nationality to French, against a pledge to honour no less than fifteen million dollars worth of bonds. It was the latter sum that Saligny was so insistently demanding, and when Juarez took no notice of his importunities, he urged his superiors to hasten direct action.

The Mexican decision to suspend foreign payments, which was made public on 19 July, precipitated a crisis. When the news reached Europe, a series of hurried discussions took place between the Governments of Great Britain, Spain and France. On 31 October a Convention was signed in London committing the three Powers to despatch a joint expedition to Mexico. According to this instrument their object was to secure redress for the wrongs inflicted on their nationals and a firm guarantee that Mexico would in future comply with its financial obligations. To this end they agreed to earmark contingents strong enough to seize positions on the Mexican coast and to carry out any other military operations that might be advisable. At the same time they bound themselves not to seek 'any acquisition of territory nor any special advantage', not to interfere in the internal affairs of Mexico and not 'to prejudice the right of the Mexican nation to choose and to constitute freely the form of its government'. These terms sound explicit enough, but in fact they concealed, on the French side, far-reaching ulterior aims.

While the War of the Reform was raging in Mexico, Napoleon's interest in the revival of monarchy in that country was being sharpened by the ceaseless activities of a group of Mexican royalists in Europe. It will be recalled that a small but influential section of Mexican conservatives had never been reconciled to the republican idea. Without wishing to revert to Spanish rule, they believed that Mexico could only be rescued from the misfortunes and humiliations to which it had been subjected since independence by a strong centralised monarchy, preferably headed by a European prince. It was the solution which Lucas Alamán would have preferred if there had been any practical possibility of imposing it.

The busiest and most fanatical advocate of turning Mexico into a kingdom was Gutierrez de Estrada, a former diplomat who for a brief period had held the post of Foreign Minister. In his deep disillusionment with current affairs he had published a manifesto setting out his views on the virtues of monarchy, and had been expelled from his native land for his pains. For twenty years he resided in Rome, labouring with amazing tenacity to convince the sceptical governments of Europe that it would be in their interests to intervene in Mexico to install a stable and authoritarian régime. In 1846 he secured an interview with Metternich, the Austrian Chancellor. A year later he reissued his manifesto and circulated it widely to potentates and their ministers.

It was not, however, until the Second Empire came into being in France that his perseverance was rewarded. In 1850 he had struck up a friendship with a young Mexican diplomat named José Hidalgo, whom he soon turned into a fervent royalist and a useful collaborator in his self-imposed task of importuning the European cabinets. It so happened that Hidalgo was connected with various highly placed families in Spain, including that of Madame de Montijo, mother of Napoleon's Empress, Eugénie. His next important step was to get himself transferred, in 1857, from Madrid to Paris, where he was at once received into the Emperor's circle of intimate friends. He thus found it easy to forge a link between Gutierrez de Estrada and the imperial court. As from 1858 he was actively supported in his royalist intrigues by his own chief, General Almonte, an old henchman of Santa Anna who had been second in command at the battle of San Jacinto. Napoleon and Eugénie listened eagerly to these Mexicans whose energies were devoted to the grand design of finding a sovereign for their country and who, in 1861, were reinforced by many conservative exiles fleeing from the triumph of Juarez. They succeeded in persuading Napoleon that they were voicing the true feelings of the Mexican people who, as they insisted, were only waiting the right degree of moral and material support from abroad to throw off the yoke of Juarez and his crew of godless oppressors. But before the Emperor could be prevailed upon to act there were two problems to be settled. The first was to discover a suitable candidate for the throne; the second, to secure the support of other powers, and particularly of the British, for the proposed intervention.

The exact circumstances in which Napoleon and the Mexican royalists fixed their attention on a member of the House of Austria for the role they had in mind have always remained obscure. The fact is, however, that in July 1861 Gutierrez personally sounded the Austrian Ambassador in Paris on the possibility that one of the Habsburg Archdukes might agree to be approached. When the answer came from Vienna, it was relatively encouraging. Gutierrez was informed that while the Emperor Francis Joseph welcomed the plan in principle, he remained to be convinced that the Mexican nation genuinely desired a monarchy, and that the venture would enjoy the effective support of Great Britain and France. The name of the Emperor's younger brother, the Archduke Ferdinand Maximilian, was not mentioned in this exchange, which took place before it was known in Europe that Juarez had suspended debt payments.

But when the tripartite talks about intervention began Napoleon knew that Austria had risen to the bait and had decided in his own mind that Maximilian was the right man. Whether he himself inspired Gutierrez' approach to the Austrian Ambassador is a matter of conjecture. He did however assure Gutierrez and

Hidalgo that if an allied intervention were agreed upon, they could count on his help in using it to force a royalist solution on Mexico. Simultaneously the Austrian government was given to understand that Napoleon would look favourably on Maximilian's candidature.

The motives which led the two Emperors to expedite agreement on the scheme were complex and have never been adequately explained, but it seems likely that Napoleon, apart from his dreams about the historic destiny of Mexico and the adjoining lands, saw advantage in offering Francis Joseph some reparation for the provinces torn from the House of Austria by the recent war in Italy, while Francis Joseph and his brother thought it fitting that their dynasty should recover the throne of Mexico which the Habsburgs, as kings of Spain, had occupied for nearly two hundred years. However this may be, the Franco-Austrian understanding made rapid progress concurrently with the negotiations for the London Convention. Napoleon's difficulty was that he was quite unable to move the British government from its attitude of non-intervention in the internal affairs of Mexico, and thus satisfy the very natural Austrian insistence that Great Britain, as well as France, should guarantee the success of the enterprise in which the Archduke was to be involved. Shortly before the Convention was concluded he frankly divulged to the British his plan to establish the monarchy and his support of Maximilian's candidature. He suggested that while the intervention should 'ostensibly' be directed at the redress of the powers' complaints, it should be allowed to become the pretext for helping the Mexican people to change their form of government. This Machiavellian proposal was politely ignored by Lords Palmerston and Russell and the Convention, when signed, contained the non-intervention clause on which the British ministers had been insisting.

The British were now satisfied that they had foiled Napoleon's project for setting up a monarchy in Mexico, and that the Convention would serve as a reliable barrier against his ambitions. They were, however, gravely mistaken, for the Emperor was at that very moment assuring the anxious Austrian government that although the British, for parliamentary reasons, were unable overtly to agree to any broadening of the terms of the Convention, they were in fact ready to acquiesce in his plans for putting the Archduke on the throne. This specious explanation was duly accepted in Vienna, where the outcome of the Allied expedition to Mexico was keenly awaited. It seems strange, in view of Napoleon's record for tricky diplomacy, that he should so easily have deceived the governments of Great Britain, Spain and Austria. Nevertheless the extent of his duplicity, and the depth of misunderstandings among the Powers for which he was responsible, were gradually revealed in the ensuing months.

The Allies landed without opposition at Vera Cruz early in January 1862, convoyed by an imposing array of warships. There was an interesting disparity in size between the three contingents. The largest force consisted of six thousand Spaniards commanded by General Prim, who had been standing by for some months in Cuba in case Spain should decide to act unilaterally. The French contingent, led by Admiral Jurien de la Gravière, initially amounted to no more than a brigade, but unknown to the other Allies, considerable reinforcements had already been earmarked for service in Mexico. The British contribution, seven hundred marines under Commodore Dunlop, was a pointed reminder that Great Britain was not prepared to join in any serious encroachment on Mexican territory. For the purpose of negotiating with the Mexicans, the military commanders were supplemented by Commissioners. In this capacity the French and British governments nominated their Ministers to Mexico, Saligny and Sir Charles Wyke, while General Prim acted in both roles. Though strongly critical of Juarez, Wyke had resolutely persisted through the autumn of 1861 in his attempts to reach an agreed settlement of the British claims. Indeed he had succeeded in concluding a convention with Zamacona, the Mexican Foreign Minister, by which the essential British requirements were conceded. But to Wyke's intense disgust, this settlement was rejected by the Mexican congress. On top of this rebuff, he was taken entirely by surprise when the Allies arrived at Vera Cruz, since, owing to the slowness of the transatlantic mail, he had not even been notified that they were on their way. He was, incidentally, on the worst of terms with his French colleague.

Once the Allies had landed, they had to decide how to proceed, for no detailed planning had so far taken place. Their first act was to issue a vague but grandiloquent proclamation about the purposes of the expedition. These, it said, were to obtain the necessary safeguards for their national interests, and equally 'to preside at the grand spectacle of your regeneration'. The latter phrase was capable of being interpreted in more than one way, but it was hardly likely to appeal to Mexican liberals, who considered themselves already regenerated by the Reform.

The next step was for the Commissioners to discuss the demands which, in the form of a joint note, each of them proposed to put forward to the Mexican government. There was nothing novel about the British requirements, which had been advanced many times before, but there was consternation among the other Commissioners when Jurien and Saligny announced that they intended to extort from Mexico both the fifteen million dollars alleged to be owing on the Jecker bonds and the entirely exorbitant sum of twelve millions in satisfaction of the residue of French claims.

When Prim and Wyke indignantly refused to underwrite these exigencies, a ludicrous deadlock occurred, for the Allies turned out to have no common policy and there was nothing for their soldiers to do. Without either a declaration of war or an invitation from the Mexican government the presence of these foreign forces on Mexican soil was bound to look wildly anomalous. Moreover the sickness rate from yellow fever— the dreaded 'black vomit' of colonial times—was rising steeply, and it had become imperative to find healthier quarters for the troops inland. The Commissioners also felt that the allied army was in a dangerous quandary, especially as a much larger Mexican force under General Zaragoza had arrived in the neighbourhood of Vera Cruz and, on Juarez' orders, was enforcing a close blockade. They therefore addressed a message to the Mexican government rather naively suggesting that the latter should invite the Allies to move to the region of Córdoba and Orizaba. For a punitive expedition it was an odd exhibition of impotence.

There ensued a phase of discussions, in which Prim was deputed to treat with the courteous and adroit Manuel Doblado. The two men got on well together and were soon able to report that they had agreed to a formula providing for the opening of regular negotiations on the Allied claims, which were to be held in Orizaba. The Allies, for their part, were to declare that they would do nothing to impair the integrity of the Mexican republic, and were accordingly to be empowered to occupy Córdoba, Orizaba and Tehuacán for the duration of the talks. The terms, which were embodied in a document known as the Convention of La Soledad, were hardly palatable to the French Commissioners, but in the circumstances Jurien and Saligny were forced to subscribe to them. The whole transaction was a signal tribute to Doblado's diplomatic skill. Aided by the yellow fever threat, he had manoeuvred the Allies into an amicable parley with the Juarist government, whose competence and honesty they now implicitly admitted.

In early March the depleted expeditionary force marched up from the coast, closely followed by the French reinforcements, four thousand men under the command of General Lorencez. His arrival caused further dissension among the Commissioners, and the expected meeting with the Mexicans never came off. Wyke and Prim complained that in many ways the French were acting as if the Conventions of London and La Soledad had never existed. A new element of friction was the presence in the French camp of General Almonte with the avowed mission of stirring up a conservative revolution against the government in Mexico City. These differences culminated in a furious show-down at a conference between the Commissioners on 9 April, when every kind of recrimination was hurled across the table. Since the French were quite clearly determined to let nothing stand in the way of their forward policy, the British and Spanish representatives declared, on their own authority, the intention of withdrawing their national contingents forthwith from the expedition. Their decision was acted upon without delay, and was later heartily endorsed in London and Madrid. At last, in mid-April, the French army was free to impose its masters' will on Mexico.

Lorencez assumed that this would prove a ridiculously easy task. He despised the Mexican army and was misled by Almonte's assurance that the country was on the verge of repudiating Juarez. He accordingly marched briskly on Puebla, where he expected an eager welcome from its clerically inclined population. But barring his advance was General Zaragoza's army, which he found occupying strongly fortified positions on a hill called the Cerro de Guadalupe. Without hesitation Lorencez hurled his infantry against the centre of the Mexican line, but the defences held and the ground before them was littered with dead and wounded Zouaves. After suffering a thousand casualties the French abandoned the attack and retreated ignominiously to Orizaba. As battles go the clash at Puebla was a small affair, but in moral terms Mexico had won a resounding victory. Its anniversary has ever since been saluted as a popular holiday: the ballroom of the national palace in Mexico City is hung with a huge panoramic painting of the battle, and Zaragoza's equestrian statue proudly adorns the highway to Puebla. At neighbouring Huejotzingo, the Indians celebrate the Shrove Tuesday carnival

Building on the Zócalo, Mexico City (*J. March-Penney*)

Augustinian Monastery of Acolman

(*J. Allan Cash*)

by dressing up in gaudy parodies of French uniforms, amid the deafening discharge of antique muskets.

In Paris the reaction was one of intense irritation, coupled with a burning impatience to avenge the defeat. It was bad enough that Napoleon's plans had undergone so disconcerting a setback, and worse that the veterans of Sebastopol and Solferino had been humbled by a scratch force, including a battalion of Zacopoaxtla Indians from the Sierra de Puebla. The French government lost no time in raising their forces in Mexico to the strength of an army corps and General Forey was appointed to replace the unlucky Lorencez.

Ten months, however, were to pass before he was poised to resume the advance. In the meantime the awkward turn which events had taken caused profound embarrassment in Vienna. Francis Joseph and his ministers had already begun to feel distinct misgivings about the involvement of the Archduke Maximilian. They were understandably worried by the lack of a British guarantee and by the failure of the Mexican royalists to assert themselves. They were assailed by suspicion that Napoleon was not playing straight with them. They therefore warned Maximilian not to commit himself too deeply. But unfortunately the Archduke's fascination with the Mexican mirage had never ceased to grow since the day when he undertook, under certain conditions, to become a candidate for the throne.

While only in his thirtieth year, Maximilian was by no means devoid of talent and experience. He had governed Lombardy, the most sensitive of the Austrian dominions, with tact and energy for two years until Napoleon provoked the war which resulted in its loss to the Habsburg empire. He had also commanded the Austrian Navy. He was intelligent, well-read and liberally minded. His addition to seafaring had given him a wider interest in the outside world than was normally developed by princes of his family. He was endowed with a fertile and romantic imagination which led him to ponder restlessly over unpractical designs. At the same time he possessed the typical virtues of the Victorian age. Hardworking, dutiful and conscientious; dignified, honest and kindly, he would certainly have made an admirable sovereign of a constitutional kingdom. But he lacked political insight and a hard sense of reality, and was in no way suited for the ruthlessly competitive atmosphere of Mexico. He never displayed the tougher qualities of statecraft. His judgement was frequently at fault and he clung obstinately to wrong courses and decisions.

His reserved and defensive manner conveyed a somewhat unmerited impression of weakness of will and character, while an exaggerated sense of loyalty encouraged unscrupulous people to assume that he could be manipulated for their own ends.

In appearance he was tall and slight, with a luxuriant blond beard. He was married to the twenty-one year old Charlotte, daughter of the first King of the Belgians (Queen Victoria's Uncle Leopold). As befitted a Coburg princess, this young woman was remarkable for her lively and ambitious disposition and for the vigorous interest which she took in her husband's affairs. There is no good evidence for concluding that in the Mexican adventure she exercised a dominant influence over Maximilian's decisions, but no more fervent believer in his imperial destiny could have been at hand to strengthen his resolution. Neither of them was resigned to playing a subordinate role for the remainder of their lives within the stifling confines of the Austrian empire.

The official residence of this young couple was at Miramar, a romantically beautiful castle lapped by the waters of the bay of Trieste. Here Maximilian studied with his usual diligence everything that had been written about Mexico, and while visitors came and went, conducted his correspondence with the numerous interested parties. He was in constant touch with the two Emperors, Napoleon and Francis Joseph, with the latter's ministers, with King Leopold and the Pope. From all these exalted personages he received a wealth of counsel. Not all of it was unreservedly favourable to his ambitions, but at no time was he categorically advised to have nothing to do with the undertaking. Gutierrez de Estrada, now settled in Paris as the Archduke's confidential agent and liaison officer with the French court, toiled zealously to keep up his enthusiasm. Some of his suggestions, however, were such as to arouse doubts about his sagacity in Maximilian's mind. He strenuously urged, for instance, that Santa Anna's assistance should be invoked, and was much put out when the former dictator declared that if he intervened at all, it would be on the other side.

Another embarrassment was his continued failure to persuade the Mexican prelates who had fled their country in 1860 to return to their bishoprics and prepare the faithful for the establishment of monarchy. Maximilian was alarmed by his ultra-reactionary views, and by the bishops' clamour for the total restitution of ecclesiastical properties. Nevertheless he refused to be disheartened. It is true that the disturbing news of the battle of Puebla induced him to profess a more cautious attitude towards acceptance of the throne, and in the year which preceded General Forey's resumption of the offensive he firmly maintained his insistence on the British guarantee as well as on the necessity that he should receive a genuine and unequivocal invitation from the Mexican people. Thus the weary months of 1862 passed without progress towards the crucial decision.

In 1863 events moved more rapidly. On 12 March the French appeared once again before Puebla, which was defended by an army of thirty thousand men under Gonzalez Ortega, for Zaragoza, the hero of 5 May, had died in the interval. Forey was obliged to mount a regular siege of the city, and the Mexicans fought so stoutly that it was two months before they surrendered. Meanwhile the French had shattered a relieving force commanded by the former president, Comonfort. The way to Mexico City lay open and Juarez, with no troops to protect it, retired with his government to San Luis Potosí.

Forey marched in on 10 June, among the plaudits of the conservatives and of the mob, which always appreciated a fine military spectacle. In accordance with Napoleon's instructions, he proceeded to force the political pace. Within a month he had arranged for the nomination of an assembly of two hundred and fifty conservative notables, who obediently abolished the Republic and created a Mexican Empire in its stead. They decided to offer the throne to the Archduke Maximilian, and pending his acceptance set up a Council of Regency consisting of the Archbishop of Mexico, Monsignor de Labastida, and Generals Almonte and Salas. The Assembly entrusted a deputation of eight members with the mission of laying the offer before the Archduke.

The imminent arrival of the deputation put Maximilian in an awkward dilemma. While Napoleon and the Mexican conservatives were pressing him to accept without further ado, his more circumspect advisers, including his brother Francis Joseph, besought him not to abandon his two fundamental conditions. When the delegates, shepherded by Gutierrez and Hidalgo, presented themselves at Miramar on 3 October, they got neither a yes nor a no. Maximilian told them that his acceptance must still depend on the confirmation of the notables' invitation by the Mexican nation as a whole. He added that he would also require certain—unspecified—international guarantees, but the word 'British' was not mentioned. This temporizing reply was not at all what the deputation wanted, and it withdrew discomfited. Napoleon's impatience mounted, but he had to wait for two further months while the Archduke made repeated but unavailing attempts to influence the British Government in favour of a guarantee through contacts in the City of London.

By Christmas the pressure exerted on him from Paris and Mexico City had become irresistible. Moreover he had convinced himself that further hesitation would be incompatible with his honour and the hopes which he had inspired in his Mexican sponsors. On 4 January 1864, he let it be known that he was ready to take ship for Mexico as soon as he was personally satisfied that a sufficient number of his future subjects had declared for his cause. As General Bazaine, Forey's successor, was busily engaged in extracting signatures by force from the cowed population, this could no longer be considered a serious stipulation. The sole additional assurance he now needed was that French military support would not be removed for at least six years.

From that moment Maximilian was no longer a free agent. He had placed himself irrevocably in Napoleon's hands. This fact became starkly evident when he turned to negotiate the actual terms under which France would consent to grant him military and financial aid. So far as the military clauses were concerned he had no reason to complain, for Napoleon undertook to leave at least twenty thousand French troops in Mexico until the end of 1867. But the financial arrangements to which the Archduke reluctantly subscribed imposed a crushing burden on the new Mexican empire. It was established that Mexico should receive a loan of over two hundred million francs, but the interest was to be guaranteed by the Mexican and not the French government. In the same breath Mexico was called upon to repay in instalments no less than two hundred and seventy million francs, which according to French calculations represented the cost of Napoleon's intervention up to July 1864. Nor was this all. It was proposed to exact a thousand francs per annum for every French soldier serving on Mexican soil after that date. As the last straw, Mexico was to assume responsibility for the Jecker bonds and for the excessive claims drawn up two years earlier. Such were the methods by which Napoleon and the banking ogres of the Second Empire designed to save a struggling and already bankrupt nation. The illusion which Europe cherished of the Indies as an inexhaustible gold mine died hard.

Having put his signature to the Convention of Miramar, as the document containing these terms came to be known, Maximilian suddenly faced a final ordeal. On the eve of his departure Francis Joseph demanded, as the price of his own consent to his brother becoming Emperor of Mexico, that he should renounce his right to the Austrian succession and to all his remaining rights as a member of the House of Habsburg. The prospect of the severance of his hereditary and traditional ties with Europe filled him with anguish. In a moment of intense emotional stress, he was on the point of giving up the whole enterprise. Only the most vigorous remonstrances from Napoleon, and the agonised entreaties of Gutierrez, prevented him from backing down. Even King Leopold, usually so cautious, wrote that he must above all not disappoint the Mexicans. So on 9 April, at a solemn meeting of the Council of Empire presided over by Francis Joseph himself, he signed away his rights; on the following day he ceremonially accepted the offer of the Mexican notables, again marshalled under the leadership of Gutierrez, and on the 14th he and Charlotte embarked in the Austrian frigate *Novara*, pride of the navy which he had been so happy to command. With a small escorting squadron they set sail down the Adriatic.

The voyage to Mexico took six weeks. For Maximilian and Charlotte it was a period not so much of rest as of busy preparation as they planned the shape of the future imperial court and administration. But they recovered their spirits, depressed by the strains and uncertainties of the past two years, and were full of enthusiasm for the work ahead. Their reception at Vera Cruz was not encouraging. General Almonte, the head of the provisional government, failed to arrive in time to greet them; the demeanour of the inhabitants of this city of strong liberal sympathies was noticeably aloof, and the arrangements for their onward journey could not have been called efficient. The country through which they struggled on the way to Orizaba was waterlogged and miasmal. It was only when the carriages laboriously climbed to the plateau that Maximilian was able to appreciate the natural magnificence of the land he had come to rule. Puebla gave him a joyful welcome, and the *hacendados* in their handsome charro costumes rode in to offer their allegiance. Huge crowds of inquisitive Indians assembled to gape at their Emperor, bearded like Cortés or the legendary Quetzalcoatl.

In Mexico City, which they reached on 12 June, the imperial pair were enthusiastically acclaimed by the crowds, while the clergy and the old Creole families were profuse in their assurances of loyalty. Their first problem, prosaically enough, was to find somewhere to live. The National Palace, semi-derelict after so many batterings and ransackings, was plainly unsuitable. Maximilian plumped firmly for the hill of Chapultepec, with its groves of age-old American cypresses planted by his Aztec predecessors and its glorious views of lake and volcano. The modest house which the Viceroys had built there as a summer pavilion was equally ruinous but Maximilian, who was in his element when devising schemes for building and decoration, transformed it into a very passable version of a German *Residenzschloss*. There he and Charlotte, in the first year of their rule, led a strenuous but happy existence, conscious that they had found their vocation, and quite undaunted by the magnitude of their task.

While they were installing themselves at Chapultepec, the fortunes of Juarez were at their lowest ebb. Bazaine, the unlikeable and secretive officer who was destined in the war of 1870 to surrender France's finest army to the Prussians, chased him from San Luis Potosí over the whole of northern Mexico, until he came to rest at Paso del Norte (now Ciudad Juarez) close up against the American border. This was a strategic position from which he could keep in touch with other liberal leaders who had fled to the United States and with the Lincoln administration at Washington. The end of the American Civil War was now in sight, and Juarez was rightly confident that as soon as the Southern States had been finally crushed the United States would no longer tolerate the breach of the Monroe Doctrine perpetrated by the French occupation of Mexico.

In Mexico itself there remained few pockets of resistance to Bazaine but guerrilla warfare flared up persistently even in the subjugated areas. In February 1865 he received the submission of Oaxaca, where a young general named Porfirio Díaz had obstinately upheld the republican cause. But the country as a whole was as quiet as it had ever been for the last half-century; it lay cowed in an artificial peace preserved by foreign bayonets. The towns were overawed by watchful French garrisons, and the bugles of the Foreign Legion rang out in the desert outposts.

In Mexico City matters seemed to run more smoothly. The Emperor's court was both dignified and elegant, and society had never sparkled so gaily. Maximilian took pains to get to know his subjects, whom he entertained lavishly. He also managed to create an orderly and reasonably honest government. His own energy was remarkable. Every aspect of the national life was touched by his zest for legislation and administrative planning. While his ministers laboured to complete his numerous blueprints for improvement, he sought to inspire a literary and scientific revival and to restore the faded glories of his capital. He himself traced the splendid avenue, now called the Paseo de la Reforma, which connects the city with the palace of Chapultepec. The long hours spent at his desk were varied by travels into the countryside. He spoke Spanish fluently, wore Mexican clothes and ate Mexican food. He delighted in the beauties of the landscape and in the limpid climate of Cuernavaca, where he allowed himself some relaxation and even, so people said, the company of a lovely Indian girl. For in spite of their close partnership in state affairs and family ambitions, Maximilian's personal relations with his wife were not normal. They had no children, and there was much malicious speculation about the difficulties of their private life.

There is no doubt that Maximilian's genuine affection for his adopted country, as well as his transparent honesty and good intentions, at first won him many adherents. Nevertheless he was antagonising those vested interests which had counted on using him as their instrument. On leaving Trieste he had broken his journey off the coast of Italy in order to bid farewell to the Pope and obtain his blessing. Pius IX had received him graciously, and had not raised the delicate topic of church properties in Mexico. Doubtless he believed that the new Emperor would soon yield to pressure from his reactionary supporters and repeal the Laws of the Reform. But Maximilian did nothing of the sort. He had no use for bigots, and his own liberal inclinations had been strengthened by warnings conveyed to him, directly or indirectly, by persons of proved impartiality such as Sir Charles Wyke and King Leopold's Minister to Mexico, Kint van Rodenbeek. Both these diplomats had stressed that it would be fatal for him to identify himself with the clericals and conservatives. They advised him to seek the co-operation of the former *moderado* party, men of the stamp of Gomez Pedraza and Herrera, progressives but not rabid anti-clericals.

It was a pity that these excellent people were so few and uninfluential as compared with the conservatives and the Juarists. Maximilian was assailed by the strident demands of the archenemy of liberalism, Archbishop Labastida, for the full restitution of the expropriated properties and goods. To the Emperor his attitude seemed totally irrational, and the operation, even if he had willed it, financially and politically impossible. There was no better son of the Church than Maximilian, whose dynasty was steeped in Catholic traditionalism. Nevertheless the Habsburgs had produced one emperor, Joseph II, whose secularising policy had thrown the Church in his dominions into disarray, and the Holy See was disagreeably surprised to see Maximilian following Joseph's example rather than that of earlier Habsburg champions of the Counter-Reformation.

He set his face firmly against giving back the properties, but hoped to persuade the newly appointed Papal Nuncio to acquiesce in the realities of the situation. As for the clergy, why could they not be paid by the State? But the Nuncio turned out to be obdurate. He brought with him what was in effect an ultimatum, insisting that the Church should not only obtain full restitution but should also be reinstated in the privileged position which it had occupied under the Viceroys and the early Republic. When this was hurled at his head, Maximilian lost patience. He countered with a decree confirming the expropriations and flatly defying the anathemas of Rome. For this act he received no thanks at all. The Juarists were not impressed, and the outraged Nuncio was recalled.

In less than a year after Maximilian's arrival Church and Empire had become thoroughly estranged. In the struggle between the Emperor and Juarez the clergy were now virtually neutral, but many Catholic landowners were asking themselves whether their true interests did not after all lie with the liberal nationalists. Although there was little outward sign of impending disaster, the insecure props which underpinned the Empire were collapsing as the months of 1865 sped by. The finances were already ruined beyond repair and the political scene was a compound of disaffection and indifference. The military rot was postponed till 1866.

Meanwhile the Juarists were not yet capable of taking over, for so long as Bazaine's thirty thousand men were actively employed against them, the best they could do was to harass the French and imperialists by guerrilla action. The interminable pursuit of these irregular bands was a severe drain on the French and Mexican treasuries. In Bazaine's view there was only one way to make an end of them: they must be treated as outlaws and pitilessly executed if taken in arms. He ceaselessly importuned Maximilian to issue orders to that effect, arguing that severity was the sole key to internal peace. It might also, he believed, give him a chance of complying with his master's commands to disengage the French army. Wearied and disenchanted by the refusal of the Mexican project to conform to his intentions, Napoleon's one thought was to extricate himself from his commitments. Maximilian, a chivalrous idealist who detested cruelty, resisted Bazaine for many weeks, but on 2 October he signed the decree with a heavy heart. It was a fatal mistake. Almost at once one of his Mexican officers laid hold of two republican generals, Arteaga and Salazar, and thrust them brutally before a firing squad. This act set up a horrifying sequence of reprisal and counter-reprisal, and eventually decided Maximilian's own doom. And as the savageries increased, so did the numbers of the Juarist partisans.

It was not merely the expense and the loss of prestige over Mexico that were worrying Napoleon. He was deeply concerned with the growing strength and arrogance of Prussia; he was sure that the time was near when every French soldier would be needed in Europe. Again, the United States government, with a huge and triumphant Federal army still in being, was sharply calling for the recall of Bazaine's troops. Conscious of his weak position, he wrote to Maximilian on 15 January 1866, bluntly revealing his decision to end the French occupation. It only remained, he added, for Maximilian and Bazaine to agree upon the details and dates of withdrawal. In other words, Napoleon had denounced the military clauses of the Miramar Convention. Shocked and incredulous, Maximilian and Charlotte expostulated with him in letter after letter, while confidential envoys were sent speeding to Paris. When these pleas were ignored, Charlotte prevailed on her husband to allow her to travel to Europe in a desperate effort to have the French decision reversed. She was prepared to throw herself at the feet of the Pope and the sovereigns who had once given the Mexican enterprise such fallacious encouragement.

On arrival in France, Charlotte made straight for Paris. If her father had been alive, it would have been wiser for her to start with Brussels, but alas, King Leopold was dead and his successor, her brother Leopold II, was no substitute as an adviser. Napoleon at first tried to evade an interview and sent Eugénie to call on Charlotte at her hotel. Later he relented and they had two long conversations. He listened quietly to her impassioned appeals and tirades, but although she developed her case with utter cogency, neither reason nor emotion could shake him. When she finally grasped that the decision to terminate France's involvement in

Mexico was irreversible, she left Paris in an agony of anger and frustration.

For nearly a month she retired to her old home, Miramar, where she began to show alarming signs of overstrain. On 18 September she travelled to Rome for an audience with Pius IX. Nine days later, when she was ushered into the papal presence, it was painfully obvious that her mental balance was dangerously disturbed. Her arguments lost coherence; she complained in hysterical excitement that Napoleon was conspiring to poison her. Repeatedly she rushed to the Vatican, breaking from the restraining hands of her suite. In the end a strait-jacket had to be employed, and her younger brother, the Count of Flanders, hastily summoned from Brussels, took her back to Miramar. She was suffering from an extreme form of persecution mania, for which the medical science of that time had no remedy. When the periods of clarity grew fewer, and the twilight of madness closed in, her family brought her to Belgium. There she lingered for sixty years, first in the castle of Tervueren, and after it was burned down in 1879, at Bouchout near the royal palace of Laeken. She never recovered her sanity, and death did not claim her till 1927, at the age of eighty-seven.

Maximilian anxiously awaited news of his wife's mission. Her letters, at first so sensible, then pervaded by nervous excitement, brought no consolation. Meanwhile his empire was disintegrating before his eyes. As Bazaine concentrated his troops for withdrawal, the Juarists closed in inexorably. There were no victories for them to boast of, for the northern and western states fell uncontested into their hands. In the south Porfirio Díaz had escaped from prison and was again at large. The Mexican forces loyal to the imperial flag were pitifully small and the regiments of Austrian and Belgian volunteers, from whom great things had been expected, were dissolving faster than the French regulars. Tampico was lost, and then Guadalajara.

On 18 October Maximilian heard the appalling truth about Charlotte's illness. Under the prospect of losing his wife as well as his realm his nerve momentarily gave way. Before she left Mexico they had debated between themselves whether they should put a quick end to their troubles by abdication, and it was she who had sustained the wavering Maximilian with appeals to his honour and family pride. She had exhorted him not to throw in his hand until all their resources in Mexico and abroad were exhausted. The Emperor now decided that this point had been reached; he arranged for the shipment of his papers and personal possessions and himself proceeded as far as Orizaba. There he spent a few dream-like weeks, torn by irresolution and the discordant voices of his advisers, but outwardly calm and absorbed by the natural beauty of his surroundings—the flowering shrubs, the brilliantly coloured birds and butterflies, and the sparkling streams fed by the white cone of the volcano Citlaltepetl.

His old friend and confidant, the Austrian Captain Herzfeld, begged him to escape while there was still time, arguing that only his abdication could save Mexico from another bloody bout of civil war. The British Minister suggested that he should convoke a national assembly; if a majority voted for the Republic, the Emperor could then step down with a clear conscience. But Maximilian was drifting into an exalted mood. As he recovered his courage and physical strength, the more deeply he felt that abdication would be a cowardly betrayal of the Mexicans still loyal to the empire.

These sentiments were adroitly fostered by the German Jesuit Father Fischer, a glib and sinister adventurer who had insinuated himself into Maximilian's entourage and was acting as the conservatives' mouthpiece. More robust encouragement came from Generals Miramón and Marquez, the heroes of the War of the Reform, who offered to lead the depleted imperial forces. Much as he had criticised conservative attitudes in the past, he flung himself with romantic ardour into the leadership of a lost and alien cause. Deliberately he severed his ties with the Europe which had abandoned him and which held his wife, now hope-lessly insane. Better to stand and fight in Mexico and if necessary, show the world how a Habsburg could die. Late in November he took the road to Mexico City and as he could no longer bear living at Chapultepec, established himself in near-by Tacubaya.

The French garrison left the capital on 5 February, and by 12 March the last man and gun had quitted Vera Cruz. The Emperor, whose relations with Bazaine had deteriorated to the point that he refused to grant the Marshal a farewell audience, exclaimed that he was at last free. He was much heartened by a spectacular exploit by Miramón. Hearing that Juarez had advanced the seat of his government to Zacatecas, the conservative general led a daring cavalry raid northwards in the hope of grabbing the president, and of thus changing the complexion of the war by one stroke. He very nearly succeeded. The liberal garrison was cut to pieces and Juarez escaped by a hair's breadth. But retribution came a few days later when the Juarist commander, Escobedo, in turn surprised Miramón and routed his little army. Over one hundred of the prisoners, including Miramón's brother, were shot in a gesture of calculated terrorism. With the failure of this venture the imperialist territory was restricted to a thin strip running from Mexico City eastwards to Puebla and Vera Cruz and westwards to Querétaro. But Puebla was menaced by Díaz, while the armies of Escobedo and Corona converged on the key point of Querétaro. On 19 February the Emperor rode in to organise its defence.

The imperial forces, ten thousand men at the most, were outnumbered fourfold. In political terms the prolongation of their resistance made no sense at all, and their only military function was to obstruct the inevitable Juarist breakthrough to Mexico City for as long as possible. Starting from 6 March, the investment of Querétaro lasted for seventy-one days. The surrounding heights were firmly held and early assaults repelled with ease. But Escobedo drew the ring tighter and waited for the blockade to do its work. The imperialists made two major attempts to break the siege. On 22 March Marquez, with a mission to raise a relieving force, cut his way out at the head of a thousand horsemen and reached Mexico City. But after a month spent in collecting reinforcements he turned towards Puebla, only to find it occupied by Díaz. His troops dissolved in confusion, and he himself escaped by devious routes to Cuba. Maximilian then tried a sally en masse on 27 April. His men inflicted severe losses on Escobedo and penetrated his lines. Unfortunately they had no strength left to exploit their advantage, and recoiled exhausted upon the city. Their plight was now desperate; only five thousand remained but still Escobedo hesitated to order a general assault.

The Emperor, supremely brave and resolute now that the outcome was hopeless, fixed 15 May for another sortie, but on the preceding night the issue was resolved by treachery. Colonel Lopez, an officer in Maximilian's confidence, slipped through to Escobedo and arranged for a republican detachment to be admitted under cover of darkness into the outworks of the convent of Santa Cruz, where the Emperor had his headquarters. His own men were instructed not to fire on the intruders. When the republicans had gained a foothold, they overran the town. They did not, however, catch Maximilian, whom Lopez himself, apparently assailed by last-minute remorse, assisted to avoid arrest. Accompanied only by his German aide-de-camp, Prince

Salm, he passed through the city and gained a little hill called the Cerro de las Campanas. There he was joined by Mejía and other adherents, as Miramón lay wounded in a friend's house. It was but a short respite. Flight was out of the question, and when the enemy closed in Maximilian handed his sword to Escobedo in person. It is pleasant to record that all the ceremonial courtesies were observed.

Maximilian was taken to the Capuchin convent, where he was strictly confined in a friar's cell. He was, however, allowed to retain his personal staff and to see visitors. He hoped that he might be permitted to leave Mexico, subject to a firm guarantee that he would not seek to regain the throne, but it soon transpired that Juarez had other intentions. The Emperor was notified that he was to be tried by court-martial, which could only signify that the Republicans were aiming at a death sentence. They had indeed decided to use the decree of October 1863 as the legal justification for condemning Maximilian to the same fate as had overtaken many eminent Mexicans on both sides. Juarez was no sadist; unlike certain other figures in Mexican history, he did not kill for the sake of killing. But his legalistic mind was insensitive to the claims of mercy, and he was dominated by an overriding consideration of policy. He and his government were convinced that it was vitally necessary, by making a brutal example of the Habsburg prince, to shock foreign—and especially European—powers into realising for good and all that any future violation of Mexican territory or sovereignty was doomed to disaster. And when a tardy diplomatic intervention by the Powers was addressed to Juarez, through the good offices of the American Secretary of State, it was stonily rebuffed, although the United States government had consistently given the Republicans its moral and material support. It was as well that the Americans, as the aggressors of 1846, should understand that the warning was equally intended for them. Juarez similarly rejected a number of personal appeals for clemency.

During the month which passed between his capture and condemnation, Maximilian remained admirably calm and composed. He declined to countenance plans for his escape which Salm and others had feverishly improvised. When he heard that his trial was to be staged in the municipal theatre before a court of seven junior officers, he flatly refused to appear. The proceedings therefore took place in his absence. Even if the sentence was politically predetermined, three of the judges voted for banishment and their president was obliged to use his casting vote in favour of death. The execution was fixed for 15 June, then postponed for three days. On the morning of 19 June the Emperor, Miramón and Mejía were conducted through the hushed streets of the colonial city to the Cerro de las Campanas and made to stand against a wall. Amid the grisly preliminaries of the execution Maximilian moved with perfect courage and self-possession. He insisted that Miramón should take the place of honour on his right, comforted the failing Mejía and presented a gold coin to each member of the firing squad. His final speech was a prayer that his blood might be shed for the good of Mexico. As the volley crashed out he was repeating the cry of Hidalgo—'Viva Mexico! Viva la Independencia!'

His body was taken to Austria on board the *Novara* and laid in the imperial vault—the *Kapuzinergruft* in Vienna. On the Cerro de las Campanas there stands a little memorial chapel in the Gothic style, dusty and neglected, full of withered flowers and pathetic, faded relics. It is dwarfed by a colossal concrete statue of Juarez: erected in 1967 for the centenary of the republican victory, it broods sullenly over the domes and steeples of Querétaro. Neither monument reflects the spirit of the man it commemorates.

Mexicans brought up in the revolutionary tradition are prone to
see the outstanding figures of their national history in strongly
contrasting colours. Cuauhtemoc, Hidalgo, Morelos and Juarez
are white; Cortés, Santa Anna and Maximilian are black. Of all
the blacks, no one has been more roundly and consistently
condemned than Porfirio Díaz, who gave his name to the period
of roughly thirty years known in Mexico as the 'Porfiriato'. As
time passes, a more balanced view of his record is gradually
emerging.

Like Juarez, Díaz came from Oaxaca, and his origins were
almost as humble. Born in 1830, he sprang from Creole and Mixtec
stock. As a young man he followed Juarez' leadership in his
native state and was proscribed by Santa Anna at the same time
as his chief. He eminently distinguished himself in the War of the
Reform and emerged as one of the stoutest and most resilient foes
of the Empire. We have already noticed him commanding the
republican forces at Oaxaca, where he was defeated and captured
by Bazaine. Escaping from his prison in Puebla by sliding down
a rope in true romantic style, he regained the southern mountains
and gathered another army. Shortly before the Empire's collapse
he led it to the taking of Puebla and on to Mexico City, where,
elated with victory, he greeted Juarez on his re-entry into the
capital in the summer of 1867. But greatly to his surprise, he
received the most grudging and perfunctory thanks from the
President for his endurance in adversity and exploits in the field.
From that day on his loyalty to his leader evaporated and he
employed all the resources of his astute and ambitious nature to
become the ruler of Mexico. It took him, however, nearly a

decade to achieve his aim. His first bid for power was to stand against Juarez for the presidency in the election of 1867, and when this failed miserably he retired to a *hacienda* near Oaxaca which the grateful state government had placed at his disposal.

No doubt Juarez was right in scenting trouble from the future dictator. But Díaz was not the only general to nurse a grudge against the President, who was often guilty of a strange lack of sensitiveness towards individuals, especially when they clashed with him on matters of principle. Having reimposed civilian control, Juarez was determined not to allow it to be undermined again by militarism. He therefore cold-shouldered the military chiefs and disbanded the greater part of the republican army. The rest he placed under the command of a general of his own choice, Sostenes Rocha, on whose loyalty and efficiency he knew he could depend. Rocha dealt ruthlessly with a whole series of outbreaks by disgruntled veterans of the two wars, so that Juarez' next four year term could be devoted to the work of peaceful reconstruction. He tackled this task with his usual methodical diligence. With the help of a brilliant Secretary of the Treasury, Matías Romero, he gradually reduced the finances to order, while Gabino Barreda, the Minister of Education, began to organise a system of public instruction on strictly secular lines. Industry and commerce gradually revived, and as a symbol of the new era of security and progress, a railway line was pushed through from Vera Cruz to Mexico City in the face of formidable natural difficulties. It was a real triumph for the British engineers who designed it, and for the Mexican workmen who laboured on the steep gradients and in the steamy heat of the coastal plain.

This programme was already pointing the way towards the modernising policies of the 'Porfiriato'. Meanwhile a significant change had occurred in the shape of internal politics. Ever since the foundation of the Republic power had been disputed between two opposing parties or factions, one of which, the clerical-conservatives, had now virtually disappeared as a political force. Only the liberals were left, with the result that the voters' allegiances were being transferred from ideological causes to rival personalities in the liberal ranks. So long as Juarez was the dominant personality all was well, and political stability was assured. But not even he found it altogether easy to maintain his authority under a federalist constitution designed to restrict the presidential powers and to provide safeguards for local and individual rights. After so many years of disruption there was obviously a compelling need for a firm central government capable of imposing a uniform and salutary discipline on the whole of this vast, amorphous country.

In particular, it was necessary to curb the influence of the regional bosses, who in their way were just as dangerous as the generals. During his wanderings in northern Mexico as a fugitive from Bazaine, Juarez had been within an ace of succumbing to the jealousy of these provincial magnates, one of whom, Santiago Vidaurri, had actually deserted to the imperialists. It was essential for the president to keep the political machine under his control and not permit it to be manipulated by such persons for their own purposes. Although Juarez never lost his confidence that democratic processes could be made to work in Mexico, and considered himself bound to respect the constitution, he was forced, in the interests of national unity, to resort to less than democratic methods in order to steer the voters into the government fold. Once these practices had been adopted, even on a discreet scale, and had become, so to speak, part of the recognised electoral procedure, they could not easily be discarded, and under a less scrupulous leader than Juarez they would inevitably degenerate into the most flagrant abuse of democracy. That is exactly what happened when Díaz became the guardian of the constitution and the controller of the electoral system.

Late in 1871 a fresh presidential election was held on the expiry of Juarez's third term. This time he was opposed not only by Díaz but also by his hitherto faithful lieutenant Sebastian Lerdo de Tejada. Thus the liberal party was split into three quarrelling sections, among which the votes were evenly divided. Congress, left to decide the outcome, settled on Juarez as President of the Republic and Lerdo as President of the Supreme Court. Díaz, exasperated by the failure of a second bid for the highest office, raised the south in rebellion and at the same time provoked a rising in the capital. Both were promptly crushed by Sostenes Rocha. Díaz's brother, Felix, was killed at Oaxaca, and Porfirio only saved himself by going into hiding in the fastnesses of Nayarit, where Lozada, the Indian chieftain who was the boss of its remote sierras, gave him shelter. The last embers of the insurrection had hardly been extinguished when Juarez, on 18 July 1872, died of a heart attack at his desk in the National Palace. As provided by the constitution he was succeeded by Lerdo, under whose leadership the restored republic lasted for another four years. The Juarists gave him their support and the followers of Díaz were glad to accept his offer of an amnesty. Díaz himself was permitted to return to Oaxaca, but not to his *hacienda,* which had been destroyed in the troubles.

Lerdo failed to make the best use of his presidency. He was an intelligent and cultured Creole who had served Juarez efficiently and, until the last episode, loyally. By temperament, however, he was haughty and over-confident. After his first gesture of reconciliation he no longer bothered to seek favour with the generals or the jealous liberal politicians who might be tempted to oust him. Even so he would probably have got through his term without incident if he had not announced his intention to stand for re-election in 1876. This development brought Díaz once again into the field. His supporters published the Plan of Tuxtepec (a town on the borders of Vera Cruz and Oaxaca), based on the principles of 'Effective Suffrage' and 'No re-election', slogans which are still reproduced between the text and the signature of every letter sent out by a Mexican government department.

Meanwhile Díaz was in the United States raising funds for his venture. Fortunately for him Lerdo was on bad terms with Washington because he had refused to permit American railway companies to extend their lines into Mexican territory. He preferred, he said, to leave a desert between weakness and strength. Consequently the United States authorities turned a blind eye on Díaz's warlike preparations. In March he crossed the frontier with a small force, captured Matamoros and advanced on Monterrey. There he encountered the formidable General Escobedo, hero of the final campaign against Maximilian, who chased him back into Texas. Undeterred by the initial failure of his classic combination of plan and 'pronouncement', he took ship from Havana to Vera Cruz, slipped ashore in a workman's disguise and rode for Oaxaca and safety in the same daring style as had marked his escape from Bazaine twelve years earlier. Some months of uncertainty and typical Mexican manoeuvring then ensued. Lerdo, confident that his generals would be able to deal with Porfirio at their leisure, held the presidential election and was declared successful. But at this point Iglesias, his President of the Supreme Court, disputed the legality of the proceedings on the grounds that certain states were still technically in rebellion against the Federal power. This was the signal for serious defections from the Lerdist ranks. In November Díaz advanced from the south, defeated Lerdo's commander, Alatorre, at Tecoac and occupied Mexico City, where he was received with jubilation.

The discredited Lerdo fled the country from Acapulco and Iglesias, who had aspired to the presidency for himself, fled too. Díaz had at last triumphed over all possible rivals.

His election to the provisional presidency followed as a matter of course. Nevertheless it was too early for him to presume to become President for life. Having proclaimed the principles of Tuxtepec, he had at least to make a show of respecting them. So when his provisional term had expired he arranged to hand over the mandate to his old comrade in arms General Manuel Gonzalez, who had helped him to win the battle of Tecoac. It was only after Gonzalez, whose notions of statecraft were rudimentary, had mismanaged his four years of office that Don Porfirio resumed the presidency, which he was not destined to relinquish until forced out by the Revolution of 1911. 1884 was the year in which he felt it safe openly to discard his own principles and consolidate his personal dictatorship.

The Gonzalez interlude remains something of a mystery. It is understandable that Díaz should have found it convenient to act temporarily through a stooge, but not one who might spoil the results of his own work through recklessness or incompetence. No doubt he calculated that Gonzalez's faults would not be imputed to himself and that if his nominee's administration got out of hand he could easily resume control and reap the credit for putting matters straight. In the event Gonzalez was permitted to finish his term. Don Porfirio did not intervene directly but kept a close watch on the scene from the governorship of Oaxaca and, subsequently, from a seat on the Supreme Court. Díaz's first three years as President had passed in a sober atmosphere of retrenchment and political appeasement. Gonzalez, however, with tacit if not more positive encouragement from Díaz, launched a number of policies with which the dictatorship was later to be identified and for which Don Porfirio has taken the blame. It was Gonzalez who first sold enormous tracts of officially 'empty' public lands on easy terms to private individuals and companies in Mexico and the United States, who first distributed lucrative railway and mining concessions to American speculators without regard for the real necessities of Mexican development, and who passed a new mining law which, contrary to the traditional Spanish code vesting the subsoil and its resources in the State, transferred these valuable rights to the owners of the surface lands. All these initiatives were pushed further under Díaz's direct rule. During Gonzalez's presidency they provoked an orgy of graft among his associates and a wide circle of corrupt officials. Despite a rapid inflow of foreign capital the state finances were being depleted by unnecessary extravagance. To the general relief, Díaz had himself re-elected in 1884 and quickly stopped the financial rot.

Don Porfirio was fifty-four years of age. The earlier part of his life had been a breathless succession of battles, hair-raising escapes, glories and sudden eclipses. Now he was the sole effective survivor of the generation which had assured the triumph of the Reform and defended it against reaction and foreign interference. Henceforth he assumed the role of elder statesman, the legendary paladin of the republic on a dozen hard-fought fields and the father of his country. While in semi-retirement he married a young girl, Carmen Romero Rubio, daughter of a close adherent of Lerdo de Tejada. This man, Manuel Romero Rubio, had accompanied his leader into exile, but later changed his mind and offered his services to Díaz. Recognising his very real political abilities, Díaz made him his Secretary of the Interior.

Through the influence of his wife the hardened military adventurer of mixed Indian descent, whose personal bravery, administrative efficiency and natural astuteness were equalled by his adaptability to circumstances, was reconciled with the conservative society which he had combated so strenuously in the past. He ended by becoming their ideal. The new generation of leaders which came to the fore in the eighties and attached itself to Don Porfirio's fortunes lacked the idealism of the men who made the reform. In theory liberalism was still their creed, but it was a liberalism vitiated by a cynical lack of devotion to the principles of the 1857 Constitution. So long as the dictatorship respected the legal and political forms of the Republic, they did not worry overmuch over the decay of democracy or the neglect of social problems. According to the tenets of the extreme—and already outdated—nineteenth century individualism which they obeyed, the state's social obligations towards the mass of the people were strictly limited. Unlike Juarez and the more enlightened of his colleagues, they professed no sympathy with the Indians, still numbering thirty or forty per cent of the population, who seemed to fit so awkwardly into the economic scheme of things propounded by the disciples of positivism and laissez faire.

Among the talented young men who owed their intellectual formation to the National Preparatory School founded by Gabino Barreda, the philosophy of Auguste Comte—cold, sceptical and materialist—was all the rage, and was given a new impulse when the atheist poet Ignacio Ramirez was made Minister of Education in Díaz's first government. It was argued that what Mexico needed for its all-important economic enrichment was the strictly scientific spirit; the visionary aspirations of the liberators and reformists might be tranquilly eschewed. Indeed the advocates of this way of thinking went too far and were denounced by their critics as anti-patriotic.

The current philosophy of material progress was no bad thing in itself. The fallacy of the positivists was to believe that the national wealth could be multiplied solely by means of a feverish exploitation of the country's physical resources and by dependence on foreign capital to provide Mexico with the apparatus of the industrial revolution. Without a serious effort to raise the economic and social level of the masses such development, though salutary and overdue, was bound to be lop-sided and to benefit only the top layer of the population, the landowners and the nascent bourgeoisie.

A good example of the unreal hopes in which scientifically minded persons were apt to indulge at the time was the prediction that the wholesale alienation of public lands would result in a huge immigration of Europeans, and that these would surely achieve a productivity of which the Indians were congenitally incapable. Such a miscalculation seems absurd to anyone who has noticed how quickly an Indian peasant can actually be transformed into a competent industrial worker, but in the nineteenth century it was perhaps excusable. No immigration of course occurred, but it is calculated that during the Porfiriato no less than fifty million hectares of national property were disposed of to private interests.

Meanwhile the rigorous application of the Ley Lerdo further reduced the area of the *ejidos* and greatly extended that of the traditional *haciendas*. More especially the stock-raising properties in the north, which did a profitable trade with the United States, grew to an enormous size. Luis Terrazas owned two and a half million hectares in Chihuahua, and in Zacatecas a sole *hacienda,* that of Cedros, covered seven hundred and fifty thousand hectares. Further to the south the dimensions were more modest, but the famous estate of La Gavia, near Toluca, measured one hundred and thirty thousand hectares, and in Hidalgo the railway ran for a hundred and forty-five kilometres through the property of the Escandons. The little sugar growing state of Morelos was divided between thirty-two owners, but included several *haciendas* of about thirty thousand hectares each. By the end of the Porfiriato more than half the territory of the Republic belonged to a few thousand Mexican families and foreign concessionnaires. The period also saw a considerable increase in the number of ranch-eros, farmers who cultivated properties ranging from a few hundred to a few thousand hectares with the aid of their families and a few employees. These formed a small but sturdily inde-pendent rural middle class.

The dispossession of the peasants was carried out methodically and callously. It was often strenuously resisted, especially by villagers who held indisputable titles dating from the colonial era, but the Indians had little chance against chicanery or brute force. Their preference for the communal system was condemned as a tiresome anachronism and an obstacle to progress. When opposi-tion became too active it was smashed by the *rurales,* the corps of picturesquely accoutred mounted gendarmes with which the dictatorship kept the peace, suppressed banditry and overawed the population. Occasional agrarian revolts on a larger scale were put down with pitiless severity.

Conditions on the *latifundios,* or great estates, varied from region to region and property to property. Obviously not all *hacendados* were inefficient, brutal or absentee. Many were capable and conscientious men living quietly on their lands and exercising a paternal authority over their Indians. But even in the best cases life for the landless peon was monotonously harsh. Wages were sometimes as low as twenty-five centavos a day; corporal punish-ment was a normal practice and most peasants fell hopelessly into debt with the *hacienda* store. Their diet was insufficient and their housing primitive in the extreme; disease was rife and a school was rarely available for their children. Church festivals, the performance of age-old ritual dances and ceremonies, and the consumption of pulque, were their only diversions. As a general rule, wages were higher and more humane treatment could be expected in the northern states, and in the more competently managed coffee, tobacco and sisal (henequen) plantations of the south, than on the central plateau. Throughout that region a large proportion of the *hacienda* lands were left uncultivated. The agricultural system was therefore on the whole uneconomic. Lands lay fallow, the Indians struggled on the brink of starvation and Mexico was obliged to import foodstuffs for its townspeople. When Díaz, at the end of his long rule, celebrated the centenary of

Hidalgo's rebellion, the standard of living in the countryside nowhere approached that of colonial Mexico, while its indigenous inhabitants had lost both their lands and their personal rights and liberties.

The expropriations weighed even more heavily on the remnants of those native peoples which had so far preserved a semi-independence and a wholly or partially tribal way of life. These included the Yaquis of Sonora, the Tarahumaras and other smaller communities of the northern sierras and a section of the Mayas in the Yucatán peninsula. The encroachments on the Yaqui lands, which were well suited to the growing of cotton and sugar, were preceded by campaigns against the wild Apaches of the United States borderlands, who year after year raided deeply into northern Mexico, attacking the farms and mines and massacring the settlers. Their last incursion into Chihuahua was made as late as 1891.

The Yaquis, who were no barbarians and only wished to be left in peace, fiercely resented attempts to deprive them of their tribal territory. Although a show was made of preserving a portion of the lands for their own use they had no faith in the intentions of the government and repeatedly rose in revolt. Under their leaders, Cajeme and Tetabiate, three thousand dogged Yaqui warriors held off nearly five thousand Mexican troops between 1885 and the turn of the century. After a cruel and exhausting struggle the tribesmen were compelled to submit. Eight thousand of them were transported to the plantations of Yucatán. Despite these misfortunes, their nation survived in sufficient numbers to provide Yaqui regiments for the revolutionary armies and to profit from the prosperity of modern Sonora. Another Federal army of four thousand men was employed in 1901 to subjugate the Mayans of Chan Santa Cruz in Quintana Roo, the last independent remnant of a native insurgent movement which had swept the whole Yucatán peninsula in the mid-nineteenth century and virtually confined the rule of the whites to the principal towns.

In sharp contrast with the impoverishment of rural life, which was the most depressing feature of the Porfiriato, other branches of the economy prospered as never before. Mexico was lifted straight out of post-colonial stagnation into the bustling activity of the late Victorian era. Díaz himself was no financial and economic genius, but his natural shrewdness helped him to choose the right men for the job of reconstruction. His most important task was to rescue the finances from their state of chronic dilapidation. As Secretary of Finance in his first administration he employed Matías Romero, who had served Juarez in the same office. After the expensive Gonzalez episode he appointed the capable Manuel Dublán, and in 1893 switched to José Yves Limantour, the most celebrated of all his ministers.

Dublán's first concern was to consolidate the internal debt. He went on to negotiate three sterling loans, two for railway construction and one for the settlement of the long-standing British debts, on which no interest had been paid since the fifties. Limantour, French by descent and international in outlook, carried on the good work of restoring Mexican credit abroad. In 1894 he achieved, for the first time in the annals of independent Mexico, a balanced budget. The initial surplus was repeated and enormously multiplied over the next sixteen years, and by the end of the Porfiriato very impressive reserves had been accumulated. Mexico had no trouble in raising further substantial foreign loans to finance its development. The interest on these was fixed in 1899 at five per cent, and was in process of reduction to four per cent when the Revolution put an end to economic stability. Even before financial orthodoxy had taken full effect, capital was flowing freely from abroad, the chief sources of foreign investment being the United States, Great Britain, France and Germany. The pithy remark 'Poor Mexico, so far from God and so near to the United States' has been attributed to Díaz, but he was presumably thinking of possible political risks rather than of the great draughts of dollars which were pouring into his country from the north.

Between 1880 and 1910 Mexico was provided by foreign capitalists with the complete framework of a contemporary modern economy—an efficient banking system, heavy and light industries, electric light, power and traction, railways and harbours, telegraphs and telephones, waterworks and drainage. There was also a heavy foreign investment in mining, agriculture and real estate, and in the early years of the twentieth century British and American interests began to acquire and exploit the oilfields. The value of this commitment is hard to calculate with accuracy, if only because the many estimates made of it differ so widely, but a total of three thousand four hundred million dollars is probably not wide of the mark. The figures for British and American investment respectively in the years 1880 and 1910 were of the order of nine million and ninety million pounds, and of thirty million and a thousand million dollars.

The pace of railway building may be measured by the increase in mileage from a mere four hundred in 1876 to eleven thousand eight hundred in 1911. In the feverish scramble for concessions the national requirements were apt to be overlooked; the duplication of lines was becoming chaotic, but in 1909 Limantour made the system more rational by acquiring control of two-thirds of it for the state. Mining too, received a massive infusion of American and British capital, with the result that exports of minerals jumped by six hundred and fifty per cent during the dictatorship. The traditional production of precious metals was stimulated by new processes and supplemented by the opening of copper, lead and zinc mines, while the exploitation of the coal and iron ore of Coahuila gave a modest start to the steel industry of Monterrey.

Construction, mining and public utilities were largely an American and British preserve, but France also played a notable part in the Porfirian expansion. Although French influence had been virtually eliminated in the years following Napoleon III's ill-fated intervention, it revived quickly under the Third Republic, a régime with which the restored Mexican Republic found itself in sympathy. It was the French who took the lead in the banking sector, in the textile, tobacco and other industries and in important branches of the retail trade. Many of the Frenchmen engaged in industry and commerce settled permanently in Mexico, identified themselves much more closely with Mexican society than their Anglo-Saxon counterparts and acquired Mexican citizenship. Their descendants still form a powerful and respected group in Mexican economic life. Another permanent element consisted of the Spaniards, who were trickling back in considerable numbers to become plantation owners, overseers on the large estates and small shopkeepers. As investors, however, they were not prominent.

Of the individual contributions made by foreign interests to Mexican development, one of the most significant and exciting was that of S. Pearson and Son, under the leadership of Weetman Pearson, afterwards Lord Cowdray. This originally modest firm of British contractors was in an altogether different category from the giant American concerns which came to dominate Mexico's economy, but its successes were no less remarkable. It displayed a sure and dynamic touch and a fine spirit of panache. In 1889 Díaz, who had heard of Pearson's work on the Hudson River Tunnel, invited him to conclude a contract for the construction of a canal to drain the Valley of Mexico and solve the perennial problem of floods in Mexico City which had baffled the Viceroys. This task was carried out in six years, and it is no reflexion on Pearson's engineering skills that seventy years after the completion of his work further subsidence of the lake-bed has revived the problem in an even more acute form: in 1969 the Federal District called in another British firm of tunnelling experts to tackle it.

Before the canal was finished Pearson had already accepted another commission to rebuild and modernise the harbour of Vera Cruz, which in turn led to his equipping the city with a complete range of public utilities. He then turned to a more ambitious project, the railway across the isthmus of Tehuantepec. The Mexican government, which had hesitated for many years between the merits of a canal and a railway, had finally decided on the latter and raised an expensive loan in London for the purpose.

After the first three contractors to whom the work was entrusted had bungled the job, Pearson took it over, rebuilt a hundred and ninety miles of line and capped each end with a brand-new port—Coatzacoalcos on the Gulf of Mexico and Salina Cruz on the Pacific. He then arranged with an American shipping company to run services to and from these points. The whole complex was inaugurated in 1907 and proved very profitable until the volume of trade was cut down by the Revolution. It was run as a joint operation by Pearson's firm and the Mexican state, but in 1918 the contract was rescinded and it passed entirely under Mexican control. Nevertheless it remains an impressive monument to Pearson's technical capacity and forethought in business, for the isthmus is the most rapidly booming area in modern Mexico.

Meanwhile Pearson was launching another enterprise of bigger scope and overriding importance: the production of oil. The main Mexican fields have been discovered at intervals along the great arc of the Gulf coastline from Tamaulipas to Tabasco, and it so happened that the American Edward L. Doheny, who in 1900 began to buy oil-bearing lands in Tamaulipas and San Luis Potosi, narrowly anticipated a similar operation by Pearson on the isthmus, where seepages had been observed on the site of his railway construction.

The race was now on. As soon as the potential output of the strikes had been confirmed, both British and Americans moved with tremendous speed. Pearson extended his concessions into northern Vera Cruz, where a series of unusually rich wells were found, and the neighbourhood of Tampico, where his interests overlapped with those of Doheny, Standard Oil and other American groups. He planted his first refinery at Minatitlán, near Coatzacoalcos, and in 1908 began to sell its products on the Mexican market. Not unnaturally an intense rivalry broke out between the Mexican Eagle, as Pearson's company was called, and its American competitor, a subsidiary of Standard Oil. Bitter polemics ensued in the world press and peace was not made between the two companies until after Don Porfirio's downfall. But in 1911, when the British investment in Mexican oil stood at fifty-five per cent, and the American at thirty-eight per cent of the total, Pearson's many endeavours had reached their climax. They were of lasting and indispensable value to the future expansion of the Mexican economy.

The great investments of the Porfirian era stimulated a rapid increase in trade, both internal and external. Limantour abolished the *alcabalas,* the antiquated system of internal tax barriers which had so long hampered commerce within the national boundaries. As for exports, their value soared from forty million pesos in 1878 to two hundred and eighty-eight million in 1911. In the earlier years of Díaz's rule the balance of foreign trade was persistently unfavourable, but the trend was reversed when Limantour took control. The annual surpluses which Mexico thenceforth enjoyed were urgently needed to cover the outflow of funds for the service of the foreign debt, and the payment of dividends to foreign investors. Limantour's critics denied that they were sufficient for the purpose; they argued that the favourable balances did not in fact compensate for the drain of capital, that new investments simply increased that drain and that Mexico was caught in a vicious circle and helplessly enmeshed in selfish foreign interests.

It is true that very large profits were being extracted from Mexico by some foreign concerns, but other ventures, especially in the mining sector, were much more risky; dividends fluctuated or were suspended for years at a time. Apart from these uncertainties, it is hard to see how, in the late nineteenth century, the Mexican economy could have been built up by any other means than by attracting foreign capital. Where domestic funds were available for investment, they fitted into the general pattern and were utilised to good effect, creating an entirely new class of Mexican entrepreneurs. Díaz was in no position to defy the prevailing philosophy of material advancement and close his country to foreign endeavour, and if he had not presided over the process of change other leaders would have taken a similar course.

Nor is it realistic to blame him for the attachment of the Mexican economy to the United States. That was the inevitable consequence of geographical realities and the economics of the two countries were to a large extent complementary. The United States, in full expansion, offered a limitless market to Mexican products and Mexico was its natural supplier. At the beginning of the Porfiriato fifty-seven per cent of Mexican exports went to Europe, but this figure had dropped to twenty-one per cent at the end of the period and the American share had risen to seventy-five per cent. The surplus which Mexico earned on its American account was used to meet the deficits incurred in trading with Europe, which continued as an important secondary source of manufactures and capital goods. What is surprising about the Porfirian era is not the high degree of American economic penetration but that the fact that it had so little effect on the dictator's behaviour when he thought that national interests had to be defended against American pressure. While conceding almost unlimited facilities to American investors and traders, he was determined that Mexico should not become a political satellite of the United States. Throughout the various phases of his career his attitude towards the United States remained cool and dispassionate. His worst disagreements with Washington on political questions occurred during the height of the investment boom, as when he first granted, and subsequently withdrew, permission for the American Navy to establish a base in Lower California. He was never a puppet of the United States, with which he maintained even relations, untainted on his side by fear or excessive trust.

It is difficult to find fault with Don Porfirio and his advisers on purely economic grounds. When all political prejudice is discounted, it is obvious that in the thirty-four years of his ascendancy much more was put into Mexico than was taken out. The 'Cientificos', as the group surrounding Limantour was called, were not a clique of cynical and rapacious opportunists. His own origins were somewhat exotic, but his collaborators—economists, lawyers and intellectuals—were for the most part Mexican patriots of high education and ability, devoted to the task of converting their backward country into a modern and internationally respected nation. Their philosophy, deriving from Comte and the British classical economists, was logical and consistent. They believed that when the economy had been sufficiently primed and equipped, it would expand by its own momentum. The process of enrichment, directed by a well-trained Mexican élite on severely rational principles, would in time cease to depend on foreign elements, and the prosperity created by the flow of goods and services from the new industries would filter down to the masses through the emerging middle class. Meanwhile it was important that the march of progress should not be impeded by political strife or diverted into an unproductive search for social betterment. Sooner or later the whole population, including the most recalcitrant Indians, would receive their share of the benefits.

The 'Cientificos' would have emphatically rejected the suggestion that their insensitive attitude towards social ills and the plight of the peasantry might vitiate their plans and bring down in ruins the whole structure of the Porfiriato. In their view there was no real danger from that quarter. They envisaged that the established order would gradually evolve into a less autocratic form of government after Díaz's death and they held that Mexico must be regenerated by pervasive economic action from above, not by the promotion of social reform from below. But their neglect of the human factor was, of course, a capital error. It was not only that they ignored the strength of the pent-up resentment which was slowly accumulating against the régime. If they had taken a closer look at the industrialised countries which they were so keen to emulate, such as Germany and Great Britain, they would have found plenty of examples of the social legislation which was putting an end to the reign of laissez faire.

Notwithstanding the prevalence of materialist doctrines in high places, there was plenty of intellectual activity under the Porfiriato. It was an especially fertile period for poetry and scholarship. Indeed Mexico experienced a marked cultural revival after so many years of barren ideological strife and of destruction of its historical landmarks. In the earlier part of the century educated Mexicans had been formed either by the Catholic traditions which had survived from Colonial times or by radical tenets derived from France or the United States. The old teachings, haphazard as they were, produced many eminent and cultivated men, but the institutions which imparted them had collapsed in the wars of the Reform and the intervention. Juarez was obliged to start from scratch. When he came into power the Church schools had been abolished and the state had nothing to put in their place; there was no organised system of primary or secondary education. The biggest casualty of this troubled period was the ancient Royal and

Pontifical University, which had ceased to exist as such. What remained of it was dispersed among a number of separate schools or faculties which struggled precariously to dispense higher education to a diminished complement of students. Outside the capital the situation was even worse: there were no universities and the attendance at the few provincial colleges was wretchedly small.

The restored republic fostered the building of state primary schools. In 1878 there were five thousand of them with a hundred and fifty thousand pupils, and about the same number of children were being educated in private establishments. This was indeed a slender base for a country of nine million inhabitants, and so it continued to be, for in 1910, when the population had reached fifteen millions, there were still only twelve thousand schools with approximately a million pupils. But at the secondary and advanced levels the new system of public instruction was remarkably effective. The National Preparatory School, installed by Gabino Barreda in the ornate colonial building of the former Jesuit college of San Ildefonso, amply proved its worth. Its curriculum gave rise to fierce controversies; the Catholics attacked it for its atheism and the old-fashioned liberals because it was so rigid and utilitarian, but despite frequent changes of programme it survived as the gate through which the best of Mexican youth passed on its way to higher professional and technical studies.

From the seventies onwards it was the ambition of Justo Sierra, the brilliant scholar and writer who presided for two generations over Mexico's intellectual development, to combine the various independent schools (Law, Medicine, Engineering, Fine Arts etc.) into a National University, but it was only in the last year of the Porfiriato that he succeeded in his aim. For his opponents the very name 'University' was a synonym for clerical reaction and should therefore be avoided. Sierra, although he professed positivism, was a humanist of the deepest culture, a master of Spanish prose and an indefatigable educator. A democrat at heart, he supported and served Díaz because he believed that Mexico could not afford to dispense with strong government.

As the years advanced Don Porfirio's government took on a more conservative tinge. The radical element receded into the background and the highest posts in the administration were shared between the 'Científicos' and representatives of the big landowning families. A sign of the times was the cautious reconciliation which took place between State and Church. In the period after 1867 the latter's fortunes had sunk very low. The laws of the Reform were strictly enforced, revenues were insignificant and the clergy, still headed by the redoubtable Archbishop Labastida, who somehow weathered all political storms, had been reduced to a few hundreds for the whole country. Many regions were no longer even visited by a priest and countless churches, deprived of their incumbents, were falling into decay or used only by the Indians for their semi-pagan ceremonies. Díaz, who was or had been a freemason, was wont to say that as an individual and father of a family he should be regarded as a Catholic but that as head of state he could profess no religion, because the law allowed him no choice in the matter. With his usual shrewdness, however, he saw that a conciliatory attitude towards the Church would suit the popular mood. He therefore quietly established amicable relations with the hierarchy, using as his intermediary Bishop Gillow of Oaxaca, a colourful prelate who moved easily among the 'Cientificos' and in conservative society.

Díaz had to move circumspectly, since the sharp anti-clericalism of the Juarez era was still rife among politicians and intellectuals. Some newspapers took a delight in smoking out clandestine monasteries and nunneries, and in denouncing overt co-operation between the Federal authorities and the clergy. But although in 1910 the census registered only four thousand five hundred priests, the Church's position in the national life had been to a great extent restored. The laws were tacitly relaxed to permit a revival of Catholic schools and the voice of the bishops was again raised, as it had been in the colonial past, to demand better treatment for the peons and to stir up the Catholic conscience on their behalf. José Mora del Rio, Bishop of Tulancingo (Hidalgo) and later Archbishop of Mexico City, took the lead in these social activities. Unfortunately they were too few to effect a change before the outbreak of the Revolution.

The years 1894 to 1910 were the apogee of the Porfiriato. Mexico was solvent, to all appearance prosperous and without doubt more tranquilly governed than at any time since the great Viceroys of the eighteenth century. The dictatorship maintained itself in power without much visible apparatus of repression. The army, which had shrunk to thirty thousand men, was more ornamental than effective. In the capital Díaz's police agents kept a discreet but vigilant eye on ambitious or disaffected persons, and journalists who outstepped the limits of what he regarded as legitimate criticism found themselves undergoing long and uncomfortable spells of prison. The *rurales* could be relied upon to squash any incipient unrest in the countryside and impressed foreigners by their success in stamping out brigandage.

Díaz was not exactly a tyrant but he was autocratic and suspicious and regarded all potential rivals with a jealous eye. At the same time he was a superb political manipulator, and his superiority in this art was in a sense a guarantee of mild government. He succeeded in making the rewards of participation in his system look much more attractive than the dubious prospects of kicking against it. The risks of opposition loomed prohibitive, but the prizes of conformity were there for the taking, especially when so much money was entering the coffers of the ruling group and percolating down to its protégés. Díaz knew well how to distribute favours to his best advantage. He gradually packed all seats in Congress, all places in the judiciary and all senior official posts with his nominees. Those who felt too proud or squeamish to collaborate were not molested or persecuted provided that they refrained from embarrassingly open opposition. They were allowed peacefully to opt out of public life and to engage freely in whatever economic or cultural pursuits they might prefer. But many liberal-minded people tended to support the régime because the situation offered no alternative form of government, and because they believed, or professed to believe, that it was merely a transient phase. Justo Sierra was a case in point, but there were many more like him. Moreover the strict observance of constitutional forms which marked Díaz's personal and absolute rule made it easier to accept. So did the general atmosphere of progress and optimism. There were infinite graduations of attitude between grudging acquiescence and hearty approval. And for those who had money and access to the good things of life Mexico was a very pleasant place to live in. For over three decades it was singularly unproductive of political martyrs.

The principles of no re-election and effective suffrage naturally went by the board. So long as Don Porfirio showed no signs of senility, the idea of his displacement—by constitutional or other means—was unthinkable. National and state elections were prearranged to suit him, with little need for violence or even corruption. In the provinces the smooth functioning of the dictator's electoral and administrative machine was entrusted at the lowest level to the mayors (municipal presidents). At a slightly higher echelon came the clan of *jefes políticos,* three hundred political bosses who could be relied on to do any dirty work that might be necessary. At the top Díaz's talent for selecting trust-worthy lieutenants was exercised with special care in his choice of state governors. These key magnates had to be humoured, but also watched in case they became too big for their boots and, if need be, played off against each other or against other big fish, such as military commanders. It was a game in which Díaz was a past master. The governors varied in quality, but some ran their states progressively and humanely. The landowners, old and new, were heavily represented among the governors; Olegario Molina, the henequen magnate who owned seven million hectares in Yucatán and served simultaneously as Minister of Fomento (Development), was a good example of the Porfirian hierarchy. Among the military men General Bernando Reyes, governor of Nuevo León, was conspicuous for his energy as well as for a certain independence of character.

Apart from Díaz's age, no threat to the stability of his régime could be discerned in the early years of the twentieth century. The only straightforward opposition came from an extreme left-wing group headed by the Flores Magón brothers and taking its name from their newspaper *Regeneración*. They were anarchists, not Marxist Socialists, by inspiration and their purpose in the long term, for they realised that it was not immediately attainable, was the destruction by violent social revolution of the Porfirian dictatorship and economic system. They set out to gain control of the nascent Mexican labour movement. This had begun tentatively to organise the workers in co-operatives and syndi-cates, and to press their demands by industrial action. In 1906 there was a wave of strikes in the Federal District, Vera Cruz, Puebla, Tlaxcala and Jalisco. In the far north the mining settle-ment of Cananea, headquarters of the American 'Cananea Consolidated Copper Company', was the scene of serious dis-orders. The miners, rioting in protest against inadequate wages and the privileges granted to American personnel, were sternly repressed by the governor of Sonora with considerable loss of life.

An even bloodier episode was the uprising at the textile factories of Rio Blanco, near Orizaba. This ended in the death of two hundred workers at the hands of the troops. By that time the Flores Magóns had fled to the United States, where they formed the so-called Mexican Liberal Party. They also published a detailed programme of the radical reforms which were to follow the abolition of the dictatorship and clear the way for the eventual establishment of a workers' state on anarchist lines. Many of these measures, which smacked more of orthodox socialism than of the ideas of Bakunin, were incorporated in the revolutionary constitution of 1917. But in 1906 the pinpricks of the *Regeneración* group did not endanger the régime; they had only a marginal influence on the events which led up to Díaz's downfall. The end of the Porfiriato was brought about by a variety of factors, some of them quite fortuitous and personal.

When Díaz was re-elected in 1904 it was decided to lengthen the presidential term from four to six years. This of course meant that if he survived he would be eighty the next time he came up for re-election. The problem of the succession was therefore becoming acute. If another strong man was needed, the obvious candidate was Bernardo Reyes. But the latter's relations with Don Porfirio had cooled. In the preceding term he had enjoyed high favour as Minister of War, but it appeared that what Díaz had in mind was that Limantour, the linch-pin of the administration and leader of the 'Cientificos', should succeed him with Reyes providing the military backing. When Reyes made it clear that this was not the arrangement that he had been hoping for, he was invited to return to his governorship. As for Limantour, it transpired that as the son of a French national he was constitutionally debarred from the presidency, and Díaz showed no disposition to alter the law in his favour. Indeed he allowed his Minister of Justice to bring this awkward fact to the public notice. Obviously he had not yet fixed his choice on any individual. The furthest he would go was to nominate a vice-president (an office which had fallen into abeyance) in the person of Ramón Corral, the man who as governor of Sonora had crushed the resistance of the Yaquis. This, as everyone knew, was no solution to the problem, because Corral possessed neither the personality nor the qualities of a president.

Meanwhile Díaz kept his own counsel and the country was none the wiser. Whether his indecision was intentional or otherwise, it did provoke a revival of political interest and speculation. This was further stimulated by an interview which the dictator granted to an American journalist named Creelman and which was published by *Pearson's Magazine* in March 1908. It informed the world that Don Porfirio's aim had been to prepare Mexico for democracy and that in his opinion the moment had now arrived for an opposition party, loyal of course to himself, to enter political life. Díaz went on to explain that he personally was ready to guide that party towards a share in the government, but he did not define how that arrangement was supposed to work. As quoted by Creelman he implied, if he did not explicitly announce, that he would not seek re-election in 1910, but when the interview was reproduced in Mexico his compatriots, astonished and excited as they naturally were, could obtain no confirmation that this was in fact his intention. Nevertheless his rather sibylline utterance was interpreted as a licence for greater freedom of criticism and for the formation of new political groupings. If, as seems unlikely, it was designed for foreign consumption only, it was a serious error on Díaz's part.

In the subsequent manoeuvring for position Reyes threw away his advantage. His son, Rodolfo, vigorously campaigned on his behalf and tried to represent him as the rising champion of liberal and democratic Mexico. A new party, the Democrats, was formed to promote the General's interests and attracted many enthusiastic adherents. But although it was only envisaged, as a first step, that he should be substituted for Corral as vice-president, he was curiously reluctant to come into the open in the role of critic, much less in that of opponent, of his chief. Despite his undoubted ambitions, his competence and relative independence of mind, he was terrified by the possible consequences of insubordination. Sensing his weakness, Díaz forced him to retire to Europe in the autumn of 1909, and the political machine which his supporters had been building up was left without a director. His place was taken by a very different character, Francisco Madero, who was the last person whom anybody could conceive as capable of overturning the dictatorship. Nevertheless he did it within seven years of embarking on a totally unexpected political career.

Madero was born in 1873. His family were rich *hacendados* and industrialists in Coahuila, which his grandfather had governed during Díaz's first term of office. He was very thoroughly educated, first by the Jesuits at Saltillo and later in French and American schools and universities. There he developed a keen interest in social and economic questions. When he returned home he ran one of the family estates with exemplary competence and careful regard for the welfare of the peons. A small bird-like figure with a lively and restless manner, he was ascetic and cranky by nature and much addicted to spiritualism. His concern with social themes gradually led to his intervention in politics. In 1905, convinced of his mission to fight for freedom and reform, he tried to organise opposition to the official candidates in the state elections, and was inevitably defeated. He bided his time till 1908 when, his hopes stirred by the Creelman interview, he brought out a book entitled *The Presidential Succession of 1910,* which attacked the Porfirian order in moderate but quite unequivocal language. Madero insisted that the principle of no re-election should be reintroduced into Mexican public life. Nevertheless, in the two editions of his work published in 1908, he refrained from calling for Díaz's resignation. He envisaged that Don Porfirio should remain as titular President until overtaken by death or infirmity, but demanded that the vice-presidency, governorships and other key posts should be progressively yielded to the Anti-Re-electionists, as his supporters were rather clumsily called.

During 1909, recruits rallied to the side of this outwardly unimpressive little man whose challenge to the dictatorship was growing daily more outspoken. He issued a third edition of his book calculated to appeal to all shades of opinion hostile to Díaz, including the disillusioned Reyists, moderate and advanced liberals and the younger intellectuals who did not accept the dogmas of the 'Cientificos'. He even made overtures to the Flores Magón faction in exile. He was now openly campaigning for the presidency in his speaking tours through the country, and in April 1910 he was formally adopted as candidate of the Anti-Re-electionist Party with Dr Vasquez Gomez, formerly physician to the Díaz family and a Reyist, running for the vice-presidency.

With the election fixed for July, Díaz was slow to take alarm. Having disposed so easily of Reyes, he underrated Madero's strength and popularity. At an interview arranged between them early in the year Madero tried to make him see reason; he still hoped to persuade Díaz to accept some arrangement which would safeguard his personal position while ensuring a smooth transition from absolutism to democracy. But Don Porfirio, though he listened politely to Madero, subsequently derided and ignored his offer. Madero, for his part, came away convinced that Díaz was a spent force. He therefore intensified his campaign. Even the capital was filled with unruly demonstrators, and he was gaining ground so fast that Díaz finally decided to take precautions. Madero was arrested on a charge of incitement to armed insurgency and imprisoned at San Luis Potosí, without, however, becoming disqualified as a presidential candidate. This was the moment which the dictator, for obscure personal reasons, chose to have a tiff with Limantour, who left for Europe on financial business and stayed absent in the crucial months which followed. But the elections were held peacefully and Díaz, unconscious of impending disaster, turned his attention to the centenary celebrations of Mexican independence which he had lovingly planned for the glorification of his country and régime.

September passed in a whirl of festivities and ceremonies, starting a little humourlessly with the inauguration of the new lunatic asylum. As the octogenarian drove in state down the Paseo de la Reforma, escorted by dragoons in plumed helmets and applauded by the crowds, few of the numerous foreign visitors suspected that the edifice of his government had rotted. The capital was resplendent with the public monuments erected in the Porfiriato—a great marble opera house in art nouveau, the Independence Column surmounted by a golden Winged Victory, the statues of Columbus and Cuauhtemoc and the hemicycle dedicated to Juarez—and with the fine Parisian-style houses of the aristocracy. There was a spectacular ball in the National Palace, an imposing military parade with Mexican and foreign contingents and a garden party for fifty thousand in Chapultepec park. Half a million people watched a pageant representing the grand occasions of Mexican history, such as the meeting between Cortés and Moctezuma and the entry of the *trigarantine* army. When the rejoicings were over Díaz announced his own and Corral's re-election, with majorities so immense as to condemn them to ridicule. He then quietly released his opponent from prison.

No doubt he calculated that Madero would vanish into discredited retirement. Scarcely, however, had he taken refuge in Texas, as Díaz had done so many years before, than he issued a declaration under the name of Plan of San Luis Potosí, in which he denounced the election as fraudulent, proclaimed himself provisional president and summoned the Mexican people to a general uprising on 20 November. There was no such response, and Madero, who had hopefully crossed the border into Coahuila, was forced to retreat in a hurry. Over most of the country his appeal provoked only minor disturbances. Better news, however, soon came from Chihuahua, where certain obscure but spirited chieftains were taking the field for Madero. Small bands of horsemen ranged elusively over the vast expanses of the state, harassing the Federal garrisons and cutting railway and telegraph lines. At this initial stage their operations were hardly distinguishable from adventurous brigandage, but they struck the spark from which the authentic fire of revolution was to blaze up.

The insurgents found an able organiser in Abraham Gonzalez, Madero's lieutenant in Chihuahua, and an enterprising military leader in Pascual Orozco, a former storekeeper, who overcame Federal detachments in several small engagements. With the local authorities in disarray, Madero again crossed the frontier and assumed political control over his unusual associates. His chief asset at the beginning was the immobility of the government's forces, which had lost the initiative to a handful of cowboys. But the insurgents lacked arms and money and Madero's brother, Gustavo, who acted as his Chief of Staff, was hard put to hold them together. Luckily revolt was spreading to other northern states, while an outbreak of different character, but equal importance for the future, occurred in that legendary region of guerrilla warfare, the marches of Morelos and Guerrero. There the movement took the form of an agrarian uprising by the workers on the sugar estates, and it was led by the formidable Emiliano Zapata. The mills and *haciendas* were going up in flames within a short train journey from the capital.

Although the rebels had no organised forces, and no treasury except the private fortunes of the Maderos, their successful defiance of the Federals, and the rapid spread of political disaffection, had already paralysed the dictator's authority in all parts of Mexico. Nevertheless this was not equivalent to a general rush to join the Maderos. They themselves were worried by their lack of resources and the uncertainty of their prospects; they feared that a stalemate might ensue. At this juncture Díaz, baffled by the impotence of his administration and army, recalled Limantour from Europe and gave him authority to negotiate with the revolutionaries.

Limantour reached Mexico City on 19 March 1911, after a meeting with Gustavo Madero and Vasquez Gomez in New York. He returned with the impression that the crisis could be solved by compromise. On taking over the direction of affairs from the ailing Don Porfirio, he dismissed Corral and sent for Bernardo Reyes. Under the protection of an armistice, his emissaries joined the Maderist negotiators at Ciudad Juarez, the Chihuahua border town, then held by the Federals but closely invested by the rebels. The former Reyists, represented by Vasquez Gomez, alleged in later years that the Maderos had by that time lost their nerve and were contemplating a transaction favourable to Limantour. Whatever the truth of their contention, the terms actually presented to the Federals were very stiff. They comprised the resignation of Díaz, the expulsion of the 'Cientificos' from the government and Congress, the cession of eighteen governorships to the revolutionaries and the payment of their expenses to date. Francisco Madero was to be recognised as provisional president. When Limantour's spokesmen refused these demands fighting was resumed, in defiance of Madero's orders, and Orozco's troops took Ciudad Juarez by storm. Two days later Zapata and his peasant army took Cuautla.

These two victories, though of minor military importance and unco-ordinated, assured the success of the revolution. No major battle had been fought; the Federal army, such as it was, was still practically intact, and the situation resembled neither a civil war nor even a classic *pronunciamento*. Nevertheless Limantour realised that the props had been removed from the dictatorship and that it was useless to continue the struggle. It was not clear what the Mexican people wanted, but they no longer wanted Díaz. He therefore authorised his representatives, who were still at Ciudad Juarez, to sign what was in effect a capitulation. It was agreed that Díaz and Limantour should resign, while Francisco de la Barra, Mexican Ambassador at Washington, became provisional president until new elections could be held.

The document was signed on 21 May. When the news reached the capital two days later, Díaz, confused in mind and tortured by an abscess in the jaw, seemed unable to comprehend the full purpose of what had happened. He ordered the troops still loyal to his person to fire on the crowds demonstrating against him in the Zócalo. This they did with such effect that two hundred people were killed. But the issue had already been decided. On 25 May Don Porfirio was compelled to sign his resignation; the next day he was taken to the station and put on the train to Vera Cruz. Four years later, when the Mexican Revolution had reached its climax of sanguinary chaos, he died in Paris, secure in his belief that he had done the best for his country.

The Years of Struggle 1911-20

The Mexican Revolution was not a world-shaking event like the contemporary convulsions which overthrew the empires of Russia and China. It was an essentially Mexican phenomenon, deriving from conditions which did not exist outside Mexico, and it took a course which was not even followed by other Latin American countries. The causes of the explosion matured among the racial, social and economic discontents which had accumulated under the Porfiriato and were partly the legacy of earlier periods of Mexican history, but it was some time before the revolutionary movement became clearly identified with the basic aspirations of the masses rather than with the more restricted aims of the liberal statesmen and thinkers who were trying to find a stable alternative to arbitrary rule. When it developed a well defined popular ideology, this too wore distinctively Mexican colours and evolved on quite different lines from the revolutionary socialism of Europe. It made room for a much wider variety of opinion than Marxism could even tolerate.

Mexicans tend to regard their Revolution not as a short episode of calamitous violence succeeded by a long period of reconstruction, but as a continuous process of reform and development which has lasted from 1911 until the present day and will not come to a stop so long as the national leaders are wise enough to be guided by revolutionary ideals. In theory, therefore, to be 'revolutionary' means to act in a dynamic and progressive manner, and it has been the consistent purpose of the Revolution to create a new Mexican society in which the contradictions and discords of the past are resolved in an atmosphere of political freedom, social justice and harmony and economic opportunity for all. Hidalgo, Morelos and Juarez are portrayed as its precursors, and the history of the last fifty years is explained in terms of the gradual application of revolutionary principles to the recalcitrant facts of Mexican life.

But this was not how the Mexican Revolution has struck the outside world. Its idealistic aspects have been obscured by the smoke and dust of the most savage of civil conflicts, the feuds of ambitious chieftains, the wreckage of the economy and accretions of picturesque folk-lore. There were times when all orderly government seemed to have dissolved into chaos and barbarism. Significantly enough, the population declined by several hundreds of thousands in the second decade of the century. Yet the ruin was by no means universal. In many parts of the country the disruption of ordinary life was not disastrous, while the sorely buffeted Mexican state never failed to uphold its dignity and international interests in the difficult circumstances of the First World War.

The first, or Maderist, phase of the Revolution, was a peculiarly unhappy one. Madero was rapturously acclaimed as liberator, but the conservative De la Barra stayed in office for six months until the elections had been held. Madero's sweeping victory scarcely concealed the fact that he had already lost ground. By November the political situation had become thoroughly confused. No concord or trust remained among those who had ousted Don Porfirio. Conservatives, Reyists and the democratic left had split up into a dozen intriguing factions. Nor was Madero the man to grasp power firmly and put an end to this carnival of political irresponsibility. It soon transpired that he had no talent for administration or for handling men. He failed to control his Ministers and came to rely to a dangerous extent on his brother Gustavo and other members of his family whom he had installed in the higher posts. The government produced no coherent programme of legislation and in day-to-day affairs relied, for lack of anything better, on the officialdom inherited from the Porfirian régime. The press misused its freedom to satirise the foibles and personal appearance of the little President, whose prestige declined rapidly when he pleased neither the vested interests nor the partisans of radical reform. He had not been in office four months when he was faced with three separate armed risings.

Indeed Zapata, the peasant leader in Morelos, had warily remained in arms. He had no faith in the ability of Madero to redeem the vague promises of agrarian reform which he had included in the Plan of San Luis Potosí. The provisional government sent General Huerta against him without avail, for when pressed Zapata had only to retire into the encircling mountains where regular troops were unable to penetrate. Madero had the operation called off, and in a parley at Cuernavaca sought to convince Zapata of his sincere intention to impose land reform. But when no such action followed his assumption of the presidency, Zapata impatiently broke with him and proclaimed his own Plan of Ayala, drafted by a Cuautla schoolmaster, which demanded the immediate distribution of *hacienda* lands. Madero made various attempts to bring him to book, by persuasion or force of arms, but they were all unsuccessful. Zapata tightened his hold on the sugar-growing region and waited for a favourable moment to extend it.

In December Reyes tried his hand at an old-fashioned *coup d'état* in Nuevo León, but he misjudged his opportunity and was hauled off to prison in Mexico City. The next challenge, in February 1912, was more dangerous. This time it came from Pascual Orozco, the *guerrillero* from Chihuahua, whose motives in rebelling were entirely personal; he considered that Madero had not rewarded him adequately for his exploits in the campaign against the Federals. He was also reputed to have been bribed to take the field by the Terrazas family, the biggest landowners in the state, but the programme on which he in fact appealed for support was modelled on the extremist ideas of the Flores Magón group. After some initial successes he was routed by Huerta, a former Porfirian commander of undoubted efficiency, but drunken and unprincipled in the extreme. When this general returned in triumph to Mexico City, it was found that a million pesos were missing from his war chest, and since he failed to account for them, Madero dismissed him from the service. As it turned out, the President's insistence on probity in his subordinates ensured his own destruction.

These events were watched with growing apprehension in the United States, where public, if not official, opinion had tended to sympathise with the revolutionary cause. President Taft had promptly recognised Madero's government and discreetly assisted it, while disclaiming any intention of intervening in Mexico's internal affairs. Tactfully disregarding Madero's fiery attacks on the encroachments of the American capitalists, he warned his compatriots not to take sides in Mexican politics. Had it not been for one unsettling influence, and that a decisive one, the support, or at least the correct and impartial attitude, of the United States might have helped Madero to overcome his domestic difficulties. Unfortunately the American Ambassador, Henry Lane Wilson, took an implacable dislike to Madero and did his best to blacken him in the eyes of Washington. He persistently denounced the President's ineptitude, his hostility to the United States and his fatal leanings towards radicalism. By manipulating or disregarding his own instructions he contrived to give the Mexicans a misleadingly harsh impression of his government's attitude towards the Madero régime. Although the revolution had not taken place without some loss of American lives and property, it was grossly dishonest of Wilson to exaggerate those incidents and to pretend that disorder was increasing, whereas the truth was that by mid-1912 peace had been restored in the whole of Mexico outside the area overrun by Zapata.

At the same time Madero had increased his majority in Congress and was tardily preparing a reform programme which, though unpalatable to the Conservatives, was calculated to strengthen his popularity. Despite the revolts his position was by no means as shaky as Wilson tried to make out. But the Ambassador succeeded in creating an unreal atmosphere of crisis in which the American press and public opinion could be induced to believe the worst about Mexico. The United States government, for its part, was forced to respond to this mood. Stern remonstrances were addressed to Madero and a substantial force was stationed on the frontier. To give the administration its due, it did not entirely credit Wilson's darkly coloured version of events, but enough harm was done to ruin Madero's reputation in the United States and to undermine his position at home. The personal feud waged against the President by this unscrupulous and overbearing representative of dollar diplomacy opened the way for the plot which was hatched against him in the latter months of the year.

Madero survived with ease another revolt in October, when General Felix Díaz, Don Porfirio's nephew, 'pronounced' against him at Vera Cruz. With his usual lenity the President reprieved Díaz from execution and lodged him in prison alongside Bernardo Reyes. In accordance with Mexican custom the prisoners enjoyed every comfort in confinement and were allowed to receive their friends. Thus there was no difficulty in organising a military conspiracy for the overthrow of the régime. Rumours of an outbreak were rife in the capital but Madero refused to pay heed to repeated warnings. As for Wilson, his political predictions had become even more unfavourable to the President and it is hard to believe that he was not privy to what was about to occur.

The uprising was fixed for 9 February 1913. On the morning of that day Reyes and Díaz were released from gaol and placed themselves at the head of rebel contingents. There followed what are known as the 'Tragic Ten Days', which recalled the bloodier *pronunciamentos* of the preceding century. They were full of unexpected twists of fortune. Reyes, making for the National Palace, ran into unexpected resistance from the presidential guard, for Gustavo Madero, alerted at the last moment, had successfully appealed to their loyalty. In the exchange of shots Reyes was killed, and Díaz fell back on the Ciudadela. By nine o'clock the rebels were on the defensive and it seemed that the President had only to call for their surrender. Unfortunately he proceeded to commit a capital error by entrusting this operation to Victoriano Huerta, the man who nursed a bitter grudge against him. Presented with this gratuitous opportunity for revenge, Huerta decided to go one better and usurp the leadership of the coup. At first he pretended to obey orders. Establishing himself in the National Palace, he began a desultory bombardment of the Ciudadela, to which the rebels replied. As in the days of Generals Bustamante and Valencia, the shot and shell killed more civilians than soldiers and much damage was done to the city. But heavy casualties were later inflicted on the loyalist troops launched by Huerta in pointless attacks on the rebel positions, while reinforcements arriving from the provinces were not engaged. Yet it was not immediately suspected that Huerta was playing a double game.

When the apparent deadlock had lasted for a week Wilson, who had been urging Madero to resign, arranged a truce between the combatants for the purpose of removing foreigners from the line of fire. Under cover of this pause Huerta indicated to Díaz that he was ready to enter into a combination with him. On 17 February the two men secretly concluded the 'Pact of the Ciudadela', by which it was agreed that Huerta should become provisional president, to be succeeded by Díaz after a decent interval and an election. It remained for the new allies to take the lives of the legal rulers of Mexico. The first to fall into the trap was Gustavo Madero. Invited to meet Huerta at a restaurant on the following day, he was kept waiting while the usurper's officers burst into the National Palace and arrested his brother and the vice-president, Pino Suarez. Then he was himself seized and rushed to rebel headquarters, where he was barbarously tortured and finally shot. As soon as Huerta was sure of the success of this double operation, he appeared on the Palace balcony and announced the restoration of peace. Later that evening he celebrated his formal reconciliation with Díaz and the Reyists at the American Embassy, where the secret pact of the day before was publicly ratified and Wilson presented Huerta to his assembled diplomatic colleagues as the saviour of Mexico. Madero and Pino Suarez were persuaded to resign by the promise of a safe conduct and the Foreign Minister, Pedro Lascurain, who played a sadly equivocal part throughout the crisis, obliged Huerta by acting as president for an hour. This he occupied first in appointing Huerta in turn as his Foreign Minister and then in resigning himself in the general's favour. Having performed this shameful parody of constitutionalism, Huerta felt free to dispose of his prisoners, who had ominously been retained in close captivity. Their friends and relatives, who correctly feared the worst, besought Wilson to intercede, but he replied, with appalling effrontery, that it would be improper for him to do so. He contented himself with advising Huerta to act as he thought fit for the peace of his country. The general hesitated no longer and his two enemies, while ostensibly in transit from one prison to another, were 'shot during an attempt at rescue'.

It is hard to find any redeeming feature in Huerta. His military reputation rests on his repressive exploits against the Mayans of Chan Santa Cruz and Orozco's cowboys. In the February crisis he showed himself a master of cruel and ruthless intrigue, and some foreigners found his forceful energy attractive and reassuring. On the advice of their diplomatic representatives, Great Britain and other European countries decided to recognise his government. President Taft, however, rejected a similar plea from Henry Lane Wilson before bequeathing the thorny Mexican problem to his Democratic successor, Woodrow Wilson. Huerta proved a disappointment to those who counted on him to impose a neo-Porfirian order on Mexico, for his régime was soon exposed as a vulgar tyranny. Essentially he was a reversion to the type of the military presidents of the early independence period, but he altogether lacked their style and polish. In his personal habits he was brutish and sodden. He established a reign of terror in the capital, replacing Ministers and governors of Reyist or Maderist persuasion by his military cronies. Congress, which had been tricked or bullied into acceptance of his presidency, was dissolved and then packed with his nominees, while Belisario Dominguez, a senator who presumed openly to denounce him, was assassinated by his henchmen. As all opposition at the centre was cowed, it was left to the three great northern states to resume the revolution which Madero had begun. Neither Coahuila, nor Chihuahua, nor Sonora was willing to recognise Huerta's authority.

The first to declare against him was Coahuila, in the person of its bearded and pompous governor, Venustiano Carranza. This unlikely candidate for revolutionary fame had been a senator in Díaz's time and had subsequently adhered to Madero, a fellow landowner in the same state. Styling himself First Chief of the Constitutionalist Army, he issued a proclamation under the title of Plan of Guadalupe, calling for Huerta's resignation and the restoration of legal government on Maderist lines. Sonora followed suit by decision of its own legislature, which brushed aside the state governor, Maytorena, and accepted Carranza's political leadership. The First Chief was unlucky in his initial campaign. Harried by the Federals, he left his general, Pablo Gonzalez, to continue the struggle as best he could and himself sought refuge at Nogales, on the Sonora-Arizona border. There he established a secure base of operations under the protection of the Sonoran forces, the best disciplined of the constitutional armies and the most effective in the long run. They were led by Alvaro Obregón, a former school teacher and factory worker with a cool head and a real gift for military command. He and two other prominent members of the Sonoran group, Adolfo de la Huerta and Plutarco Elias Calles, were destined to become Presidents of the Republic.

The situation of Chihuahua was quite different, but equally encouraging for the constitutionalists. Its governor, the Maderist general Abraham Gonzalez, was caught by Huerta's troops and flung under a moving train, but he was amply avenged by the volcanic character who personifies this epic but confused phase of the Revolution, Doroteo Arango, better known as Pancho Villa. Born about 1880 in the wilds of Durango, Villa grew up as a vagrant outlaw, the obscure hero of countless minor scrapes with authority. The Revolution jerked him out of his precarious existence as a cattle thief and made him a captain of horsemen. In 1910 he joined Madero, for whom this scarcely literate semi-bandit seems to have nourished a genuine affection, at the head of a small band. In his first campaign against the Federals, while operating under the orders of Pascual Orozco, he revealed the qualities which were to make him so formidable a leader of light cavalry—his mastery of rapid manoeuvre and tactical surprise amid the vast panorama of the northern battlefields, his faculty of unerring decision, his sharp judgement of the characters of friend and foe and the personal magnetism which inspired such devotion and awe in his followers.

His next appearance in the field was in support of Huerta, when the latter was engaged, on Madero's behalf, in suppressing Orozco's subsequent revolt. Although he again acquitted himself more than creditably in battle, he offended Huerta by his contemptuous indiscipline, was court-martialled for insubordination and condemned to death. Rescued at the last moment from the firing squad by Madero's personal intervention, he was removed to prison in Mexico City. It did not take him long to bribe himself out and return to Chihuahua, taking the traditional route of escaping patriots by sea and through Texas. A month after Huerta seized power, he swam his horse across the Rio Grande and soon raised an army of his former troopers. One by one he wiped out the Federal garrisons and by midsummer was master of the state. With Obregón advancing on his flank, he began to nibble his way southwards. Both commanders formally recognised the First Chief's authority, but Villa preserved greater independence of action. For the next six months, however, there was not much change in the military balance. The Federal forces were fighting with renewed spirit and Villa was unable to break through their strongly entrenched position at Torreón, the centre of the cotton-growing district of La Laguna. Once he captured the town, only to be expelled in his turn.

Apart from the region controlled by Obregón, the north was a scene of chaos, criss-crossed by the forays of innumerable local chieftains and sub-chieftains, who plundered and killed with sublime disregard for the true interests of the constitutionalist cause. Indeed this was the life which Villa had left before he found himself in command of tens of thousands of men. It was touch and go what treatment private property might receive. Much of it was systematically looted and bartered in the United States against ammunition and supplies. But more often an armed band would ride up to a flourishing *hacienda* at nightfall and leave it in the morning a pile of smoking and corpse-strewn ruins. The British manager of an estate belonging to the Martinez del Rios, enlightened landowners in Durango, has left a fascinating record of some of these eerie visitations, when his fate would depend on the whim of a drunken or sadistic ruffian. He was well acquainted with Villa, who on one occasion in his earlier career, insisted as an indulgent gesture in sharing his bed, spurred, hatted and accoutred. But Villa, though utterly callous and prodigal of human life, was capable of generous actions and not devoid of a certain hazy idealism. The same could not be said of some of his subordinates, men like Rodolfo Fierro or Tomás Urbina, who were monsters of unnatural cruelty, revelling in the mass slaughter of prisoners and innocent persons. Alongside these brutes Villa attracted to his camp a substantial body of intellectuals and men of practical experience who actually preferred him to the First Chief. With all his crudity and savage behaviour, they saw in him the promise of a clean break with past evils. In the pedantic Carranza, on the other hand, they detected fundamental weaknesses of character—insincerity, conceit and jealous self-seeking.

A more significant rivalry, however was that which was developing between Villa and Obregón, the 'Centaur of the North' and the scientific student of war as it was about to be practised on the battlefields of Europe. Far to the south, the third focus of the Revolution attracted a smaller retinue of outsiders, for both its aims and methods were peculiar. Zapata also vaguely acknowledged Carranza's supremacy, but there was little sympathy or co-operation between Morelos and Sonora. The Zapatists went their own way, building up their commonwealth of Indian peasants and gradually extending its boundaries towards the environs of Mexico City. As it spread, it brought a simple kind of social revolution. The landlords and their administrators were killed or expelled and the lands parcelled out. The excited peons were guilty of fearful atrocities but their movement lacked the daemonic energy and mobility of the northerners.

While contending with its internal enemies, Huerta's government was also fighting a long diplomatic duel with Woodrow Wilson. The new President, with his rigid moral convictions, soon conceived a deep abhorrence for the dictator, his unconstitutional behaviour and his murderous practices. To Ambassador Wilson's repeated requests for recognition, he replied that Huerta would only deserve this favour if he held a free election in which he himself did not figure as a candidate. He added, however, that the United States would be glad to mediate between the government and the Constitutionalists. No doubt he hoped that although Huerta could hardly be expected to agree to his conditions he might conveniently be edged out by the process of mediation. M anwhile he recalled the Ambassador and clapped an arms embargo on both sides. This last measure had little material effect on either of the combatants, because Huerta was receiving munitions from Europe while his opponents were liberally supplied, in defiance of legal enactments, by their well-wishers across the border. The President also despatched the Democratic politician John Lind to Mexico City with a mission to explore the prospects of mediation. His instructions were to press for an armistice and an early election, and to threaten recognition for the Constitutionalists if Huerta failed to comply. Suspecting that the threat was bluff, the general stalled, but finally promised an election in October.

On the first of that month Villa took Torreón for the first time and Huerta, feeling that his rule was crumbling, countered by dissolving Congress and imprisoning one hundred and twelve recalcitrant deputies. This action outraged Wilson, for whom the last straw was Huerta's announcement, when the election had been held, that it could not for technical reasons be considered valid and that he intended to stay in power as provisional president. From that moment Wilson was determined to bring Huerta down by all possible pressure short of armed force. His public statements were so hostile to the régime that Mexicans were tempted to conclude that he was indeed contemplating intervention, while in Europe the United States was being quite unjustifiably accused of annexationist aims. The immediate reaction of his compatriots was to rally to Huerta's support; for the first time he acquired a measure of popularity. Wilson was at the same time distressed by the cool reception of the overtures which he was making to Carranza. The wily First Chief was not interested in any form of American good offices. He knew that it was political damnation for any Mexican régime to appear to assume power by patronage of the United States and therefore confined himself to insisting on the acceptance of his nascent administration as the legal government of the country. Wilson was not prepared to go so far as long as the military situation was uncertain and there was no chance of invoking a free vote from the Mexican people, but he decided, in February 1914, to raise the embargo in favour of the Constitutionalists. This act tipped the balance against Huerta.

On 3 April Villa captured Torreón for the second time. Another Constitutionalist force headed towards Tampico, where the oil companies demanded international protection for their installations. The interests involved were mainly British. Indeed the fuel derived from the Mexican Eagle's fields had acquired a crucial importance as a result of the Admiralty's decision to switch from coal to oil, and the British recognition of Huerta, to which Wilson had taken indignant exception, was largely due to the somewhat questionable belief in Whitehall that his régime was best fitted to guarantee the industry's safety. But the warships of several nations were hovering off Tampico, with the American Admiral Mayo in command. Obviously the situation was explosive, and the arrest by the nervous Federal authorities of a small party of American sailors who had strayed into a forbidden area of the docks touched off the inevitable incident. The sailors were released and the Mexican commander duly apologised, but the significance of the affair was inflated beyond all reasonable proportions by American insistence on a ceremonial salute to the flag, what the Mexicans call a *desagravio a la bandera*. It seemed as if Wilson was deliberately exacerbating a petty quarrel in an attempt to provoke hostilities. At all events this ridiculous issue of national prestige ruined relations between the United States and Mexico for many years and nearly precipitated immediate war. When Huerta refused the salute the American Atlantic fleet was concentrated in the Gulf of Mexico and preparations were made to confiscate a large consignment of arms which was about to be delivered at Vera Cruz in a German merchant vessel, the *Ypiranga*.

Since an operation of this kind could not have been carried out at sea without a violation of international law, the Admiral was ordered to occupy the port and seize the cargo after unloading. At first no resistance was encountered, but fighting soon blazed up between the American landing parties and the cadets from the Mexican Naval Academy, who were joined by the townspeople. The city was bombarded and the casualties ran into hundreds. In the confusion the *Ypiranga*, the ostensible cause of the trouble, slipped out of harbour and later discharged its load at Coatzacoalcos. Flaming protests were received at Washington from both Huerta and Carranza, and Wilson, who was horrified by the tragic outcome of his policy, was relieved when Argentina, Brazil and Chile offered to mediate between the two countries. A conference was convoked at Niagara Falls and eventually submitted impeccable recommendations. By that time, however, Huerta's downfall was imminent and they were ignored by the United States government as well as by the Constitutionalists. The Americans remained in occupation of Vera Cruz and cut off the flow of customs revenue to the treasury in Mexico City.

The Federals now gave way on all sides. Advancing from Torreón, Villa won another victory at Zacatecas, while Obregón, sweeping even more rapidly through Sinaloa and Jalisco, occupied Guadalajara and Querétaro. In the hour of success the latent animosities between the leaders were starkly revealed. Carranza managed to check the further southward progress of Villa's troop trains by the simple expedient of interrupting his coal supplies, but at the cost of a fatal breach with the general of the 'Division del Norte'. When Obregón rode into Mexico City on 15 August, Villa was not at his side. The capital changed hands without a fight, for Huerta had already abandoned the contest and embarked, as Porfirio Díaz had done three years previously, on the *Ypiranga*.

His disappearance put an end to the dictatorship but ushered in a phase of naked civil war. This was preceded by an uneasy pause. Obregón, who was alone capable of composing his chief's dispute with Villa, journeyed northwards at the risk of his life and bearded the frustrated and suspicious chieftain. They agreed to summon a convention for the settlement of the differences between the three factions of Constitutionalists and persuaded the Zapatists to join them. The delegates, civilian and military, met at Aguascalientes in October but failed to find a solution after five weeks of windy debate. The best they could do was to appoint as provisional president one Eulalio Gutierrez, an honest but powerless general from San Luis Potosi. Politically the convention was a victory for Villa, who had himself nominated Secretary for War and held the unfortunate President firmly in his clutches. By virtue of an understanding with Zapata, he was also in a position to assert his military superiority. So, by one of those bewildering shifts in the balance of internal power which characterise the unsettled periods of Mexican history, Carranza was dislodged, again without a battle, from Mexico City and retired under the protection of Obregón's forces to Vera Cruz, which the Americans had meanwhile evacuated.

The capital awaited with anxious forebodings the approach of its new masters, as at the wildest moments of the wars of independence. First came Zapata's mysterious and deeply dreaded squadrons, filtering silently through the high passes into the valley. They were followed by Villa's veterans, the 'Dorados', packed into long convoys of battered boxcars with their horses and their ubiquitous female camp-followers, the *soldaderas*, triumphant, trigger-happy and roaring out the infectious songs of the revolution. The two elements joined, but they did not mingle. As it happened, the excesses committed by the soldiery were less horrific than might have been expected, and it was noted that the Zapatists were much the better disciplined. That December in Mexico City witnessed the brief apotheosis of the peon. After centuries of subjection the underdog was in control. But neither Villa nor Zapata had the slightest conception how to use their victory, and they were indisposed to listen to sage counsels from the intellectuals about the shaping of Mexico's future. The civilian element of the ephemeral Gutierrez government, which included some able and respected figures, melted away in discouragement. Gutierrez himself succeeded in escaping from Villa's armed tutelage and eventually submitted to Carranza. It became obvious that the peon chieftains had nothing to offer Mexico but anarchy.

What was needed was not the domination of an armed horde, but the promise of a system which would satisfy the Indian's innate sense of order and justice and the Spaniard's deep respect for legality. Carranza and his supporters were well aware of the need to demonstrate their capacity for statesmanship and sound government. From their base at Vera Cruz they controlled more territory than the chieftains in Mexico City, and they reiterated their claim to be regarded as the sole legitimate government of the Republic. During their short sojourn on the coast they did not waste their time. While Obregón reorganised his forces and fused them with the remnants of the Federal army, Luis Cabrera, the First Chief's principal civilian adviser, drew up a comprehensive scheme of reforms known as the 'Additions to the Plan of Guadalupe'. This document outlined the broad principles of the social and economic legislation which the new democratic government intended to introduce, and a succession of decrees gave effect to the more urgent features of the programme. Of fundamental importance was the decree of 6 January 1915, entitled 'Law of Restoration and Donation of Ejidos' which, as its name suggested, committed the state not only to the restitution of lands illegally filched from the village communes, but to the further distribution of *hacienda* land as the need arose. It opened the way for the enormous expropriations of private property to which each twentieth century President has resorted. Carranza also bid for the support of the urban workers, to whom he promised an ample programme of labour legislation. He established good relations with the union leaders, revived the so-called

'Home of the World's Workers', which had been founded in Mexico City under Madero's auspices, and encouraged the planting of similar centres in the provinces. He let it be understood that these reforms were but the prelude to a radical revision of the constitution of 1857.

This constructive activity was accompanied by striking military successes. Finding the capital untenable, the chieftains evacuated it in January and Obregón moved in, thus driving a wedge between Zapata and Villa. He then cautiously advanced westwards and took up a strong defensive position at Celaya in the Bajío. There, in mid-April, was fought the decisive battle of the civil war. Villa, impetuous as ever, made a bad mistake in wasting his splendid cavalry in a series of costly frontal attacks on barbed wire and machine guns. He plunged into action without waiting for the arrival of his professional chief of staff, General Felipe Angeles, who happened to be delayed on another mission. This officer, an artilleryman of high professional attainments and singularly attractive character, had preferred Villa to Carranza and remained loyal to him to the end. But his absence at this critical moment was fatal. Obregón, secure behind his entrenchments, repelled every onslaught from the Dorados, who retired with crippling losses. In the following months they were driven inexorably northwards and repeatedly defeated in battle. Although Villa kept a precarious hold on Chihuahua, he no longer posed a serious threat to Carranza's supremacy and his operations reverted to the level of banditry.

The sweeping nature of Obregón's victories did not altogether please President Wilson, who would have preferred to preside, in moral impartiality, over a reconciliation between the warring elements of the former Constitutionalist alliance. But in the embittered state of American-Mexican relations this aim was clearly unattainable. Moreover the outbreak of the first World War forced the President to pay less attention to Mexican affairs. In 1914 he was still inclined, with a strange disregard for the realities of Mexican life, to favour Villa for president. The personal representatives whom he continued to despatch to Mexico in the hope of influencing the contending parties were apt to report that Villa was a more flexible customer to deal with than the rigidly intransigent Carranza, with his tiresome insistence on immediate recognition and the overriding importance of Mexican sovereign rights. But in 1915 Villa's star was on the wane and Carranza could no longer be ignored or snubbed. In order to preserve the illusion of bringing the parties together, the United States persuaded five Latin American states to join them in inviting representatives of all the Mexican factions to a conference on neutral ground, the primary purpose of which would be to set up a provisional government. Not surprisingly Carranza declined to participate, and the exercise ended, in October 1915, with the reluctant recognition of his government by the United States and the Latin American countries concerned. In addition, all deliveries of arms to Villa were cut off. Carranza had won a gratifying diplomatic victory.

Despite this development the enmity between the two countries persisted and reached new heights during 1916. It was cleverly inflamed by Villa, who saw a remote chance to retrieve his fortunes by involving the Carranza régime in war with the United States. Should he fail to emerge from the resultant confusion on the crest of a nationalist wave, like a latter day Santa Anna, he would at least have gained the satisfaction of injuring the Americans, who, in his opinion, had so signally betrayed him. In January his men held up a train in Sonora and murdered sixteen American engineers on their way to reopen a mine; in March he staged a spectacularly provocative raid on Columbus, New Mexico, in which more Americans were killed and much property was destroyed.

Preoccupied as he was with the menace of war with Germany, President Wilson was obliged to bow to the public cry for reprisals, which rang even louder in an election year. Nevertheless he was unwilling to send troops across the border without Carranza's prior consent, for which he correctly applied. This was a wonderful opportunity for the First Chief to reap the fullest possible credit for his defence of Mexican sovereignty. Without flatly refusing Wilson's request that General John J. Pershing, the future commander of the American army in France, should be allowed to pursue the Villistas into Mexico, he imposed so many hampering conditions on his operational freedom as to ruin his chances of ever getting to grips with them. Every real or fancied infringement of these restrictions evoked a furious diplomatic protest, with a consequent increase in friction. An ominous incident occurred in April when an American patrol clashed at Parral in southern Chihuahua with Carranzist troops and forty Mexicans were killed. Carranza thereupon demanded the immediate withdrawal of Pershing's expedition. Negotiations for a compromise broke down, and two months later a further encounter cost the Americans over thirty killed and prisoners. Wilson mobilised the National Guard and called for the release of the prisoners, which the Mexicans wisely conceded. At this point the tension began to relax. The United States government set its face against a war which would have concerned no major American interest and tied up the whole of the inexperienced forces of the Union in Mexico. The wrangling between the two countries was sensibly referred to a mixed commission on which the Mexican delegates could indulge their genius for obstruction to their heart's content. This body reached no conclusion, but no sooner had it been dissolved in January 1917 than Pershing's last contingent was removed from Mexican territory.

An attempt was also made from a different quarter to embroil Mexico in war with the United States. Imperial Germany, then at the height of its struggle with the Allied Powers, was resigned to American entry into the World War, but the Mexican situation seemed to offer the chance of a diversion which might prevent the United States from intervening effectively in Europe. In February the British intelligence services opportunely intercepted the text of a note which the German Foreign Secretary, Zimmermann, had instructed the German Minister at Mexico City to deliver to Carranza. In the event of war between Germany and the United States, it proposed an alliance between Mexico and Germany and promised German aid in recovering the territories ceded to the United States by the Treaty of Guadalupe Hidalgo and subsequent arrangements. It also discussed the possibilities of inducing Japan to change sides in the war and open yet another front against the United States across the Pacific.

The superficial attractions of the offer were obvious. It appealed to Mexican nationalism in its overheated state and if it had been made six months earlier it might conceivably have succeeded in its object. Moreover many Mexicans were disposed to admire Germany—a sentiment which has outlived Hitler as well as the Kaiser. But apart from the hazards inherent in the proposals, Mexican relations with the United States were slowly returning to normal and Carranza's government was almost wholly preoccupied with the adoption of the new Constitution. He therefore rejected the German offer out of hand. The note, which was published by the United States government on 1 March, aroused great anger among Americans and was a powerful factor in determining Wilson's declaration of war.

Quite apart from these international complications, which

Carranza handled with skill and obstinate courage, the state of Mexico in 1916 was deplorable. It resembled the situation which Juarez had faced in 1867, with the important difference that whereas Juarez's prestige was unchallenged and his authority virtually unquestioned, the First Chief was by no means universally liked or esteemed. Nor was his hold on the country assured. Despite Obregón's victories Villa and Zapata, as well as a score of minor dissidents, were still in the field. The new caste of revolutionary generals and governors, mostly of obscure origin, who had replaced the obedient magnates of the Porfiriato, did very much what they pleased in the provinces. The government frankly lacked the resources to control these despots, for Limantour's financial structure had been shattered, and the administration undermined by habits of corruption, indiscipline and violence. The economy was grievously damaged and its only encouraging feature was the high price obtainable in wartime for Mexican primary products. The unrestrained printing of paper money had deprived wages, already depressed by the creeping inflation of Porfirian times, of any real value.

In these conditions firm government was impossible and no Federal government could have brought about a rapid restoration of order and prosperity. The Carranza régime, with all its imperfections, could hardly be held responsible for fostering or tolerating abuses which only the patient progress of several decades was destined to eradicate. There was little it could do in its weakness to bring immediate relief to sufferers from want and the oppression of local tyrants. It rightly concentrated on the job of building the framework of Mexico's new revolutionary institutions, without which the process of reconstruction could never have got under way.

The Constitution of 1917, which owes its existence to Carranza's initiative and for which he will always be remembered, was necessarily based on its predecessor of 1857 and incorporated two-thirds of its text. This was common ground for all who contributed to the compilation of the new charter. The remainder derived its inspiration from a variety of sources, Mexican and foreign, revolutionary and pre-revolutionary, from the traditions of the Reform and modern Socialist models. Carranza's advisers, led by Luis Cabrera, produced the first draft, which was not markedly radical in content. This was referred to a constituent convention which met at Querétaro in November 1916. The delegates to this assembly were freely and for the most part honestly elected from the areas under Carranza's control but, as might have reasonably been expected, the followers of Zapata and Villa were not considered eligible. Care was taken to ensure that all were dependable supporters of the First Chief. Even so they were broadly representative of revolutionary opinion and when discussions began they showed that they were not prepared simply to underwrite Carranza's draft as presented to them.

The radicals, headed by Francisco Mugica, chairman of the main committee, insisted on far-reaching amendments which gave the final product a distinctly advanced flavour. It was generally understood that this tendency reflected the views of Obregón, who for sound political reasons preferred to stay in the background, and there was nothing that Carranza could have done to reverse it. Nevertheless the speed with which the work was conducted indicated that the area of agreement was wider than that of discord. The long document was completed in two months and promulgated on 5 February by decree of the First Chief. By any standards of constitutional debate this was a remarkably smooth piece of work by the delegates, and a tribute to the serious spirit in which they approached their task. Thanks to their efforts Mexico has eventually evolved as a radical democracy, welcoming to free enterprise but inspired and controlled by a strong sense of social purpose.

Paradoxically enough, the powers of the president were increased by the new constitution. It might have been assumed that with the experience of the dictatorship behind them the constituents would have chosen the opposite solution, but since Don Porfirio had effectively demonstrated how the more restrictive terms of the previous charter might be transgressed, it was thought preferable to provide for a strong executive capable of checking anarchic trends in politics and of holding the loosely knit country together, so long as his tenure of office was strictly limited by the principle of no re-election. The role of the legislature, on the other hand, was drastically reduced to a point which is considered unacceptable in many democratic countries. But the Mexican Congress has rarely distinguished itself by independence of thought and action, and its subordination to the executive does not appear excessive in Mexican eyes. Another convenient power specifically conferred on the president was that of deporting at his sole discretion any foreigner whose presence he considered undesirable.

The clauses relating to the ownership and use of land, waters and the subsoil were of prime significance. They were grouped together under the famous Article 27, which defined property not as a right but as a social function, and thus made the private occupation and exploitation of land subject to regulation by the State in the national interest. The article restated in modern terms the old Spanish theory that the ownership of all natural resources was vested in the Crown; it now passed to the nation and was declared inalienable. This meant that the grant or sale of land no longer conferred on the concessionaire or purchaser an absolute and unconditional right for the extraction of minerals or oil. Before digging or drilling he was obliged to apply for a permit, which might or might not be granted, and he became liable for whatever taxation the government might care to impose. Although Carranza privately assured foreign interests that Article 27 would not be applied to them retrospectively, they were naturally worried by the threat to their rights and immunities and the inhibitions on their future expansion. For the time being, however, the issue was not pressed and remained in uneasy suspense.

The same article also spelled out the provisions of the decree of 6 January 1915 about the communal *ejidos* and defined the status of small rural proprietors. But just as the assertion of the national ownership of the subsoil did not herald an immediate attack on the position of the established oil and mining companies, so the agrarian provisions of the article were not yet applied on the grand scale against the landowners. Only about two hundred thousand hectares were distributed under Carranza's rule. The execution of agrarian reform was entrusted to a commission which worked with a slowness and lack of zeal unpleasing to the radicals. As an *hacendado* himself, Carranza had little enthusiasm for expropriations, and his attitude was shared by the numerous upstarts of the revolution who had succeeded in laying hands on estates for themselves.

Article 123 (which has a street in Mexico City named after it) was an immensely long chapter devoted to labour relations and social welfare. The Mexican workers' rights of association and general ability to protect themselves against exploitation, which had been minimal under the dictatorship, were recognised and promoted by Madero, but in an unmethodical fashion. They were now suddenly equipped with an elaborate and advanced labour code based on the legislation prevailing in the most enlightened foreign countries. It was an extraordinarily comprehensive charter of the workers', the employers' and the State's rights and duties, but in the conditions of 1917 it was more a statement of principles which would take effect in the future than of measures which would be introduced without delay. So unstable and impoverished a country was little prepared for drastic social innovations. Thus the detailed regulations and safeguards could only be enforced gradually. Nevertheless the article established a sound basis for the ordered development of Mexico's modern industrial society and of the present social security system, which was launched in the forties by Avila Camacho's government. In the short term much eloquent talk was heard about the unique achievement of the Mexican revolutionaries in enshrining the sacred rights of labour in the national constitution, and there was substance in this claim, although at first the gap between the ideal and reality was conspicuously wide.

But if wages, working and living conditions improved slowly, the trade unions were brought into the main stream of Mexican life and were soon exerting a political influence of their own. The first union leader to make a name for himself was Luis Morones, an electrician who was one of the founders of the original 'House of the World's Workers'. This flashy and domineering individual later became the evil genius of the labour movement; he exploited it for his own ends and amassed a huge fortune by shamelessly crooked methods. But in the early stage of his career he was a zealous and effective champion of the workers. Carranza threw him into prison for his part in fomenting a general strike, and after his release he helped to organise the unions in the CROM (Confederación Regional Obrera Mexicana), a powerful body which decided to put its weight behind Obregón.

The Constitution confirmed the State's duty to provide free elementary education of a strictly laic character. This in itself was no essential advance on the policy of Juarez, but it was accompanied by a stringent prohibition on similar activity by the Church. The triumph of the Revolution caused a sharp revival of anti-clerical sentiment. The constituents felt that the Church had identified itself too closely with the dictatorship and its undoubted tendency to favour Huerta, as representing the forces of order, had caused much resentment. Hence the laws of the Reform were refurbished and built into the Constitution, where they still remain, anachronistic but unmodified. In some respects the legislation was made even more restrictive. The very fabric of the churches was now declared to be State property; religious processions and ceremonies in the open air, to which the Indians especially were much attached, were banned; clerical dress was not permitted to be worn on the street and foreign priests were excluded from the ministry. The Archbishop of Mexico, Moya y del Rio, protested energetically but in vain. It was some consolation for Catholics, however, that the laws continued to be very laxly applied, and the horrors of persecution were postponed for nearly ten years.

In March 1917 the First Chief at last took office as legal president. He was at the top of his power and prestige, the victor over dictatorship and anarchy and the architect of the Constitution. If he had completed his term by guiding Mexico into a peaceful and uneventful era of reconstruction he might have taken his place alongside Juarez as one of the few outstanding Mexican patriots who have won more fame by their constructive achievements than simply by their feats of demolishing tyrannical or outdated systems of government. As it happened, the three years of his presidency produced only disappointment and frustration. His government failed to carry out the reforms foreshadowed by the Constitution of Querétaro or even to give the impression that it aspired to do so. Its inaction was partly the very natural result of the exhaustion which succeeded six years of war, but it was also due to Carranza's personal inability to give direction and impart enthusiasm to the national effort. He too was tired, and as he grew older the didactic and overbearing side of his character which offended so many of his contemporaries became less easy to condone. His courageous perseverance degenerated into narrow obstinacy and intolerance of criticism or even advice.

For all his determination to vindicate Madero and overthrow Huerta, he was not a revolutionary at heart, but a man of the nineteenth century, a typical northern landowner of liberal principles but conservative tastes who had been carried to power on the shoulders of radicals. He belonged to neither of the two broad categories of revolutionary—the intellectual idealists with their sense of social mission or the rough military chieftains with their frankly opportunist outlook and violent habits. Still less was he fitted to appreciate the true force of the popular longing for change and betterment which underlay the success of the Revolution, or to conceive of the Revolution itself as a lengthy and logical process of national evolution. For him 1917 should have marked a return to pre-revolutionary normality, not the beginning of a new and lasting adventure.

The pacification of the country made slow progress. Villa continued to raid in Chihuahua and Felix Díaz rebelled in Oaxaca. There were plenty of minor outbreaks of dissidence elsewhere. In 1919 the seizure of the American Consul at Puebla by an insurgent band brought Mexico and the United States again to the verge of war. But the same year saw the end of Zapata, who was ambushed by a peculiarly nasty trick. A colonel in the government forces opposing him sent word that he and his detachment wished to desert to the rebels, and as an earnest of his intentions attacked and wiped out another unsuspecting body of government troops. He then invited Zapata to a meeting and when, duly impressed by this demonstration of sincerity, the chieftain turned up at the rendezvous with a small following, he was murdered on the spot.

Such acts of treachery were only too common in the Revolution, and the dignified Carranza met a similar fate only six months later. He brought destruction on himself by his evident unwillingness to relinquish power. The country assumed that when his turn ended he would automatically be succeeded by Obregón, who was patiently waiting in the wings, and spend the rest of his days in comfortable and honoured retirement. But he preferred, with incredible folly, to try to thwart Obregón, the most popular and influential of all Mexicans, and to perpetuate his own rule. When it transpired that he intended to promote the candidature of Ignacio Bonillas, the Mexican envoy to the United States, in the hope that the election of this stooge president could be contrived by official manipulation of the votes, Obregón decided that he must be deposed.

Carranza played into his hands by attempting Federal intervention in Sonora, on the pretext of a railway strike. This state was Obregón's fief and governed by his fellow Sonoran and close associate Adolfo de la Huerta. The inevitable rebellion followed, accompanied by the equally inevitable political manifesto, this time called the Plan of Agua Prieta. Carranza stood no chance against the powerful Sonoran clan. When Obregón escaped from Mexico City and put himself at the head of the movement, his outworn régime collapsed without resistance. Taking the gold reserve with him, he boarded the presidential train for Vera Cruz, just as Díaz and Huerta had done before, but abandoned it half-way when he heard that the state authorities intended to detain him. With a small group of companions he took to the saddle and struck out northward through the Sierra de Puebla, hoping to

237

make his way along devious tracks to the coast. The local military chieftain, Rodolfo Herrera, offered to escort him to safety, but had him shot to death through the flimsy walls of the hut where he was sleeping in the mist-wreathed hamlet of Tlaxcalantongo.

Pancho Villa, his most dangerous adversary, survived him for three years. When the Sonorans took over the government they offered an amnesty and lands to him and the remnant of his Dorados. In a fantastic reversal of roles, Villa became an *hacendado*, receiving the princely domain of Canutillo on the confines of Durango and Chihuahua. He did not long enjoy his repose from the wars. One early morning in 1923, as he drove to the *hacienda* in his fine new Dodge from the house which he kept in the little town of Parral, he and his bodyguard were mown down by killers sworn to avenge the innumerable victims of his butcheries. Above the rostrum of the Mexican Chamber of Deputies the names of the nation's heroes are inscribed in golden letters. Until three years ago, that of Villa was missing; the scars of his cruelties were too raw. Its addition, in 1967, to the roll of honour is a reminder that his memory has been divorced from ugly reality and passed into the realm of myth.

Chapter Eleven

The Revolution (II)

Slump and Recovery 1920–46

For the next fourteen years the Sonoran presidents and their nominees ruled Mexico in no less autocratic a fashion than Porfirio Díaz. Obregón and his successor, Calles, were clever and forceful men, hard-headed realists who reimposed order on the country and restored conditions in which Mexicans could once again go about their tasks in relative security. They firmly asserted the central government's authority over the semi-independent regional despots. In their methods of disposing of malcontents and potential trouble-makers they were considerably less squeamish than Don Porfirio, who had governed in a more sophisticated climate. The brutality and corruption which prevailed in high places were of a blatancy unparalleled in the old dictator's time. Political assassination was rife, and the cynical Obregón was reputed to have calculated the exact price of every former insurgent leader who might be prepared to drop his pretensions to power in return for money, property or one of the many lucrative offices in the president's gift. A new race of rich *políticos* with a vested interest in the régime came into existence. These pillars of the 'revolutionary' establishment acquired a large stake in industry and commerce, plantations and mines; cultivated polished manners and built themselves enormous villas in Cuernavaca or the suburbs of the capital, encrusted with startling fancies of bogus Hispano-Mauresque decoration. They were not imbued with an excessive enthusiasm for democratic procedures and social reform.

Adolfo de la Huerta acted as provisional president for six months until Obregón could be legally elected. He took office in

November 1920 and, like so many of his predecessors, he found Mexico insolvent. Pending a revival of the economy there was no prospect of a substantial increase in the revenues and Mexican credit abroad could not have been shakier. Foreign opinion tended to equate the Mexican Revolution with Bolshevism. Moreover the United States refused to recognise the Obregón government. The Democrats, who were still in power in 1920, had reacted to the murder of Carranza with the same moral abhorrence as they had displayed in the case of Madero. Their Republican successors took a more progressive line. They explained to Obregón that they might consider recognition if the Mexican government gave proof of a genuine disposition to resume the service of the foreign debt, to settle the innumerable claims outstanding for injuries inflicted on American interests before and during the Revolution and to clarify the status of the oil companies' titles.

Obregón was confronted with similar but less acute problems with other nations. Thus, even if he had himself been moved by conviction or temperament to launch a sweeping and expensive programme of reform in fulfilment of the promises in the Constitution, he would have been frustrated by international difficulties as well as by domestic weakness. His own bent, however, was away from social upheaval. He preferred to move with bourgeois caution, implementing the aims of the Revolution only in so far as they did not impede economic recovery or disturb the political balance. His agrarian policy was typically circumspect and betrayed his northern origin. He came from a region where communal *ejidos* were a rarity and individual properties, great and small, the rule. He was no fanatical enemy of the *hacienda* system and personally favoured the independent *rancheros*. It was also obvious to him that the initial result of a wholesale dissolution of private estates would be a sharp decline in agricultural production.

He therefore kept distributions of lands for *ejidos* to the minimum necessary for maintaining revolutionary morale. They were also made subject to a complicated procedure which discouraged rapid progress. The initiative in applying for grants was left to the timid and inexperienced villagers themselves and could easily be blocked by the intervention of influential persons with the authorities or by bureaucratic delays in the agrarian commissions and the courts. Thus by the end of Obregón's presidency the total extent of lands in communal ownership still amounted to only one hundredth of what remained in the possession of private landlords. The *hacendados*, for whom the only compensation offered lay in government bonds of very doubtful value, fought the expropriations by all means in their power. Many had been impoverished, but few ruined, by the depredations of the revolutionary armies. The *ejidatarios,* on the other hand, lacked the capital, the equipment and the skill for making the best of their newly acquired plots.

In most economic matters Obregón had little room for manoeuvre. He was compelled to operate the system which he had inherited from Díaz and Limantour, and which ten years of Revolution and serious, but sporadic, damage had not changed in its essentials. It was not a system devised to suit a revolutionary and sensitively nationalist régime. When the dust subsided it was seen that the oil industry, the mines, the public utilities, the railways and the banks were still in foreign hands. But the harmonious relations which had prevailed in Díaz's time between the owners and shareholders of these enterprises and the Mexican government had been marred by continuous friction and mutual distrust. Any modest endeavour by Mexico to exert a measure of control over the key industries in the national economy was sure to be misinterpreted and opposed by the foreign interests concerned, while Mexican public opinion was only too ready to denounce as treasonable the most sensible moves by its own administration to conciliate those foreigners and find a sound basis for future co-operation with them. The political risks which Obregón faced at home were perhaps more daunting than the frigid attitude of the United States government.

Nevertheless he had no alternative but to persevere and seek a settlement of the various issues. In 1922 a resumption of payments to foreign bondholders was negotiated with American bankers. Meanwhile a keen controversy was being waged about subsoil rights. Obregón confirmed Carranza's assurance that Article 27 of the Constitution would not be applied retrospectively, and the Mexican Supreme Court conveniently recorded a judgement enunciating the doctrine of 'positive acts'. This meant that if a company had made overt preparations—such as the erection of equipment—to exploit a holding acquired before the Article took effect, its rights and operations were immune from government action. But the Americans were not so easily satisfied. They pressed hard for these guarantees to be embodied in a formal treaty—a demand which no Mexican government could have accepted. Obregón did however suggest that this and other

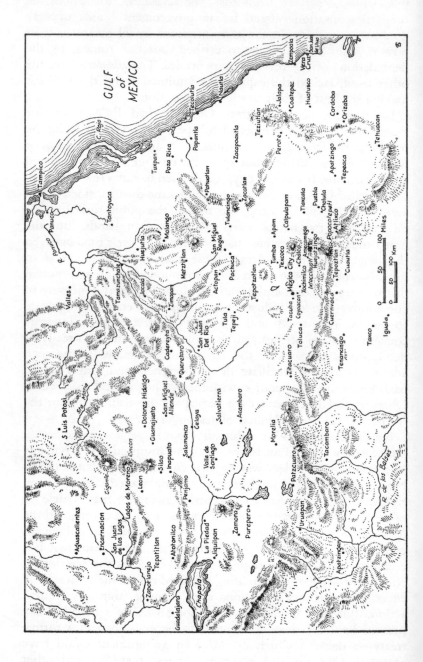

outstanding questions might be reviewed by the two sides without official commitment.

This proposal was accepted and the talks were held in Mexico City during the summer of 1923. After much discussion the Americans professed themselves content with the informal guarantees offered for oil properties acquired between 1876 and 1917. Thus the position was temporarily stabilised. It was also decided to set up two mixed commissions to assess the mountainous arrears of claims and counter-claims which had been accumulating during the past fifty years; one of these was to concern itself solely with damages resulting from the Revolution. By the end of August the atmosphere had so improved as to permit a renewal of diplomatic relations. In 1924 a number of similar commissions were appointed to deal with the claims of European countries. For ten years the work of these various bodies pursued its dilatory and acrimonious course until it was found less exhausting to conduct it through normal diplomatic channels. Even today a few hardy revolutionary claims still linger in the files of certain Embassies, but the vast majority have been settled or dropped in the intervening years. The masterly technique employed by the Mexican Foreign Ministry in resisting the claimants' exigencies can best be appreciated by a glance at the results. According to the simplest reckoning, the inflated estimates submitted by foreign governments on behalf of their nationals were patiently whittled down until the lump sums eventually accepted for distribution to the sufferers totalled exactly 2.64 per cent of demands running into hundreds of millions of pounds.

Obregón's bid for international respectability and the favour of the United States succeeded in the nick of time, for in December 1923 he was faced with widespread rebellion. The movement which now challenged Obregón was a haphazard but dangerous coalition of interests which happened to be opposed to him for one reason or another. It was headed by the military commanders in Vera Cruz, Jalisco and Oaxaca, a sufficiently formidable combination. Further away in Yucatán local conservatives seized and executed the loyal governor, Felipe Carrillo Puerto, who had alarmed them by his zeal for agrarian reform.

In addition to those who revolted from pure opportunism, many prominent individuals, including José Vasconcelos, the outstandingly brilliant and successful Secretary of Education, felt serious doubts about Obregón's sponsorship of Calles, his

Secretary of the Interior, for the presidential succession in 1924. They found him personally distasteful and correctly foresaw that he would prove the harshest of dictators. The leadership of the dissidents was assumed by a third key figure in the administration, Adolfo de la Huerta, who after exercising the provisional presidency had given excellent service as Secretary of the Treasury. It was he who had steered the tricky negotiations with the Americans to their satisfactory conclusion. But as Obregón's oldest political henchman he bitterly resented the preference given to Calles, his rival from Sonoran days, and was easily persuaded to resign his office in order to campaign against him. His alliance with the generals put an end to electioneering and for three months there was hard fighting in the style of 1915.

At first the government forces were hard pressed and nearly lost Mexico City. They recovered when the United States came to Obregón's assistance with lavish supplies of arms and even aircraft. The rebels were decisively beaten in Jalisco and Vera Cruz and there was plenty of work for the firing squads. De la Huerta, who was allowed to escape to California, was reduced to earning his living for a while as a singing teacher. Having once nourished operatic ambitions, he was fortunately well qualified. His removal from the political scene, and the summary execution of his military champions, brought Calles into the presidency without further trouble. The ten years of his ascendancy which followed were not entirely undisturbed by insurrections, but these were tame affairs, easily squashed and in no way comparable to the great *pronunciamentos* of the past.

By contrast with Obregón, in whom ruthless ambition was disguised by an open and affable nature, Plutarco Elias Calles was an unattractive figure. Ponderous and secretive, pitiless to his real or fancied enemies and not particularly loyal to his friends, insatiable in his appetite for wealth and power, gross and corrupt in his personal habits, he brought little but discredit on the Revolution and the Mexican nation, which he exploited shamelessly for his own ends. He was a man of little education and no refinement. A Sonoran of partly Lebanese origin, he taught in a primary school before joining the revolutionary forces. He showed no mean talent as a commander and excelled as a political organiser, specialising in the suppression of opponents by murder and intrigue. The sinister grip which he began to fasten on the country during his spell as Secretary of the Interior developed in his presidency into a full-blown and unpleasant tyranny. His sole, though by no means negligible, virtue was the hard realism which he shared with Obregón.

Through the maintenance of internal order, the promotion of an energetic programme of public works and the encouragement of native Mexican industry, he conferred undoubted material benefits on his country. He also pushed on with the distribution of lands to the *ejidos* at twice the rate of his predecessor. Despite these very real advances, the Calles era was an unhappy one in terms of the depressing deterioration in the political and moral standards of the ruling clique. It seemed as if the idealism of the Revolution was being suffocated in the toils of a system in which contemporary observers detected affinities with Fascism. In temperament, however, Calles resembled Stalin rather than Mussolini. Although he had less scope for tyranny, the comparison is not altogether fanciful.

In his Sonora days Calles had described himself as a Socialist, but when he came into power he showed no interest in State ownership of the means of production. On the contrary, he fostered the rise of a new group of revolutionary capitalists among his own supporters. While leaving the economy free, he clamped a tight totalitarian control on other national activities. Until 1928 he manipulated the labour movement through his close alliance with Luis Morones of the CROM, to whom he gave ministerial rank and carte blanche to eliminate the smaller unions. Only the CROM received official protection and encouragement. Its notorious inner committee, the Grupo Acción, bullied the workers into submission by the same strongarm methods as the president's agents employed in the wider political field.

In 1926 Calles moved into action against the sole institution in Mexico which retained its independence of his system, the Church. The attack which he launched on it was more serious than any previous exhibition of anti-clericalism, because it endangered the very survival of the Roman Catholic religion as a formative influence in people's lives. The Church was no longer rich or powerful. The modest renascence which it had enjoyed in the Porfiriato had been blighted by civil war and by the uncompromising restatement of anti-clerical policy in the Constitution of 1917. It was incapable of arousing political opposition to the government, much less of deflecting it from its revolutionary course. In fact it was sagely lying low. Nevertheless the régime found it irksome that every Catholic family should harbour a degree of scepticism about revolutionary principles, if not a basic disbelief in them. No doubt religion would sooner or later wither away, but in the meantime it was expedient to keep alive the myth that progress and enlightenment were being balked at every step by the baneful forces of reactionary obscurantism. Calles was in no real need of a scapegoat; he was simply exasperated by the Church's inherent inability to fit into his pattern.

The pretext for the offensive against religion was furnished by the imprudence of that least revolutionary-minded of Mexico City dailies, *El Universal*, in drawing attention to the protest raised by Archbishop Moya on the original promulgation of the anti-clerical classes of the constitution. Calles chose to regard this as a deliberate provocation and directed that these provisions should be strictly enforced in future. Numbers of foreign clergy were deported forthwith and the remaining Catholic schools closed. The bishops were powerless to oppose these measures, but they refused to comply with the government's demand that the appointment of Mexican-born priests should be made subject to registration by the civil authorities. They urged that a regulation of this kind would deprive the Church of its spiritual freedom. Finding Calles adamant, they obtained authority from Rome to resort to a course which smacked of mediaeval contest between Pope and King. Priests were ordered to withdraw from the churches throughout Mexico and to abstain from administering the sacraments, in the expectation that popular indignation would compel the government to climb down.

But although Catholic sentiment was indeed deeply wounded, the government was unmoved by moral pressure and remained as obdurate as the hierarchy. The stalemate lasted for three years. The Church's interdict perhaps weighed more heavily on Catholics in the towns than in the country, where the Indians continued to use the churches for their traditional fiestas without benefit of clergy. But it was in the rural and staunchly Catholic west— Jalisco and Michoacán—that resentment boiled over into rebellion. There Catholic guerrillas, known as the Cristeros from their rallying-cry of 'Viva Cristo Rey', began to harass the impious authorities, selecting as their particular targets the village schoolmasters, who often offended the parish priests and their flocks by their scorn for religion. The outrages committed by these fanatical countrymen were amply repaid by the atrocities of the soldiers sent to repress them, and many prominent Catholic laymen became the victims of vicious reprisals for crimes of which they were completely innocent. The work of the Church was driven underground and such priests as circulated clandestinely, celebrating Mass, administering the sacraments and imparting instruction behind closed doors, did so at the peril of their lives. The revolting public execution, in the heart of Mexico City, of one of these brave men, the Jesuit Father Proa, shocked Mexico and the world. It also prompted the newly arrived American Ambassador, Dwight Morrow, who worked hard and success-fully at the difficult task of establishing relations of confidence with Calles, to seek ways of breaking the deadlock. Thanks to his patient mediation contact was resumed between the government and the bishops, and in the summer of 1929 each side made small concessions which enabled the priests to return to the churches. The Cristero rebellion petered out.

Unfortunately this arrangement brought no reconciliation, only an uneasy truce which satisfied nobody. It was not until the presi-dency of Cárdenas, himself no friend of the Church, that the State abandoned the policy of active, though intermittent, persecution for an attitude of frigid tolerance. Up to 1934 the Catholics were further squeezed by measures which reduced the total number of priests in the country to a few score. Some of the provincial bosses outdid the central authorities in their anti-religious excesses. The governor of Tabasco, Tomás Garrido Canabal, a thoroughly evil assassin and debauchee, virtually uprooted Catholicism in his state. His followers, the 'Red Shirts', pulled down the churches and machine-gunned their congregations. Graham Greene's description, in *The Power and the Glory* and *The Lawless Roads,* of the squalid terror exercised by this and similar monsters was not in the least exaggerated.

With the approach of the presidential election of 1928 Mexicans asked themselves how Calles, now well settled as dictator, would arrange the succession. The principle of no re-election demanded that he should step down; it also forbade the return of Obregón. Nevertheless these two proceeded to conclude a bargain which flagrantly flouted the express aims of the constitution. They decided, in a spirit of mutual loyalty solidly founded on self-interest, that Obregón must succeed Calles; and when this became known, it was of course assumed that when the time came for the next change Calles would again follow Obregón. Mexico was thus faced with the prospect of an indefinitely prolonged alternation of power between these two revolutionary dinosaurs. Each equally feared the other and knew that he was not at the moment strong enough to risk an attempt to dispose of him. Consequently each was obliged to respect the alliance with the other as indispensable for the perpetuation of the system which they had jointly built up. It was accordingly announced that the principle at stake must be interpreted as referring only to consecutive terms of office, and the constitution was simultaneously amended so as to extend the term to six years. No other candidate was permitted to stand for election. When General Francisco Serrano, a dissipated but popular hero who had served as Obregón's Secretary for War, threatened to do so he was arrested and put to death, along with his principal followers. It was a fearsome indication of the lengths to which the Obregón-Calles combination was prepared to go in order to eliminate its rivals.

Many politicians found it hard to believe that Calles had really relegated himself to the background and resigned himself to waiting six long years before resuming the reality of power. Among these was the labour boss, Luis Morones. He knew that Obregón disliked him and his organisation and would have much preferred Calles to stay in office. When he realised that, for inscrutable reasons of his own, Calles was determined to step down he withheld the CROM's support from his successor, but allowed him to be elected unopposed. This was the situation when, on 17 July 1928, Obregón was shot dead at a banquet by a young cartoonist named Toral who had been allowed to approach his table with a portfolio of drawings. This unexpected stroke of fate caused a tremendous commotion. Public opinion was not disposed to accept the official version of the event, which was that Toral was a fanatical Catholic who had acted entirely on his own. Suspicion inevitably fastened on Morones, or on Calles himself, and was accentuated by the immense pains taken by the President to substantiate the official explanation. But whatever the motives of the crime might have been, it left Calles in supreme and undisputed control of Mexico, without partner or rival. The only point in doubt was whether he would again presume to tamper with the constitution in order to retain the presidency for himself.

He was not long in making up his mind. On 1 September he summoned all the notables of the régime to hear his last annual message to Congress, on which the responsibility for electing a provisional president now devolved. He announced to his curious but apprehensive audience that Mexico must no longer be governed by the former military chiefs of the Revolution. He urged the legislature to assert its democratic right to choose a civilian head of state and declared, amid delirious applause, his intention of retiring into private life. The statement was welcomed in the United States and Europe as proof of Calles's mature political wisdom, but his compatriots were not deceived. When the rhetoric had been discounted, they rightly concluded that Calles was simply informing them of his preference to exercise power in future through a puppet president, and this was indeed what occurred. During the murdered Obregón's six-year term the presidential chair was occupied by no less than three successive puppets, none of whom was permitted to enjoy the dignity for more than two years. They were Emilio Portes Gil, Pascual Ortiz Rubio and Abelardo Rodriguez.

In order to leave no doubt as to where the reality of power resided, Calles had himself called the Supreme Chief (Jefe Maximo), thus going one better than Venustiano Carranza. He continued to take the policy decisions, to inspire legislation and to dictate appointments. Patronage stemmed from his house and not from the National Palace. For the purpose of strengthening his hold over the nominal head of state and the regular organs of government he invented an institution which has since become a settled and indispensable element in the revolutionary scheme— the official political party. This was a most important innovation. As has been seen, a party system of a kind had operated in the early Republic, but it withered away in the Porfiriato and was not revived in the early years of the Revolution, when people accepted the same general ideology but were deeply divided by personal allegiances. The Partido Nacional Revolucionario (PNR) founded by Calles was not designed to compete with other parties on the same terms and by democratic methods, but to eliminate all effective competitors from the start. In an election it was fully supported by official funds and enjoyed privileges from which opposition candidates, if they dared to present themselves, were debarred.

Under the new dispensation the state became the instrument of the party, which grouped together all active political forces and embraced all shades of revolutionary opinion. Membership was made compulsory for ministers, governors, generals, judges, senators and deputies, while all state employees were required to contribute a proportion of their pay to the party chest. At the controls of the machine sat the Supreme Chief, wielding total power but inhibited by no constitutional responsibilities. In its outward aspects the system owed much to Communist and Fascist models, and was introduced at a moment when Marxism was attracting the sympathies of numerous Mexican intellectuals and labour leaders. But the resemblance lay in organisation and not in ideology. The PNR's origin must be sought in the need which Calles felt to perfect in institutional form the techniques of personal government which he had learned from Obregón and, ultimately, from Don Porfirio. In the hands of subsequent presidents it has been adapted to serve more democratic ends.

Morones and the CROM were pointedly excluded from the party fold. Although Morones had been a valuable ally during his presidency Calles was irritated by his performance in the crisis of 1928 and decided to cut him down to size. He was determined to prevent the labour movement from developing into an independent political force. Without official backing the CROM lost its predominance and the unions dissolved into a multitude of squabbling factions which neutralised one another. The party's first convention in 1929, which was called primarily for the purpose of selecting the official candidate for the next ephemeral presidency, provided the Supreme Chief with further opportunities of suppressing dissent. He vetoed the delegates' choice of Aaron Saenz, supposedly a safe Calles man of irreproachable revolutionary antecedents who subsequently abandoned politics for industry and became Mexico's richest sugar producer. He indicated that he would prefer Ortiz Rubio, a colourless figure possessing none of the qualities of Saenz or even of the outgoing Portes Gil, the lawyer from Tampico who would have made a very adequate president without Calles at his elbow.

This piece of effrontery brought an opposition crusader into the field in the person of José Vasconcelos, a bitter enemy of all aspirants to re-election since Díaz. This refreshingly non-conformist product of the Revolution combined a fiery enthusiasm for its social and cultural ideals with an unfashionable attachment for Mexico's Hispanic past. As Secretary for Education he had dotted the countryside with elementary schools and infused new life into the National University. The uncompromising integrity which he opposed to the malpractices and insincerities of the Calles era inspired universal admiration. Yet he was helpless against the party machine. His campaign, in which he tried to emulate the exploits of Madero in 1911, altogether failed to shake the dictator's hold, and Ortiz Rubio was declared elected by a million votes to twenty thousand. Vasconcelos retired to the United States, where he occupied his time in writing a major treatise on aesthetics.

The next four years passed uneventfully. In September 1932 Calles discarded the wretched Ortiz Rubio, whose subservience to the boss had made him a figure of fun, and replaced him by Abelardo Rodriguez, a north-westerner like himself and the owner of many profitable business enterprises in that region. He himself lived a leisurely existence at Cuernavaca, where golf alternated with poker and whisky sessions. The Revolution was plainly running out of steam; the agrarian and other radical programmes were nearly at a standstill and there were signs of friction developing between the younger party members, steeped in ideas deriving from Russia and Republican Spain, and the comfortably settled parvenus who surrounded the Jefe Maximo. Sensing that something must be done to give the impression that the Revolution was once again on the march, Calles delivered one of those enigmatic speeches which left his hearers uncertain of their exact import but uneasily conscious that he was dissatisfied with their performance. He stressed the need for a fresh national effort and recommended that this should take the shape of a Six-Year Plan, to coincide with the next presidential term. His advocacy of a Plan was bound to appeal to the Left, fascinated as it was by the spurious glamour of Stalinism. The Right, on the other hand, was assuaged by his growing distaste for collectivism in agriculture and his express preference for a system of individual peasant ownership. He suggested that the main lines of the Plan should be drawn and approved by the party convention in December 1933, at the same time as it endorsed his own nomination of the future president.

This time the Chief's favour fell on General Lazaro Cárdenas, a thirty-nine-year-old native of Michoacán. The new official candidate was not one of those military chiefs who had grown fat on the pickings of the Revolution. He had remained unusually diligent and devoted to duty. He was dour and reserved in manner and austere in his tastes, but his total honesty and simplicity of character did not impair a lively talent for political manoeuvre. His record as soldier and administrator was impeccable, and his reformist sympathies made him acceptable to the radicals. Since, however, his fortunes had been linked with those of Calles since 1915, he was not expected to take any course which might displease his patron. When he took office he found that his ministers had been chosen for him by Calles. They included the disreputable scoundrel Garrido Canabal, scourge of the Catholics in Tabasco, who was appointed Secretary for Agriculture.

But Cárdenas soon showed that he was made of different stuff from the three puppets who preceded him. Although the result of the election was of course determined in advance, he had shrewdly stumped the country as if victory depended on the effectiveness of his campaign, addressing himself directly to the peasants and workers and enhancing his own prestige at the expense of the aloof and arrogant Calles. When listening to the grievances of simple people he never appeared to be in a hurry and his easy, popular approach vastly appealed to the masses. On his return to the capital he knew he could depend on their loyalty. His first acts as president reflected his puritan temperament; he quitted the presidential apartments in Chapultepec Castle and cleaned up the overblown night life of the capital, the gambling houses and brothels in which many of Calles's friends held financial interest. When labour troubles broke out, he sided demonstratively with the strikers and denounced both the employers and the ineffectual and corrupt unions which were hand in glove with them. He promised to resume the large-scale distribution of lands.

Alarmed by this display of independence, Calles publicly warned the President that if he persisted in his temerity he risked sharing the fate of Ortiz Rubio. Cárdenas reacted with vigour. With the support of the majority of Congress, he dismissed the ministers foisted on him by the Supreme Chief, appointed another team and took the appropriate military precautions. In order to placate the Catholics he expelled Garrido Canabal from the country and dissolved his Red Shirts. Calles's strongest adherents were weeded out from governorships and military commands, while Portes Gil was brought back to conduct a similar purge in the party. Dismayed but impotent, Calles watched this whirlwind of activity from various provincial retreats. He returned to Mexico City in December 1935, amid rumours that he was planning a desperate attempt to regain power. His presence provoked much public excitement and a few disorders, but it was evident that he had no support from the army or among the people. In April Cárdenas ended the suspense by putting him on an aeroplane and depositing him in the United States. For good measure he packed off Morones as well, and no decent Mexicans regretted their departure.

The draft Six-Year Plan approved by the party convention was a hastily prepared amalgam of social and economic projects and of no practical value to Cárdenas, who had worked out his own ideas for setting the Revolution again in motion. He attributed its loss of momentum to the failure of its leaders, the bosses and the intellectuals, to keep in touch with the masses and to give them a proper sense of participation in the government of the country and in a continuing process of reform. He decided that the party, and through it the state with which it was so closely linked, must be reshaped on the broadest possible basis. He distinguished four main 'sectors' in the national life which most truly represented democratic forces and popular aspirations—the Army, the peasants, the industrial workers and a fourth element, less easily defined, which consisted of government officials and white-collar workers in general. These were the main groups of which the party, as well as the membership of government and Congress, should in future be composed. Cárdenas felt that a coalition of those forces, under the political direction of leaders elected by their own sectors as organised within the party, would be strong enough to defeat any form of reaction and to prevent revolutionary backsliding. He did not judge it necessary to find a place in the new scheme of things for the landowner and the capitalist.

Cárdenas's closest sympathies lay with the countryfolk. Indeed he was inspired by an almost religious mystique of the soil, with a strong bias in favour of collectivism. He was never happier than when visiting the rural backwaters, as he did in the course of endless informal peregrinations. He was eager to make amends for the Revolution's slowness in satisfying the peasant's hunger for land. Since Zapata's death no sincere and effective champion had arisen to redress their grievances. There were many local agrarian organisations, but they spoke with no authority in Mexico City. What Cárdenas did was to bind them together in one powerful and officially sponsored league, the CNC (Confederación Nacional de Campesinos).

He performed a similar service for the labour movement, which he found in disarray. The eclipse of the CROM and the expulsion of Morones had brought to the fore a new leader, Vicente Lombardo Toledano, the descendant of Italian immigrants and the complete antithesis of Morones. He was an intellectual of very strong Marxist tendencies, a splendid orator and fluent writer, who had shone as Senator for Puebla and as a teacher of law in Mexico City. When the CROM went to pieces he formed a group of unions which later decisively supported Cárdenas in his showdown with Calles. It expanded rapidly and won official recognition as the CTM (Confederación de Trabajadores Mexicanos).

The Cárdenas régime owed its exceptional coherence and solidity to the co-operation between these two mass organisations of workers and peasants, which overshadowed the other two sectors. Moreover it was soon found that the smaller professional army which replaced the amorphous levies of the Revolution had no need of an elaborate political structure, and Cárdenas's successor, Avila Camacho, eventually abolished it as a separate sector of the party. As for the fourth or 'popular' sector, it developed on a smaller but influential scale as a civil servants' union.

Although these organisational changes were not completed in a day, they enabled the president to embark without delay on the radical projects which he had conceived as fulfilling the purposes of the Six-Year Plan. For the first time since the beginning of the Revolution, a sustained assault was delivered against the *hacienda* system. All over the country gleeful squads of political agitators and government surveyors were engaged in parcelling out private estates. In many regions the selection of properties for distribution was quite arbitrary, often reflecting personal animosities or the whims of local party officials. One *hacendado* might find himself stripped of his lands overnight, or on the eve of his harvest; another, by skilful temporising, might succeed in postponing the evil hour indefinitely. As might have been expected, however, it was the government's policy to take the irrigated and more easily cultivable holdings for the benefit of the *ejidos* and to leave the marginal land in private possession. There was little point in cutting up the vast cattle ranches of the north, but the new surge of expropriations engulfed quantities of plantations producing valuable export crops—cotton, sugar, coffee and henequen—together with their industrial equipment. Here it was not simply a question of turning the land over to the *ejidatarios* to cultivate by the traditional methods; it was necessary for the government to create a fresh type of co-operative *ejidos* with a minimum of technical competence in the growing and marketing of commercial crops and to invest heavily in these ventures.

The first experiment of this kind was applied to the prosperous cotton estates of the Laguna region near Torreón, and was much criticised for waste and mismanagement. There was plenty of truth in these charges, but despite the early shortcomings of the co-operatives the government was working on the right lines. If the *hacienda* was to be condemned for social reasons and on the grounds that it was economically unsuited to the needs of the twentieth century, the only conceivable substitute was the peasant co-operative managed on modern and efficient lines. Although the haste with which these changes were brought about caused great resentment and the initial results were disappointing in terms of agricultural yields, the programme was relentlessly pressed forward. In 1940, at the end of Cárdenas's presidency, more than one fifth of the total available land had passed into the possession of the *ejidos*, but the toughness of the old order was evident from the fact that over two fifths was still held by big landowners. Allocations to *ejidos* were to continue throughout the succeeding presidencies, and the process is not complete at the present day. Revolutionary doctrine professes that the great estate, the *latifundio*, is always a bad thing, while the *ejido* is the form of rural unit best suited to Mexican conditions. When all is said and done, however, it is indisputably the small landholder, the *ranchero*, to whom the greatest credit is due for the contemporary expansion of Mexican agriculture.

Cárdenas was less sure of himself when it came to applying his collectivist principle to industry, and especially to Mexican enterprises. Nevertheless he brought in a Nationalisation Law authorising the expropriation of private concerns, and their conversion into workers' co-operatives, in cases where the employers had failed to carry out their obligation to grant their employees what the authorities considered to be adequate social benefits under Article 123 of the constitution. While it was recognised that it was beyond the capacity of the average firm to concede anything approaching the full range of the benefits specified by law, the government set up as the sole judge of the reasonableness of the workers' demands and of the firm's ability to meet them. Consequently, and under the stimulus of strikes, a number of industries were taken out of private hands and transferred to the work-people, with a disastrous effect on their profitability. The campaign was therefore not pushed too far. His more orthodox economic advisers warned Cárdenas not to risk confusion in the economy, and his sole attempt to collectivise a major industry, the national railways (those in which Limantour had secured a majority holding for the State) ended in fiasco. But in principle he continued to prefer that an industry should be owned and operated by the workers, on a profit-sharing basis, than by the State. While he often listened to Marxist voices and allowed Communists to run riot in the Ministry of Education, he was himself no Marxist, but a dedicated Mexican nationalist with advanced social views.

Nationalism and social justice were the motives which inspired the act for which Cárdenas will chiefly be remembered, the expropriation of the oil industry, and overrode any objections of principle which he may have felt to its ownership by the State. There is no evidence, however, that he planned the expropriation in advance as a deliberate stroke of policy. Although he was predisposed to regard foreign capitalists in the worst possible light, he certainly did not envisage that the British and American companies could be forced or manoeuvred into withdrawal from Mexico during his presidency. He had no desire to provoke a quarrel with the United States. The very real improvement in the relations between the two countries which Ambassador Dwight Morrow, an enthusiast for the beauty and culture of Mexico, under a suspicious Republican administration and in the chilling atmosphere of the Calles régime, was consolidated by President Roosevelt, whose Good Neighbour policy in the western hemisphere seemed to promise that the United States would never again be tempted to use force in order to maintain the privileged position of its nationals. He did not therefore call in question the guarantees given to the American companies by Obregón in 1923, which Morrow had successfully defended against a threat by Calles to revoke them. They also covered in practice the properties of the Mexican Eagle Company, now owned by Royal Dutch Shell.

At the same time Cárdenas sympathised with endeavours by the unions to extract concessions from the companies, and these soon precipitated a crisis. In 1936 the Syndicate of Petroleum Workers, which was affiliated to Lombardo Toledano's CTM, demanded a collective contract involving substantial wage increases as well as numerous social benefits listed in Article 123. They also insisted that the companies should employ union members in secretarial posts with access to confidential information on management policy. The companies were willing to bargain but not to yield all along the line. At the President's behest discussions were prolonged for six months until May 1937, but since no agreement had been reached by the end of that period, the Syndicate called a strike and the oilfields ceased production.

At this point Cárdenas took the matter out of the Syndicate's hands. He declared that what Mexican law termed an economic conflict was in progress; in other words a crisis of national importance had arisen calling for compulsory arbitration by the government. He appointed a high-level commission to guide the regular Board of Arbitration in its work. The findings of this body were highly prejudicial to the companies' case, because it produced figures purporting to show that the rate of profit earned from their operations in Mexico was far higher than that derived from similar operations elsewhere, while the disparity in wage rates was equally unfavourable to their Mexican workers. The commission accordingly advised the Board that the companies could easily afford to pay better wages and more substantial benefits.

In August they were ordered to comply with virtually the whole of the Syndicate's demands, including a twenty-seven per cent wage increase. Their reply was to submit an appeal to the Supreme Court requesting the annulment of the order; they submitted that apart from the cost of the demands, which they could not possibly afford, they could not reasonably be expected to tolerate interference from the unions in their functions of management. The Court took six months to give its ruling. While studying the issues it was subjected to intense political pressure, in which the President himself joined. No effort was spared in whipping up popular sentiment against the companies. On 1 March, the Court ruled in the Board's favour and the companies were given a week to pay. In a dispute involving the constitutional rights of labour, as opposed to questions of ownership and exploitation, it could hardly have decided otherwise.

At this late stage the companies hurriedly sought a compromise. They offered a wage increase only slightly lower than the Syndicate's claim on condition that the arrangement should be regarded as final and not lead to further demands. Having won the judicial battle and forced the foreign interests to acknowledge their social responsibilities in Mexico, Cárdenas was disposed to accept both the offer and the condition, and so informed the companies. He was not yet thinking in terms of expropriation. But when settlement seemed certain the companies committed a fatal mistake by insisting that the presidential undertaking should be ratified in a formal agreement. Until this was forthcoming they declined to make any payment.

At this juncture Cárdenas suddenly lost patience with them; he regarded their demand for a formal document as an affront to the national dignity and their refusal to pay as flagrant disrespect for the law. On 15 March he broadcast to the nation his decision to nationalise the industry. The companies still affected to believe that he was bluffing. It was inconceivable to them that the Mexicans, with their limited financial and technical resources, could seriously be hoping to exploit the fields and market the oil on their own, and they relied in the last resort on diplomatic intervention by the United States and Great Britain. On the supposition that Cárdenas's announcement was a final move in the bargaining process, they offered to pay the full wage claim. Their approach was ignored and the expropriation decree was signed on 18 March.

The President's action was greeted at home by enthusiastic and almost unanimous applause. Irrespective of their political opinions, his compatriots felt that he had vindicated Mexican honour and liberated the economy from an oppressive and humiliating stranglehold. Nevertheless the Anglo-Saxon reaction was awaited with some anxiety. Fortunately for Mexico, London and Washington failed to present a united front. The British government took an intransigent line which uncritically reflected the extreme resentment harboured by the directors of Royal Dutch Shell against Mexico. The note which it addressed to the Mexican government on 8 April was didactic and injudicious. While admitting a country's right in principle to expropriate a foreign-owned concern in the national interest and in return for prompt, adequate and effective compensation, the Foreign Office impugned the whole basis of the Mexican case in international law, as well as the impartiality of the Mexican judicial organs, and demanded the restitution of the Mexican Eagle's properties. If the aim was to secure a satisfactory settlement, the communication could not have been worse framed. After an acid exchange of juridical arguments the Mexican government, in which the Foreign Minister was the pro-British Eduardo Hay, broke off diplomatic relations.

The State Department, on the other hand, approached the problem with tact and caution, and with an eye to the requirements of the Good Neighbour policy. It resisted the companies' demands for forcible action, merely reminding the Mexican government of its duty to provide fair compensation, on the understanding that this would not be expected to cover the estimated value of the reserves in the subsoil. Even so it needed several years of bargaining, and the impact of a world war, to produce the settlement which was finally concluded in 1942, under the presidency of Avila Camacho. This stipulated the payment by Mexico of nearly twenty-four million dollars, plus interest, a sum amounting to less than one-tenth of the value originally placed on their properties by the American companies. One of the latter, Sinclair Oil, had already compounded privately for eight and a half million dollars. The Anglo-Dutch interests had to wait a little longer, but paradoxically obtained a more favourable settlement. As soon as relations between Great Britain and Mexico were resumed in November 1941, negotiations were opened through the diplomatic channel, and lasted for just under six years. Mexico eventually agreed to pay eighty-one million dollars, plus interest, in fifteen annual instalments, but the debt was happily acquitted some years before the date envisaged.

When viewed in retrospect, the expropriation was an unmixed blessing for Mexico and a salutary warning to foreign interests of the hazards of building industrial empires overseas. It is more difficult to assess the balance of rights and wrongs in the dispute at the time when it occurred. The Mexican attitude, well founded as it was in law and social policy, was marred by a strong element of xenophobia and blackmail. On the other hand the charges against the companies—that they were disrespectful of Mexican law and sovereignty, that they had for many years extracted large profits from their exploitation of the Mexican subsoil without ever ploughing anything back into the economy, and that they were indifferent to the poverty and illiteracy of their workers— could not easily be refuted. They were certainly insensitive to Mexican feelings and their handling of the final crisis was curiously inept. Their complacency about the future inability of the Mexicans to run their own oil industry is more excusable, for in 1938 it was scarcely possible to predict that Petroleos Mexicanos, the modest national company set up by Cárdenas before the expropriation to develop wells on state lands, would ever blossom into the booming concern which it became in the fifties.

But the early record of Pemex, though not brilliant, did not justify the gloomier forecasts of the foreign experts. Initially its progress was hampered by the boycott of its products in world markets organised by the expropriated companies and by the difficulties which it encountered, for the same reasons, in importing new equipment. It was stultified by the lack of technical knowledge among its Mexican staff and by the gross malpractices which prevailed in the Syndicate. Political influences encouraged incompetence and waste. It was eight years before production of crude oil exceeded the level of 1937. In the circumstances, however, this performance was not to be despised, and it enormously improved after President Alemán, in 1946, cleaned up the industry and introduced efficient standards of management. Even more important was the help which it received from the United States from the war years onwards.

The echoes of the oil controversy died away in the months preceding the outbreak of war in Europe. Mexico's traditional isolation from European issues had already been disturbed by the Spanish civil war, and the thousands of Republican refugees fleeing from Franco's advance, to whom Cárdenas, an avowed enemy of Fascism, had extended willing hospitality, incited Mexican opinion against the Axis Powers.

This influence was combated by the strenuous propaganda efforts of Franco's agents and the German and Italian Legations. Their campaign met with a sympathetic response from the Mexican Sinarquists. Sinarquismo was a political movement which originated in Guanajuato about 1937 and flourished chiefly in the region where the Cristeros had operated. Its ideology flatly contradicted and condemned all that the Revolution stood for. Much to the embarrassment of the Church hierarchy, the Sinarquists professed an outmoded and aggressive form of Catholicism and flaunted the most anti-democratic and authoritarian principles. Their activities were more irritating than dangerous, but they spoiled the image of national unity in face of external pressures which Cárdenas so successfully presented in 1938. Cardenas's natural reaction to the European crisis was to draw closer to the United States, which under Roosevelt's leadership was pursuing an enlightened policy in inter-American affairs and whose attitude towards Mexico was scrupulously correct. But his task was complicated by old animosities as well as by the ideological confusion resulting from the conclusion of the Soviet-German pact of August 1939. So long as that arrangement persisted Lombardo Toledano, then at the height of his power, led the labour movement and the left-wing intellectuals in slavish conformity to Soviet policies and in militant opposition to a rapprochement between Mexico and the United States. Nor was there at first much enthusiasm in Mexico, either on the Right or on the Left, for the fight which Great Britain and her allies, with moral and material support from the United States, were waging against the Axis. There was of course no basic dislike in Mexico for the Germans, who were popularly respected for their martial qualities and preferred to the 'imperialists'.

All these factors influenced the selection of the official candidate for the presidential election of 1940. Radical elements in the party, now rechristened the PRM (Partido Revolucionario Mexicano), were inclined to support General Francisco Mugica, the veteran who had presided over the constitutional debates in 1916, but

Cárdenas indicated that he himself would prefer his Secretary of War, General Manuel Avila Camacho. The latter was duly adopted and elected, by the usual sweeping majority, over the opposition candidate, General Andreu Almazán.

The contest, however, was far from dull. It marked the emergence of a regular opposition party in the shape of the PAN (Partido de Acción Nacional), and it was clear from the course of Almazán's campaign that the scanty vote with which he was credited did not reflect the very considerable support accorded him by the middle classes and all those dissatisfied with the leftist trends of the last six years. In order to spike his opponent's guns, but also in complete sincerity, Avila Camacho made his famous declaration, 'I am a believer', in reply to a journalist's question about his attitude to the Church. This established in advance his reputation as a moderate and helped to deflate the plans for a *coup d'état* which his opponent's partisans were openly preparing.

Once installed in the presidency he amply justified his predecessor's choice. A quiet burly man of unpretentious manner and sound judgement, he soon brought the discordant factions under control. Although lacking in political experience, he handled the very delicate situation of 1941 with an unerring touch, ably backed by two outstanding ministers, Ezequiel Padilla at the Foreign Ministry and Miguel Alemán at the Ministry of the Interior. In his attitude to the belligerents he avoided the temptation to sit on the fence, waiting to see which side was likely to win, as most of his compatriots would have liked him to do at the time. Instead he associated Mexico unreservedly with the plans for hemisphere defence and economic co-operation which the United States was engaged in putting into effect. Mexican neutrality was slanted heavily against the Axis, and after Hitler attacked the Soviet Union the President had no further trouble with the extreme left about his conduct of foreign policy.

The new harmonious relationship between Mexico and the United States was formalised in November 1941 by the signature of a 'General Agreement'. In addition to the settlement of oil and agrarian claims and the conclusion of a commercial treaty, the Mexican peso was pegged to the dollar, the United States undertook to purchase agreed quantities of Mexican silver and credits were arranged through the Export-Import Bank for the development of Mexican industries and their adaptation to defence needs. At the same time Mexico renewed relations with Great Britain and after Pearl Harbor severed all ties with Japan and the Axis. In all their public statements the President and Padilla identified Mexico with the Allied cause and stressed its economic commitment to aid the war effort, but without contemplating active belligerence.

It was not long, however, before hostilities began to affect the Mexican seaboard. German submarines moved into the Caribbean and the Gulf of Mexico and for several months paralysed shipping movements in the area. After two Mexican tankers had been torpedoed and sunk with loss of life, Avila Camacho obtained the approval of Congress for a declaration of war, which took effect from 14 May. Despite a continued lack of patriotic enthusiasm, Avila Camacho succeeded in producing a satisfactory display of national unity. This was symbolised by the appearance of all six living ex-Presidents, including Calles and Cárdenas, in his company at the Independence Day ceremonies in September. An important post was found for Cárdenas as military commander of the Pacific Zone, and he was subsequently raised to the new office of Secretary of Defence.

Another occasion of great symbolic as well as practical value was the meeting of Avila Camacho with Franklin Roosevelt at Monterrey in April 1943. It was the first time that a President of the United States had ever entered Mexico. The importance of the Mexican contribution to the Allied victory should not be underestimated. Although the national army—streamlined, retrained and equipped with modern weapons through Lend-Lease—was assigned to a purely defensive role and saw no service in the field, tens of thousands of Mexicans resident in the United States were drafted into its forces and fought with distinction on all the battle fronts. The navy patrolled the long coastlines and the air force sent a squadron to take part in the final assault against Japan. But it was as a supplier of strategic materials, foodstuffs and manufactures that Mexico really pulled its weight. It was the American war industry's main source of a number of rare but indispensable substances such as graphite, antimony and cadmium, and there was an enormous increase in the production of more conventional metals—copper, lead, zinc, mercury. All over the country marginal mines were being reopened and new resources exploited, while a fresh influx of American capital and technical aid stimulated an industrial boom. A further useful contribution to the United States war economy was made by Mexican surplus manpower, the two hundred thousand *braceros* who were contracted to work on American farms and in various forms of unskilled labour.

The abnormally rapid expansion of the economy brought inflation in its train, and with it an ugly surge of profiteering and corruption. Avila Camacho's government took a number of sensible measures to control this trend and to utilise to good effect the very considerable inflow of funds resulting from the sudden rise in exports. One was the conclusion of a long overdue agreement with the bondholders for a definitive settlement of the foreign debt, nine-tenths of which was written off in the process; similar negotiations were started with the holders of Mexican railway bonds. A state development bank, the Nacional Financiera, was founded to channel funds into industry, and has since become one of Mexico's most effective institutions.

Popular discontent with food shortages and runaway prices was difficult to allay. In order to increase food supplies the government closed down the agrarian programme, guaranteeing private estates of moderate size against expropriation and only creating new *ejidos* if it was certain that they would become immediately productive. There was less emphasis on the distribution of land than on the introduction of new agricultural techniques. Meanwhile the President made a momentous step forward in the welfare field by his inauguration of a social security system for industrial workers, as enjoined by Article 123. Some years elapsed before this scheme got into its stride, but it was widely extended in the mid fifties and now counts as another striking example of the successful initiatives taken during Avila Camacho's presidency. He dealt firmly with attempts to exploit wartime hardships for political ends. This entailed action against Lombardo Toledano, who was edged out of his key post as secretary-general of the CTM and never recovered the political influence which he had exercised under Cárdenas and at the beginning of Avila Camacho's term. His removal effectively discouraged the efforts of Mexican Marxists to erode the PRM's authority.

A sharp watch was also kept on the newly established Soviet Embassy, which was developing into the headquarters of Communist political and propagandist infiltration into the whole of Latin America. The appointment as Ambassador to Mexico of a very senior and dynamic Soviet official, Constantine Oumansky, who in 1939 had held the same post in the United States, demonstrated the importance which Moscow attached to penetrating the Latin American world. Under the suspicious eye of the American

Embassy (itself numbering over seven hundred persons), Oumansky opened a large and lavishly hospitable mission which acted like a magnet on Mexican left-wingers. But after eighteen months of furious activity he was killed in a flying accident and the Soviet drive lost its impetus.

The moderate policies associated with Avila Camacho involved no neglect, as his critics alleged, of revolutionary ideals. On the contrary, the mere fact that they were framed and pursued in a less partisan spirit tended to make them more effective. It was he who initiated the last of the three big advances in education which distinguished the second phase of the Revolution. The first of these programmes was carried out by Vasconcelos under Obregón's administration, and did noble pioneer work in implanting elementary schools in the villages. The second, which was launched by Narciso Bassols, the near-Communist Secretary for Education under Abelardo Rodriguez, widened the scope of elementary instruction and much improved the pay and status of the teachers, but caused widespread offence by its political content. Through an amendment to the constitution, State education was officially characterised as 'socialist', textbooks and teaching methods reflected Marxist doctrine and aggressive anticlericalism. Under Avila Camacho a reaction set in. Indeed the new Minister, Vejar Vasquez, reversed the trend too abruptly for revolutionary tastes and the President replaced him by Jaime Torres Bodet, diplomat by profession, a great scholar and poet and later Secretary-General of UNESCO and for the second time Secretary for Education. His attack on illiteracy achieved far better results than the preceding campaigns and was continued energetically under the next president, Alemán. If the problem has not yet been completely solved, it is because the phenomenal growth of population has outpaced government planning and mopped up the very large resources devoted to education.

Besides bringing instruction to the people, the Revolution released a torrent of intellectual energy. Writers and artists responded vigorously to the agonies and enthusiasms of the time. Discarding European models and the forms which had been fashionable during the Porfiriato, they allowed a strong national spirit to pervade their work. The outside world was for the first time made aware of the existence of an individual Mexican culture, rooted in its own ancient traditions but enlivened by the exciting experiences of the twentieth century. This period was the heyday of the muralists—José Clemente Orozco, Diego Rivera, David

Mexico City: The University Library   (*J. Allan Cash*)

Across the inner bay at Acapulco   (*J. Allan Cash*)

The modern Monument to the Mexican Races in Mexico City
(*J. Allan Cash*)

The volcano of Popocatepetl (*J. Allan Cash*)

Alfonso Siqueiros and their followers—who each in his way strove to interpret the course of Mexican history and the significance of the Revolution. Although the last two were great artists, they were also violent political propagandists and their appeal tends to fade when a longer and more dispassionate view is taken of the themes they depict. Only Orozco transcends the issues of his lifetime and achieves universality, as in the cycle of frescoes with which he decorated the church of the Hospicio Cabánas at Guadalajara, a glorious classical building attributed to Tolsa. But the wealth and originality of the Mexican painters of the era can only be appreciated by a visit to the Museum of Modern Art in Mexico City.

Their achievements are paralleled in music by Manuel Ponce, Silvestre Revueltas and Carlos Chavez, to name only three of the numerous composers who have drawn inspiration from the melodies and instruments of pre-Columbian and colonial times. The Revolution itself, in its epic and human aspects, provided inexhaustible material for a school of novelists, who reproduced their personal experiences with the brutal lucidity of a film: in the works of Martin Luis Guzmán, for example, the reader meets an extraordinary mixture of history, autobiography and imaginative writing. The age was also particularly rich in poetry, which has never received the sympathetic treatment it deserves from Anglo-Saxon critics, and in the encyclopaedic scholarship represented by the Caso brothers, Antonio and Alfonso, and Alfonso Reyes. For the outsider, one of the most interesting features of this period, when politics were often so unsavoury and the government so arbitrary and autocratic, was its cultural maturity and the freedom of expression which the creative minority enjoyed.

Chapter Twelve　　　　　**Modern Mexico (1946–69)**

The presidency of Avila Camacho was a period of transition between the heroic era of the Revolution (including the phase of acute radical nationalism represented by Cárdenas) and the world of today. In the twenty-three years following the accession of Miguel Alemán to the presidency four administrations, the last of which has not yet run its course, have laboured to build a modern industrial state round the framework of Mexico's revolutionary institutions. Each has had its distinctive colour and has advanced at its own pace. The personalities of the four heads of state have differed widely from one another, but they have all succeeded in injecting new life into the national effort and maintaining its momentum. The main characteristics of the period have been stability in internal affairs and a fantastic acceleration of economic growth and social change. The radical transformations of the mid-twentieth century in Mexico can only be compared with those that resulted from the Spanish conquest, and were carried out against the background of an increase in the population from twenty to some forty-eight millions, of whom at least seven millions are crammed into the Federal District.

Mexicans are rightly proud of their success story. Indeed few countries have enjoyed so smooth and at the same time so lively a rhythm of national development in the troubled years since the end of the second world war. Once a byword for backwardness and unreasoning strife, Mexico has now been free for over thirty years from violent revolution, dictatorship, chronic insurgency and social disorder and other ills for which Latin America has become justly or unjustly notorious. By Latin American standards, and by those of other continents as well, this is no mean feat.

The Presidents

The four presidents who have governed the country in these years are Miguel Alemán (1946–52), Adolfo Ruiz Cortines (1952–8), Adolfo Lopez Mateos (1958–64) and Gustavo Díaz Ordaz, who is due to complete his term in December 1970. In spite of differences of temperament and approach to the problem of administration, these men have all conformed to a new type of head of state and government which has emerged in contemporary Mexico. They have all been *mestizos* of middle-class origin, and have had little in common with their predecessors. In the first place they have been civilians. Secondly, none of them played a significant part in the revolutionary or post-revolutionary struggles. Lastly, while sincerely adhering to the theories of the Revolution, they have tended, by inclination or the force of circumstances, to show less interest in ideology than in practical affairs, and above all in the development of a modern economy. In fact it had already become apparent during the presidency of Avila Camacho that revolutionary principles would in future have to be more broadly interpreted, in the interests of good government and orderly growth, in order to release the national energies to their fullest extent and to create confidence abroad, thus attracting the necessary co-operation from foreign countries, and especially from the United States. All four presidents have been essentially pragmatists.

They have also maintained a remarkable continuity of purpose and even of method. This has been assisted by the observance of a certain pattern in the presidential succession. Thus Alemán, who had acted as Secretary of the Interior under Avila Camacho, handed over to his own Secretary of the Interior, Ruiz Cortines. The same transition took place from Lopez Mateos to Díaz Ordaz, while the former had served as Secretary of Labour in the previous government. Such continuity is also strengthened by the retention of one or more Secretaries of State in the same office from one administration to another. For instance, Díaz Ordaz kept his predecessor's Secretaries for Finance and Labour and recalled to office as Secretary for Foreign Affairs the former Secretary of Finance under Ruiz Cortines. The principle of no re-election does not apply to Cabinet Ministers, for there is properly speaking no Cabinet system in Mexico. Ministers are not elected but chosen personally by the President, and rank theoretically as his personal secretaries. They are not responsible to Congress and are not required to account for their actions in either House. Hence the reins of power are firmly held by the President, though the actual functions of co-ordination normally devolve on the Secretary of the Presidency, a central figure in the administration and fully equivalent in importance to the head of a key department.

The conversion of post-revolutionary Mexico into a nation on the verge of economic 'take-off' was initiated with immense energy by Miguel Alemán, a vigorous and quick-witted lawyer from Vera Cruz, brimming with vitality and self-confidence. The party machine carried him to certain victory over the former Foreign Secretary, Padilla, who nevertheless obtained a fifth of the votes cast. Shortly before the election the official party had changed its title for the second time and became known as the PRI (Partido Revolucionario Institucional). The new name marked a shift of emphasis in the balance which it struck between the dynamism of the Revolution and the more conservative invocation of respect for the settled institutions of the Republic. It seemed to confirm that Mexico had chosen the middle road and was surely moving, in its own way, towards political maturity.

But Alemán did not try to hasten such evolution. The essential feature of his government was rapid and large-scale industrialisation and the exploitation of all Mexico's abundant natural resources. His policy involved not only the fullest encouragement of business activity and private investment, but also a very heavy commitment by the State in the economic infrastructure of the country. While individual enterprise was given a free hand to make money as quickly as possible, Alemán inaugurated the series of vast development programmes which have continued until the present day. Cárdenas had dreamed of such projects, but in his time there had been no hope of financing them. In 1946 domestic capital was accumulating and the State revenues and reserves had greatly increased since the war. Nevertheless the expansion planned and carried out by Alemán and his successors could never have taken place without a regular succession of large loans from foreign and international agencies, among which the World Bank and the Inter-American Development Bank are the most prominent today. It is a tribute to the high reputation earned by Mexico in the world's financial markets that these have been steadily forthcoming. Furthermore, the indebtedness thus incurred has been punctiliously repaid.

Alemán was much criticised at the time for his fondness for

expensive and pretentious schemes. Such, for instance, was the construction of the enormous University City in the Pedregal, the barren lava outflow on the southern fringe of the capital. It was argued that Mexico's educational needs could have been met by less showy architecture and a less lavish outlay. But in fact the campus designed for thirty thousand students rapidly became inadequate for the growth of a student body which is now approaching the hundred thousand mark. The truth is that Mexico's economic and human problems are so immense that they demand imaginative solutions on a grandiose scale. Alemán saw that half measures would be useless and fixed the pace for development which his successors have in general maintained.

The flamboyant and successful dynamism of Alemán's administration was unfortunately marred by increasing corruption. Lavish spending by the State, intense competition for government contracts and the prevailing atmosphere of expansion in commerce, finance and industry furnished every incentive to get rich quick. While huge fortunes were being made on all sides, it was inevitable that some of the money in circulation would stick to the fingers of the officials and particularly of members of Alemán's entourage. Although Mexicans often profess a cynical indifference to the enrichment of persons in authority, it was felt that venality was getting out of hand and must be arrested.

The inner machinery of the PRI duly went into operation and produced as official candidate for the presidential election of 1952 a man who could be relied upon not to tolerate financial laxity. Ruiz Cortines, the elderly government servant who was entrusted with the mandate to clean up the mess, did his job quickly and so efficiently that an evil which had become endemic in Mexico went definitely into decline. Probity in high places is now the rule, and though the word *mordida*, or bribe, has hardly disappeared from the Mexican vocabulary, even petty graft has become less universal. Ruiz Cortines continued to govern with sober wisdom and competence, developed the social services and gave the vote to women. He also weathered a devaluation which did not seriously slow up the pace of economic reform.

His successor, Lopez Mateos, radiated youthful energy and enthusiasm, but his charm was combined with a very firm character. He ran into trouble in the early part of his term, and 1959 and 1960 were years of some difficulty for him. His first problem was to curb a wave of strikes which broke out all over the country in protest against the rising cost of living. As Secretary of Labour in the previous administration, he had reduced such unrest to a minimum, and he now coped skilfully with the challenge to his authority. When the strike spread to the National Railways, he broke it by a show of armed force and in the ensuing years the government has had no further conflict with organised labour.

The Trade Unions are controlled by leaders who have close links with the PRI and are therefore little inclined to quarrel with the president. Indeed the persistence with which the veteran Fidel Velasquez and other Union bosses hang on to office has become a standing joke in Mexico. But their close association with party and government does not mean that they fail to stand up for the workers' rights. In bargaining with the employers they are perfectly effective and wages and working conditions in modern Mexican industry are strikingly good. A major industrial dispute has become a rare occurrence.

Lopez Mateos' firm handling of the situation did not diminish his popularity. Personally 'simpático' and regarded as left of centre in politics, he had an easy way with the masses and was certainly the best liked of contemporary presidents. His sincere concern with social affairs, and especially his rapid development of the Social Security system, was much appreciated, while his wife was much loved for her tireless efforts to relieve the poor and hungry. The president was also a great traveller, always on the move throughout the country, distributing land and inaugurating public works in a glare of publicity.

Another anxiety which disturbed his government sprang from the situation in neighbouring Cuba. The advent to power of Castro inflamed the hopes of a small minority of Mexican left-wingers, but there was no serious danger of a Castro-type movement taking root in Mexico. Mexicans felt that their own revolution had justified itself, that their country was making tremendous progress and that there was no possible attraction in plunging into Marxist experiments which in no way suited Mexican requirements or the national character.

Nevertheless there was some alarm among the propertied class and, what was more worrying, the success of Castroism in Cuba gave rise to widespread fears in the United States that its example would fatally affect other Latin American countries and particularly Mexico. Although the susceptibility of Mexico to Cuban subversion was grossly over-estimated, businessmen began to lose faith in the Mexican economy. For a while funds were leaving Mexico and less investment was forthcoming from abroad. It was a trying time for Lopez Mateos, but in due course it became clear that Mexico was virtually immune to the Cuban virus and confidence was restored. The president wisely decided that this was the right moment to project abroad the image of Mexico as a stable and prosperous country. He accordingly embarked on a series of tours in other continents which amply served their purpose. In return several heads of foreign states visited Mexico, where President Kennedy and General de Gaulle were given triumphant receptions.

When Díaz Ordaz took charge in December 1964, he found Mexico in a more flourishing condition than at any time during its existence as a nation. He was known as a very able administrator of somewhat dour temperament and with a ruthless way of dealing with difficult problems and people. He chose an outstandingly competent team of Ministers and heads of State corporations. Certain leading figures were retained from the preceding régime , including Antonio Ortiz Mena, Secretary of the Treasury and a governor of the International Monetary Fund, whose direction of Mexico's finances has been brilliantly successful. As Secretary for Education he took Agustin Yañez, one of Mexico's leading novelists and a former governor of Jalisco, and as Secretary for Foreign Affairs Antonio Carrillo Flores, son of the gifted composer Julian Carrillo, who had served successively at the Treasury and as Ambassador at Washington. Independent Mexico has never been ruled by such an array of talent. In its political complexion the government had shifted to right of centre.

Díaz Ordaz began quietly. His first year was spent on financial retrenchment at home, and he announced no plans for foreign travel on the scale favoured by his predecessor. When he did leave Mexican soil, it was to confer with President Johnson and to visit the countries of Central America, where, curiously enough, no Mexican president had ever ventured. He made it clear that economic co-operation and integration with the Latin American nations would be a basic element of his foreign policy. He also promoted a conference of Latin American and Caribbean States which, after several meetings in Mexico City, concluded a treaty, signed in 1967, for the prohibition of nuclear weapons in the area.

In internal matters Díaz Ordaz preached the necessity of national unity and discipline as the safeguards of further social and economic progress. But as early as the second year of his term a lack of harmony was already apparent in the president's relations with certain prominent personalities. A notable example was

Carlos Madrazo, his own choice as Secretary-General of the PRI, whose independence of mind cost him his job. Another was the Rector of the National University, Dr Chavez, a distinguished cardiologist who, for reasons which have not been adequately explained, lost the president's confidence and was forced out of office after scenes of disorder in which he narrowly escaped injury from an unruly band of students. It was said that the Rector's sympathies were too far to the left to be palatable to Díaz Ordaz.

A greater political stir was created by the President's dismissal of Ernesto Uruchurtu, who had served as Mayor of Mexico City for the past thirteen years and come to be regarded as an immovable institution. He was justly famous for the efficiency with which he had kept the public services of the capital abreast of the rising flood of population. Allegedly he used brutal methods in ejecting a settlement of squatters from the path of a new highway, but as he had often behaved in a similarly high-handed fashion— and without discrimination between rich and poor—the public concluded that the real reason for his fall was that Díaz Ordaz thought he was getting too big for his boots.

Viewed against the background of Mexico's economic progress and growing international prestige, these incidents were insignificant and scarcely affected Díaz Ordaz's position. The student riots which broke out in the capital during the three months preceding the Olympic Games of October 1968 were a much more testing affair for the president. These ugly outbursts of violence, the sternly repressive measures which the government was eventually obliged to take, the heavy casualties incurred in the final decisive clash between rioters and security forces, quite apart from the fact that the tragedy was played out under the critical eyes of the world's press assembling for the Games, seemed to call in question the régime's confident claim that Mexico had outgrown the instability which foreign opinion obstinately associates with all Latin American countries.

In the event, however, the riots neither invalidated this claim nor seriously prejudiced the president's reputation. He surmounted the crisis with credit, proving that he was capable of coolly facing a political challenge and, when it was defeated, of rapidly relaxing the tension. There has been no recrudescence of the troubles of 1968, which can now be regarded in their proper perspective and essentially similar to more or less simultaneous manifestations of student unrest in the United States and Europe. So far as Mexico was concerned, there was clearly no support in the country as a whole, and particularly among the peasants and industrial workers, for a social or political revolution. Indeed, the indications are that Mexico can reasonably expect to live through another period of peaceful change, increasing prosperity and fruitful development of its national institutions. If this conclusion is correct, it will be salutary to take a closer look at the factors— internal and international—which favour an optimistic view of the country's future.

The Economic Scene

The most significant of these factors is the transformation of the Mexican economy, which has been carried out in the face of formidable difficulties. The very nature of the country presented a tremendous challenge to the planners. Only fifteen per cent of its surface is said to be cultivable. Vast areas have been stripped of their topsoil by primitive or improvident agriculture and the wanton destruction of forests. The eroded wastes of the Mesquital, sixty miles north of Mexico City, or of the Mixteca Alta on the way to Oaxaca, suggest a lunar landscape. The north consists largely of irreclaimable desert and the south of dense jungles and swamps. Communications are difficult for obvious geographical and climatic reasons and even with modern equipment are costly to construct and maintain. The same applies to all major public works and to the exploitation of the subsoil.

Moreover, in the mid-forties, the industrial structure was basically the same as at the end of the Porfirian epoch, and the economy in general had hardly recovered from the shattering effects of the Revolution. There was also the intractable human problem to be solved. Apart from the explosive increase in the population, how was Mexico to find the necessary supply of trained managers, technicians and workers to staff its expanding industries? The social and educational framework then seemed quite incapable of turning them out in sufficient numbers and quality. For all these reasons it would have been impossible, thirty years ago, to forecast the extraordinary flowering of economic activity which began in the forties and has continued with ever-increasing tempo until the present day.

Each administration has boldly tackled the difficulties. The most dramatic and effective of the development programmes is that which has equipped Mexico with hydro-electric power and systems of irrigation on a gigantic scale. Despite its arid appear-

s

ance, the country is by no means waterless. The problem is to trap the ample rainfall of the wet season and turn it to good account before it pours off the uplands and expends itself uselessly in sea and swamp. This has been done by the construction of dams and yet more dams, large and small. The extent of the achievement can only be appreciated from the air: the sun flashes on myriad patches of water, from the village reservoirs to the great inland lakes formed by the Infiernillo dam on the Balsas river or the Nezahualcoyotl dam in tropical Chiapas. The imposing barrages which generate electricity also change the face of the countryside. In the north-western states of Sonora and Sinaloa, a long chain of artificial lakes stretches from north to south along the foothills of the Sierra Madre, releasing the flood waters into a network of canals which have converted a scrubby and unproductive waste into a kind of Mexican Holland, rich in wheat, cotton, sugar and a variety of vegetable crops for export as well as for internal consumption. Nevertheless the country's water resources are insufficient to satisfy the growing demands of the Federal Electricity Commission, which is already including a series of nuclear power stations in its plans for the last quarter of the century.

Electrification is well and truly on the march, but of equal importance with it has been the development of the oil industry. After its shaky beginnings Pemex was thoroughly reorganised under the Alemán administration and quickly attained a high standard of managerial and technical efficiency. Production rose steeply, keeping pace with industrial expansion. It is claimed that existing proven reserves will cover national consumption for at least the next twenty-one years and that there is no cause to worry about the drying up of exploitable reserves in the foreseeable future. National needs thus appear to be assured, though it is unlikely that there will be any surplus for export. The elaborate system of pipelines and pumping stations carrying the oil and what is equally vital, the natural gas, from the fields to the industrial areas is as impressive as the dams and the power grid.

The main axis of the oil industry is now the isthmus of Tehuantepec and the neighbouring regions of Vera Cruz and Tabasco. The reserves lie under the marshy green carpet of the coastal plain, their presence detected only by an occasional flare, or beneath the shallow waters of the Gulf of Mexico. The huge refinery at Minatitlán and the new petrochemical complex which is being built around the extension of the port of Coatzacoalcos are startling proof of the dynamism of the Mexican economy.

Near-by are the sulphur domes, very necessary for the production of the fertilisers of which Mexican agriculture was for so long starved. Sulphur has for many years figured as a valuable export commodity, but doubts about the availability of reserves recently caused the government to impose export controls and to promote the 'Mexicanisation' of the industry till over eighty per cent of the deposits were in Mexican hands. Pemex itself follows a sensible policy of buying equipment unobtainable in Mexico from a variety of foreign sources, without depending on one country for its essential supplies. Thus tankers have been ordered from Japan, and it is an ironical reflection on old quarrels that Pemex has for several years been Great Britain's best Mexican customer for machinery and capital goods.

Despite the preponderant role of the State in planning and financing programmes of public works, services and communication, the Mexican economy is less socialised than those of many democratic countries in Europe. Broadly speaking, the public sector is confined to the three great state-controlled corporations, known in Mexico as the 'decentralised agencies'—Pemex, the Federal Electricity Commission and the National Railways—the assets of which have been expropriated, against compensation, from foreign interests at various dates up to 1960. The Mexican government has shown little enthusiasm in recent times for taking over the industrial properties of its own citizens. To the big three must be added certain other important companies which are entirely state-owned or in which the State holds a majority of the shares, such as the airline Aeronaves de Mexico and the steel firm Altos Hornos de Mexico. The State also has a minority holding in a wide range of concerns.

The rest of industry remains in the private sector. Indeed Mexico is the entrepreneur's paradise, and very large fortunes are common in industry and commerce. There is no question of a tiny group at the top. Rich men are to be found among the rapidly multiplying middle class all over the country. Take, for instance, Monterrey, a manufacturing city of a million or so inhabitants, where a great industrial empire in steel, glass, textiles and beer has been built up by the Sada and Garza Sada families, a prolific and wealthy clan united by intricate patriarchal and financial relationships. Curiously enough, steel-making is divided between the State-owned company and a number of private steelmasters, an arrangement which looks paradoxical but works very well. Production is unlikely to rise above five million tons a year until the mid-seventies, but the discovery of great deposits of iron ore in Michoacán and Colima points the way to tremendous future development. Mining, Mexico's traditional industry, is undergoing revival through the application of new techniques and the successful search for fresh reserves of lead, zinc, silver, copper and other minerals. An entire mountain of manganese has been located in a remote part of Hidalgo. Here again the government is encouraging 'Mexicanisation' whenever possible.

In the field of transportation, Mexico makes most of its own railway equipment and the first all-Mexican cars are being produced by a Monterrey firm which has shipped the whole machinery of a Borgward plant from Germany for the purpose. For the rest, a wide choice of standard American, German, Japanese and French models are assembled at a number of modern factories, among which the Ford, General Motors and Volkswagen plants are conspicuous. In 1969 about seventy per cent of the components were made in Mexico and the government insists that the proportion should be gradually increased. The same system prevails for tractors and diesel engines.

This modern industrial edifice is superimposed on an agrarian community which presents a very different picture. Much has been written about the poverty of the countless villages of the Mexican countryside, about the plight of the Indians and the sharp contrasts between industrial development and rural backwardness which strike the traveller's eye. It is true that while the standard of living among the new middle class and the urban workmen is swiftly improving, progress is slower in the countryside, where the peasants are slow to abandon primitive practices and so far enjoy few of the benefits which the industrial population derives from effective Trade Unions and well-run social services. The inefficiency of the *ejidal* system, under which the communally owned village lands are parcelled out to be worked by individual families and subdivided from one generation to another, instead of being operated economically as co-operatives, is justly criticised. So is the relative lack of machines and fertilisers, and the insufficiency of credit for the farmers. But the gloomy picture painted by some foreign sociologists of a rural population doomed to irredeemable squalor and neglect is quite misleading. The countryside is not simmering with discontent and despair. Still less does it aspire to violent change on the Cuban model.

No one denies the existence of wide patches of rural squalor and malnutrition, especially in the remoter regions which are difficult of access and inhabited by people still hampered in their development by attachment to traditional Indian culture or even ignorant of Spanish. They are as deplorable as the slums and shanty towns which still disfigure the capital and other large cities. But they are by no means the general rule. The best answer to the prophets of gloom is to point to two simple but undeniable facts. The first is that agricultural production has increased so significantly that in 1969 nearly fifty million of Mexicans were far better fed than twenty millions were in 1941 (the year in which the writer first went to Mexico), while the country has at the same time become a net exporter instead of an importer of foodstuffs. The second is that the picturesque but dilapidated villages, which a quarter of a century ago had hardly changed in three centuries, have now acquired, for all their tumbledown appearance, electricity, piped water, an access road and a school. These are the basic necessities on which contemporary administrations have patiently concentrated.

The present administration is, like its predecessors, imbued with the spirit of social responsibility towards the Indians which is an essential element of the philosophy of the Mexican Revolution. It is acutely aware of the need to devote more attention and resources than hitherto to the problems of the countryside, where the rate of growth still lags behind that of industrial advance. There is still plenty of land waiting to be exploited or reclaimed, and good results may be expected from further irrigation and the current expansion of the fertiliser industry. The main obstacle to more rapid progress is not so much the lack of land, or even of machinery and technical knowledge, as the low productivity of the *ejidos*. It is the so-called small proprietor, the private owners of farms of three hundred hectares or upwards, who must be given the credit for the better feeding of the people and the growing of commercial crops for export.

Despite regular distribution of land to the *ejidatarios*, which slowed down under Alemán and Ruiz Cortines but were resumed on a massive scale by Lopez Mateos and Díaz Ordaz (eight and a half million hectares in the latter's first three years), the performance of the communal farms continues to disappoint the government's hopes. The transfer of lands from private to *ejidal* ownership all too frequently involves a drop in production. The *ejidatarios* are slow to adopt modern methods and even when the contrary is the case, they sometimes find it hard to buy seeds, fertilisers and equipment. Government credit institutions are not yet adequately meeting the demand and the private banks, while ready to help in principle, are reluctant to commit their funds when security is precarious. It is hard to see a quick way out of the intricacies of the agrarian problem, complicated as it is by political pressures—a really spectacular distribution of lands is sure to earn the president a standing ovation in Congress. Meanwhile half the population still live on the land. Those who quit the soil in response to the growing demand from the factories adapt themselves easily to industrial life, in which their natural skill as craftsmen stands them in good stead. If a peasant moves to the town and obtains a profitable job, he can soon aspire to middle-class status for himself or his children, as urban society has become essentially fluid and offers endless opportunities to the enterprising.

For year after year Mexico has enjoyed a strong economy and boom conditions, and barring a major depression in the United States and the western world as a whole, there is no need to fear that its material progress will be seriously curtailed. It is a buyer's market par excellence. A hard currency, a growth rate of seven per cent, freedom from runaway inflation and the absence of exchange control are among the advantages which have made the country a magnet for foreign investors and exporters. Mexico has no difficulty in obtaining a loan or floating a bond issue in the world's capital markets and the national complacency is duly flattered by the spectacle of so many foreign clients competing for its favours. Although only ten per cent of Mexico's total investment is now derived from foreign sources, the development programme has depended heavily on the provision of large scale and long term credit from abroad and it is very fortunate that the firmness of the economy has put Mexico in so favourable a position for bargaining with foreigners. The Mexicans are able to pick and choose their sources of loans and capital goods, while the foreigners have to cut their prices to the minimum and strain their credit facilities to the utmost. This enviable state of affairs is a temptation to excessive borrowing, which the Mexican government has wisely resisted except during the last phase of Lopez Mateos' term of office, when the president's ebullience temporarily forced the hand of his habitually cautious advisers. But the brakes were applied in time by the present administration, which has since taken care to keep foreign indebtedness well within bounds.

In practice exporters to Mexico have to confine themselves to capital goods and certain vital raw materials, since the national policy, concerned as it is with promoting new industries and diversifying production, has been highly protectionist. Other foreign products encounter formidable barriers in the shape of tariffs and import licensing. Consequently the process of substituting domestic products for imports could hardly fail to be successful. At the same time the highly priced Mexican articles are not generally competitive abroad and there is still too much reliance on exports of traditional crops and minerals. It has not proved easy to find external markets for Mexican manufactures, and much improvement is called for in industrial techniques and business methods to make them attractive in price and quality. Some hopes are pinned on the expansion of trade between the Latin American countries themselves which is expected to result from the opening up of the Latin American Free Trade Area. Meanwhile a favourable balance of payments is maintained by proceeds from tourism amounting to two million dollars a day and steadily increasing.

The enormous majority of these tourists are of course Americans, while three-quarters of the total foreign investment in the country comes from the United States and well over sixty per cent of Mexico's trade is with its northern neighbour. No wonder, therefore, that Mexican attitudes on this subject are much affected by anxiety, always latent and often loudly voiced in left-wing quarters, about the domination of the economy by the United States. Nevertheless this situation has become less of an obsession in recent years. Mexico is no helpless satellite and directs its own economic course. Dependence on the United States, which in fact has brought more benefits than disadvantages in its train, is slowly but surely decreasing, and Mexican legislation has been shown to be perfectly effective in preventing anything like a foreign stranglehold on the economy. Also the tact and goodwill of foreign investors has been equalled by the flexibility with which the Mexican authorities apply their own regulations. Broadly speaking, investors are required to comply with the rule that fifty-one per cent of the capital of a new joint venture should rest in Mexican hands. But this does not mean that wholly-owned subsidiaries of foreign firms, or firms with a foreign majority holding, are being called upon to make a sudden and radical change in their capital structure. The process is gradual, and the government's criterion is the usefulness of the firm's current contribution to the Mexican economy. Nevertheless even enterprises like Ford and General Motors are said to be shaping their plans with a view to eventual 'Mexicanisation'.

Political Evolution

The stability of Mexico owes much to its peculiar political system. The highly centralised and even autocratic presidential régime, based on the principle of no re-election and fortified by an all-powerful party organisation commanding a general measure of popular support, has amply justified itself. Moreover this system, though imperfectly democratic, has the virtue of being uniquely Mexican and of thus appealing to the strong patriotic sentiment of the Mexican people. It is sufficiently familiar and elastic to satisfy the ordinary citizen, who is convinced that the sound policies which it has produced have saved Mexico from economic setbacks and serious political upsets.

The great changes of the last quarter of a century have been accomplished in conditions of internal tranquillity. There has been no dramatic confrontation of personalities or principles, no succession of stirring events, no abrupt reversal of policies or alternation of power. The long undisputed reign of the PRI has deprived political life of its exciting uncertainties and relieved the country's leaders of many of the electoral and other worries which normally distract democratic politicians from the serious business of administration. It also offers to all Mexicans a focus or rallying point for the deployment of their patriotic energies and gives them a sense of real participation in the work of their rulers. It is the accepted heir to the revolutionary tradition as well as the guarantee against the recurrence of past chaos and the perilous attractions of Marxism or other non-Mexican solutions. The party's influence is omnipresent; it pervades and to a large extent directs the country's institutions.

Nevertheless the PRI is far removed from totalitarianism: it is the party of the masses and not, as in Fascism or Communism, of a coercive élite. It is pledged to uphold the constitution and the laws, and scarcely restricts the generous range of democratic freedoms to which the Mexican citizen is accustomed. It enjoys popular confidence because it has managed to include in its ranks representatives of all the important sectors of the national life and of a wide variety of political tendencies, from the moderate right to the advanced left. Indeed, the terms 'right' and 'left' have little significance where capitalists, trade unionists and peasants march under the same party banner. All persons holding state or government appointments are automatically members of the PRI, and for individuals prominent in economic life there are undoubtedly advantages to be gained by openly supporting it. Nevertheless it is perfectly possible to be a successful banker or industrialist, and yet be known to hold dissenting political views, so long as they are not pushed to the point of active opposition to the president. The latter acts as overlord of the party and personally exercises control over its hierarchy and organisation.

If the system is not totalitarian, neither is it democratic as democracy is understood in Europe and the United States. A new president is elected every six years and elections are held regularly for the renewal of the Senate and of the Chamber of Deputies. But in these trials of strength the opposition parties stand no chance of winning, although they are officially licensed and constitutionally enjoy freedom of action and expression. Since all Ministers and State Governors are members of the official party, it receives full support and encouragement from the authorities of the Republic and every conceivable facility is placed at its disposal. Its opponents, on the other hand, are hampered by a variety of methods, both crude and subtle, of discouragement and obstruction. Its sources of funds are infinitely more abundant and it can rely on a near-monopoly of communications media. Press, broadcasting and television overwhelmingly represent the point of view of the government and of the official party, for the private interests which own them are not prepared to risk official displeasure. There are plenty of ways, such as the withholding of newsprint, in which the government could if it wished make life difficult even for these hard-headed entrepreneurs. The PRI is not immune from the milder forms of criticism in the newspapers, but this is quite a different matter from a full-scale onslaught by a major organ of opinion on the alliance between government and party. Such an occurrence would be unthinkable; so would a direct attack on the president himself. The Mexican head of state is not obliged to defend himself against open criticism, although as head of government he bears a unique responsibility for the acts of his administration.

As regards downright malpractices, such as the corruption and intimidation of voters, or the spoiling of opposition votes, it is a debatable question how far they are still resorted to by the PRI. They are of course officially frowned upon, and there is no doubt that they are on the decrease. But they do still occur, especially in the less sophisticated parts of the country where the pistol-packing political boss is not yet extinct. Thus, in spite of the deference paid to the principle of free elections, the scales are heavily weighted in favour of the PRI. In the presidential elections of the last twenty-five years the opposition candidate has never been able to master more than a quarter of the votes given to the official candidate, and on the last two occasions the PRI's majority was even more impressive. In the Chamber of Deputies, the opposition parties have only fifteen seats out of two hundred. On such a showing the prospects of dethroning the PRI look decidedly thin.

The climate of opinion, however, is slowly changing in favour of giving other parties a chance of developing a healthy and constructive opposition. The splinter parties on the left of the PRI, with their Marxist complexion and insignificant following, are incapable of offering serious competition. The ageing Lombardo Toledano, impressively leonine in appearance and still excelling as an orator, is a wreck of his former political self and carries no weight. The only possible challenger is the PAN (Partido de Acción Nacional), which is commonly described as a right-wing party. This label is not altogether correct, since the party's policies, if it ever came into power, would be almost indistinguishable from those of the PRI. But it has taken a long time to live down its origins in the near-Fascist Sinarquismo movement, from whose ashes it sprang in 1946, as well as the taint of clericalism which made it suspect to good 'revolutionaries'. The chief obstacle to its acceptance has been the charge levelled at it by the PRI that it is basically anti-national and that its ultimate purpose is to undo or discredit the conquests of the Revolution.

In fact nothing could be further from the minds of the PAN's leader, Adolfo Christlieb Ibarrola, and the small but active group of deputies which supports him in the Chamber and has at least succeeded in enlivening its debates. In the Mexico of 1969 it had long ceased to be politically disreputable to uphold the cause of private enterprise and the virtues of the Roman Catholic Church. The PAN believes that one day it will succeed in splitting the monolithic PRI and gaining adherents in the mass. But so far no PAN candidate has been elected by a majority of constituents; they owe their ten seats to a system of partial proportional representation (a small concession to democracy) introduced by the last electoral law. And it caused a political sensation when, in 1967, a member of the PAN was voted in as Mayor of a provincial capital—Hermosillo in Sonora.

From time to time there are signs that all is not well within the

PRI itself. Ambitious young members complain that their advancement to office is blocked by the local bosses and placemen who are suspicious of democratic practices and are uninterested in reforms at the grass roots or anywhere else. Such dissensions were spotlighted during the present administration by the Madrazo affair. When he came into power President Diaz Ordaz appointed as Secretary-General of the PRI Carlos Madrazo, a young and forceful state governor, with a mandate to put new life into the party. But he set about his task with such energy that he soon upset the establishment and was consequently replaced.

The wound, however, was not healed. Madrazo had attracted a considerable following, especially among the younger people, both within and outside the PRI, and he refused to keep quiet. He has remained on the sidelines, sniping at the party for its reluctance to reform itself and at the government for what he considers its slowness in tackling educational and economic problems and the agrarian question. He has not formed a splinter party, still less does he sympathise with the PAN, but his criticisms have loosened the PRI's hold. At any rate they have reduced political complacency and given the lead for more independent thinking. More truly democratic processes are likely to be introduced in the coming years, but without any essential weakening of the presidential authority. As for the supremacy of the PRI, it will be only relaxed gradually as the powerful national interests which still regard the maintenance of the present system as a necessary condition of the country's progress cease to consider it so indispensable and plump for a less strictly controlled evolution.

All recent governments in Mexico have pinned great hopes on their educational policy as a stabilising factor in the national life. They have pressed on doggedly towards the 'revolutionary' goal of universal literacy and have grasped that if Mexico is to remain the land of opportunity which it now is, an adequate professional or technical training must be made available to the hundreds of thousands of young people who come forward every year to obtain the benefit of higher education. State universities and technical institutes have proliferated and the national system has been supplemented in many cities by privately financed colleges, such as the Technological Institute of Monterrey, the standards of which are comparable to those of the Massachusetts Institute of Technology, and the Universidad Ibero-Americana in Mexico City, which has a Jesuit as its Rector. The result of this effort is that Mexico is meeting from its own human resources the demands of its modern economy and administration.

But as the student riots proved, the very success of the spread of education, so eagerly fostered by the post-war administrations, brought disquiet in its train. Young people in Mexico have been suffering from much the same frustrations as their contemporaries in the United States and other rich and sophisticated nations. In spite of the great increase in facilities for higher education, Mexican universities and colleges can hardly absorb the flood of new pupils released from the schools, while overcrowded conditions and the strain on the teaching staff have given rise to distrust and impatience with authority and the feeling that students are not getting a square deal. Although not of political origin, these discontents have been shrewdly fanned by left-wing agitators looking for a chink in the government's armour and confused by sympathies for extraneous causes like those of Cuba or the Vietcong. If Mexico's reputation for political harmony is to be upheld, it will be essential for the president who takes over from Díaz Ordaz to devote special care to the grievances and requirements of the younger generation.

Foreign Relations

After the second world war Mexico took its place on the international stage. Previously Mexican foreign policy had been defensive: its main object had been to guard the integrity of the national territory and to promote national interests within a fairly narrow sphere. In later times two major developments in world affairs favoured the emergence of a distinctive style of Mexican diplomacy and a steady increase in its effectiveness. They were the concentration of the great international issues within the competence of the United Nations and the elaboration of the inter-American system. As the Mexican government never tires of repeating, its policy is based on the twin principles of self-determination and non-intervention. Mexico's passionate adherence to them stems from the searing experiences of the nineteenth century, when it twice suffered aggression from powerful states. Today they possess absolute validity in Mexican eyes and provide a simple standard of guidance for the national diplomacy in bilateral affairs and in the intricate controversies of the United Nations.

At the United Nations devotion to these principles has placed

Mexico firmly in the anti-imperialist camp. Mexican delegates faithfully support resolutions designed to put an end to colonialism in all its forms. But in doing so they have demonstrated that their opposition to imperialism and colonialism is not simply an excuse for twisting the tails of certain great powers. They have carefully avoided identifying themselves with the international aims of the Communist countries, and consistently stressed that on fundamental issues they are to be found on the same side as the United States and Great Britain. Their attitudes are tempered by common sense and a strong and even pedantic sense of legality. Thus Mexico still refuses to grant diplomatic recognition to Communist China or to Franco Spain, on the ground that the legitimate governments of those countries were overturned by illegal force. Nor is Mexico ever likely to contribute a contingent to a United Nations force engaged on a peace-keeping mission, because in the Mexican view that would involve a violation of the sovereignty of the country concerned. In questions where the principles are hard to apply, such as that of Gibraltar, Mexico prefers to abstain from voting. In general Mexican support is almost invariably forthcoming for moderate and reasonable proposals.

In the world as a whole Mexico is respected as one of those medium powers, like Sweden or Canada, whose collective influence affects the preponderance of the great powers and the nuisance value of many of the small ones. Its role in the American hemisphere is more significant, as befits a country with the third largest population and the fifth largest territory in the continent. Mexican representatives made a powerful contribution to the successive conferences at which the complex system of inter-American consultation and co-operation was slowly constructed.

Within the Organisation of American States, Mexico often takes a highly individual line which runs counter to initiatives and recommendations sponsored by the United States and supported by a majority of members. It has steadfastly refused to break off diplomatic and commercial relations with Cuba, because it believes that to treat that country as an outlaw only delays its eventual return to the American fold, and the formal links maintained with the Castro régime might one day make it easier to heal the rift between Cuba and the other American nations. In deference to the principle of non-intervention, Mexico has resolutely set its face against any kind of infringement by the OAS or its individual members of the sovereignty or territorial integrity of an American country. Thus, in 1961, Mexican opinion was out-raged by the abortive invasion of Cuba at the Bay of Pigs. Mexico also strongly condemned the intervention in the Dominican Republic sanctioned by the OAS five years later. It would equally disapprove of similar action in any country of Central or South America, even if it were taken to forestall or counteract a Com-munist take-over. At the same time Mexico applauded President Kennedy's handling of the Cuban missile crisis in 1962, and its security authorities effectively frustrate Cuban attempts to use Mexican territory as a channel for infiltrating agents and sub-versive material into the rest of Latin America.

Mexico's independent stand in these matters has not damaged its relations with the United States. The United States respects Mexican motives, and the two countries have agreed amicably to differ. There has been no interruption of the flow of aid and invest-ment from American sources. In its dealing with the other mem-bers of the Alliance for Progress the United States government likes to point to Mexico as the shining example of how a Latin American country has used aid and its own resources wisely to put its economy in order. The heads of the two states have formed the habit of meeting regularly: President Lopez Mateos was on excellent terms with President Kennedy and President Díaz Ordaz established an equally valuable relationship with President John-son, who was enthusiastically acclaimed in Mexico City in 1966. Their governments have ironed out a number of small but tire-some problems, mostly relating to frontier affairs, and have embarked on a series of great projects of mutual benefit in irriga-tion and the construction of desalination plants. Nothing caused more pleasure in Mexico than the return to it, in 1967, of the territory of El Chamizal, a small strip of land which had been absorbed into the United States by a shift in the channel of the Rio Grande. Both Presidents attended the ceremony of transfer. As a result of wise diplomacy on each side, there are now very few real points of friction subsisting between Mexico and the United States, though Mexican voices can always be heard de-claiming against American imperialism or the dire effects of economic and cultural penetration by the *gringos* of the north.

Such attitudes, however, are gradually becoming artificial or outmoded, for even the most virulent critics of the Yankees are influenced to a deeper extent than they would perhaps like to admit by American manners and habits of thought. Great credit for bringing the two countries together must go to the highly polished and professional performance of Mexican diplomats and jurists, such as Luis Padilla Nervo, Manuel Tello and Antonio Carrillo Flores, but the new spirit of understanding is chiefly due to the fact that two generations of the Mexican élite have largely finished their education at American universities and technical institutions, and have remained imbued with respect for American culture and achievements.

The spirit of confidence exhibited by Mexico in its dealings with the outside world was exemplified by the enthusiasm with which it welcomed the choice of Mexico City for the venue of the Olympic Games in 1968. This decision encountered criticism abroad on the grounds that the altitude would endanger the athletes' health and affect their performance, that the Mexicans did not possess the capacity for large-scale organisation and that it would be wrong for a country faced with pressing social problems to spend large sums on the Games.

The government was determined to show that these criticisms were wide of the mark. Disregarding the climatic objections, which later turned out to have been much exaggerated, it built a monumental array of sporting installations, the last word in modernity, laid down a fine new network of communications and greatly amplified the capital's tourist facilities. These arrangements were placed in the hands of Ramirez Vasquez, architect of the splendid Museum of Anthropology which contains the national collection of pre-Columbian art, while the former president, Alemán, bore the brunt of the publicity effort in foreign countries as head of the National Council of Tourism. An ambitious series of cultural events was planned to extend over several months before the Games began. The predictions of the critics were not substantiated and the arrangements worked smoothly. The Mexicans earned high praise for their hospitality. As for the expense, it was a drop in the bucket as compared with that of the national development plan as a whole, soon to be recovered by increased receipts from tourism and in terms of the benefits derived from the improvements.

Enough has been said to establish that Mexico's national performance throughout the mid-twentieth century has been consistently high. The record of its élite has indeed been brilliant. Its statesmen, economists, bankers and industrialists compete on equal terms with their opposite numbers in the most advanced countries. The work of its educators, scientists, engineers and technicians has changed the romantic but rather ramshackle environment of revolutionary times into a thriving modern community. Their accomplishments are there for all to see, but are less well known to the outside world than, for instance, the powerful originality of Mexican architects and painters, or the achievements of Mexican scholars in the exploration and preservation of the monuments and treasures of the past. But the surest guarantee for the country's future is the vitality of the Mexican people. It is only in the twentieth century that the disparate elements of which the nation is composed have been welded into a whole, so that its talents may be concentrated in an outburst of creative energy.

Bibliographical Note

I have confined myself to a short and highly selective list of books in English which I would personally recommend to the general reader. There is of course a vast body of more specialised literature available on the history, civilisation and contemporary life of Mexico.

Pre-Columbian Period

The progress of archaeology has been so swift that most of the basic works on the early cultures are already out of date, but Sylvanus G. Morley's *The Ancient Maya* (Stanford University, California, 1947) and George C. Vaillant's *Aztecs of Mexico* (London, Pelican, 1950) are still immensely worth reading. So is J. E. S. Thompson's *The Rise and Fall of Maya Civilisation* (University of Oklahoma, 1964). More compendious, but equally interesting, are Paul Rivet's *Maya Cities* (London, Elek Books, 1960); Ignacio Bernal's *Mexico before Cortés* (New York, Dolphin Books, 1963); and Jacques Soustelle's *The Daily Life of the Aztecs* (London, Pelican 1964).

The Conquest

W. H. Prescott's classic *History of the Conquest of Mexico*, originally published in 1843, is a masterpiece of dramatic writing and must on no account be left unread. Equally essential is *The True History of the Conquest of Mexico* by Bernal Diaz del Castillo (Penguin, 1963), the famous eye-witness description of the Conquest by a simple soldier. Salvador de Madariaga's *Hernan Cortés* (Hodder and Stoughton, 1942) is a fascinating biography of the Conqueror.

The Colonial Period

I know of no general history in English, although a mass of learned studies has been produced by American and other universities. Much interesting material on colonial Mexico may be gleaned from Madariaga's *The Rise of the Spanish American Empire* and *The Fall of the Spanish American Empire* (both Hollis and Carter, 1947). The Dominican Thomas Gage's impressions of Mexico are contained in his *New Survey of the West Indies*, which first appeared in 1648 and was republished by Routledge (Broadway Travellers Series) in 1928. Of the scholarly studies, I would strongly recommend Lesley Byrd Simpson's *The Encomienda in New Spain* (University of California, 1950) and John McAndrew's *The Open Air Churches of Sixteenth Century Mexico* (Harvard, 1965). They contain a wealth of information about the progress of Christianity in the early period of the colony and the treatment of the Indian population, and are much less specialised in their approach to their subjects than their title would suggest. There is a lively account of conditions in viceregal Mexico in Roderick Cameron's *Viceroyalties of the West* (Weidenfeld and Nicolson, 1968).

With regard to the **War of Independence** and the **Early Republic** there are good biographies of Iturbide and Santa Anna, both published in the United States. They are William S. Roberton's *Iturbide of Mexico* (Duke, 1952) and W. H. Callcott's *Santa Anna* (University of Oklahoma, 1936). The best edition of Madame Calderón de la Barca's *Life in Mexico*, which first appeared in 1843, was brought out by Doubleday (New York) in 1966.

I can find no work in English on the **Reform** as such, but there is a massive biography of Juarez, entitled *Juarez and his Mexico*, by Ralph Roeder (New York, Viking, 1947). The **Empire,** on the other hand, has attracted much attention. I will mention only Count Corte's *Maximilian and Charlotte of Mexico* (1928), Daniel Dawson's *The Mexican Adventure* (G. Bell, 1935) and H. Montgomery Hyde's *The Mexican Empire* (Macmillan, 1946). **Don Porfirio** still awaits an objective appraisal. Carleton Beals' *Porfirio Díaz, Dictator of Mexico* (Philadelphia, Lippincott, 1932) is a rather unsatisfactory biography.

There is also a disappointing lack of serious and comprehensive works on the **Revolution** and its heroes, although this period has stimulated much valuable specialised writing (as well as a lot of lurid and inaccurate fantasy). Anita Brenner and George Leighton's *The Wind That Swept Mexico; the History of the Mexican Revolution 1910–1942* (New York, Harper, 1943) provides a useful factual account. The true flavour of the Revolution is brought out in novels or semi-memoirs reflecting the personal experiences of the authors, such as Martín Luis Guzmán's *The Eagle and the Serpent* (New York, Knopf, 1930) and Mariano Azuela's *The Underdogs*. An admirable straight memoir is Patrick O'Hea's *Reminiscences of the Mexican Revolution* (Mexico, Editorial Fournier, 1966).

The best history of **Modern Mexico** is Howard F. Cline's *Mexico: Revolution to Evolution, 1940–1960* (Oxford University Press, 1962), and the contemporary Mexican scene is brilliantly described in Irene Nicholson's *The X in Mexico* (Faber and Faber, 1965).

Index

Note: Spanish names have been placed where possible under the paternal half of the surname. Sub-headings are in chronological and not alphabetical order.

Index